Confessions *of a* Secular Jew

ALSO BY EUGENE GOODHEART

The Utopian Vision of D.H. Lawrence
The Cult of the Ego: The Self in Modern Literature
Culture and the Radical Conscience
The Failure of Criticism
The Skeptic Disposition: Deconstruction, Ideology and
  Other Matters
Pieces of Resistance
Desire and Its Discontents
The Reign of Ideology
Does Literary Studies Have a Future?

Confessions *of a* Secular Jew

[a memoir]

Eugene Goodheart

THE OVERLOOK PRESS
WOODSTOCK & NEW YORK

First published in the United States in 2001 by
The Overlook Press, Peter Mayer Publishers, Inc.
Woodstock & New York

WOODSTOCK:
One Overlook Drive
Woodstock, NY 12498
www.overlookpress.com
[for individual orders, bulk and special sales, contact our Woodstock office]

NEW YORK:
386 West Broadway
New York, NY 10012

Library of Congress Cataloging-in-Publication Data

Goodheart, Eugene.
Confessions of a secular Jew : a memoir / Eugene Goodheart.
p. cm.
1. Goodheart, Eugene. 2. Jews—United States—Biography. 3. Jews—
United States—Identity. 4. Jews—Cultural assimilation—United States. I. Title
E184.37.G66 A3 2001   973'.04924'0092—dc21 [B]   2001021102

Manufactured in the United States of America
FIRST EDITION
1 3 5 7 9 8 6 4 2
ISBN 1-58567-146-0

For My Grandson Max

Contents

One: Coming of Age in Brooklyn

THERE'S A YIDDISH expression, *S'iz shver tzu zein a yid* (It's hard to be a Jew). "Hard but interesting," a distinguished writer once said. When I say *hard* I don't mean in the obvious sense of belonging to a pariah people that has known every conceivable indignity and atrocity. *Hard* doesn't do justice to such suffering. I mean hard in the sense of knowing what it means to be Jewish. It is not hard for the Orthodox Jew, who lives by the Book, or the Hasid, who follows his rebbe, or even the Yiddish-speaking and -reading Jew who does not believe in God or is indifferent to the question of whether or not he exists. The Orthodox Jew, the Hasid, the Yiddishist are all secure in their identity. But what of the rest of us who, when pressed, struggle to make sense of our Jewishness? The biologist Julian Huxley writes that "the Jews vary as much, if not more than any other people in the world."Alain Finkielkraut consoles us with the remark that "Judaism's very lack of definition is precious." Which is not the same as saying that there is no Jewish identity. Being Jewish for me is at once a given and a question. Ethnic identity is never unitary or coherent, and I mistrust the current obsession to turn ethnicity or race into a singular story, usually of oppression and victimization. Easy for me to say, having grown up in America in the middle of the twentieth century. The Jews of Europe and North Africa could hardly avoid the theme of oppression and vic-

1

timization. The Tunisian-born Jew Albert Memmi, in his *Portrait of a Jew,* defines the Jewish fate as a misfortune. My fate is that the migration of my parents to America enabled me to escape the misfortune. For better or worse, the variety of Jewish identity is its fate in diaspora. The Jew mixes with the country in which he finds himself and takes on its identity as well. Paraphrasing Saul Bellow's Chicagoan Augie March, I am an American, Brooklyn-born.

The legal scholar Derrick Bell admonishes his black colleagues about the dangers of being black and thinking white. We would not want to be warned about the risks of being Jewish and thinking gentile. Why would we want to deny ourselves the freedom to think and feel in whatever direction our minds and feelings take us? Just as we would not want others to define us, we would not want to tell others what it means to be Jewish, although I understand the temptation. Any answer to the question is bound to provoke a quarrel, and–here I will risk a generalization–the Jews are a quarrelsome people. I'm sure that I will be making large claims from my experience that seem self-evident to me but puzzling and even offensive to others. I will be dealing with matters that have no direct bearing on my Jewishness, in the belief that one can nevertheless find its presence everywhere in my life. If I confined myself to composing a portrait of a Jew, I would have betrayed the kind of Jew I am.

I was raised in full consciousness of being Jewish. I was sent to a Yiddish *shuleh* and I can read and speak Yiddish. But I do not consider myself a Yiddish-speaking Jew: Yiddish is not part of my essence. I am not a believer. I do not celebrate the holidays, nor do I atone for my sins on Yom Kippur. And I have transmitted virtually nothing of my *Yiddishkeit* to my children. This failure of mine became the subject of a quarrel with my father, who told me I had in effect thrown away the gift of Yiddish he had given me. My children were no longer Jews. I defended myself by pointing out the difficulty of a divorced father giving his children a Jewish education, especially when they clearly didn't want it. The environment in which I grew up virtually dictated such an education for me and my friends, but it was not reproducible. My father was unmoved and held me responsible for what he conceived to be a betrayal. So I asked him, as our argument came to a boil, whether he hadn't betrayed his heritage when he left his Orthodox father behind in the Ukraine and went off to America, where he set himself up as an atheist. "Your break with your father was greater than the break between me and my kids. You abandoned the religion of your father, the religion that's supposed to define your Jewish identity, so what are you talking about?" "No," he insisted, "I have Yiddish, it is what makes a Jew a Jew. What your children have, wonderful as they are, is nothing. They have no cultural identity." (They were his grandchildren, he was a devoted and doting grandfather, but in this argument they were only my children.)

It seemed so unreasonable, yet I couldn't escape the feeling that my father was onto something. Mind you, to an Orthodox Jew he was little more than a heathen, an *apicoiris,* and he reciprocated in his contempt for the dress of the Orthodox, the beard, the sideburns, the black coat, the ancient ways. On Yom Kippur we neither repented nor fasted. My father would draw down the window blinds of our kitchen so that we could eat to our heart's content, unobserved by the neighbors in the apartment house across the way. (My mother, an atheist like my father, has always discouraged visits to her on Yom Kippur. She doesn't want her neighbors to know that her son and daughter-in-law travel on the high holy days.)

I said that I am not a Yiddish speaker and that Yiddish is not part of my essence. Was I being truthful? In times of crisis or despair or pleasurable intimacy with a friend I often find myself thrown back to a Yiddish expression, where for the moment my soul comes to rest. My bond with my oldest friends has as its medium a Jewish joke, an intonation that my wife, who is only half Jewish and comes from a completely different tradition, recognizes as something alien, quite unlike my customary way of speaking and acting among colleagues and acquaintances. Yiddish is the language of comic despair: the perfect ineffectual vent for frustration, the resentful person's imaginative revenge against life. It has unique capacities as a bearer of the experience of suffering. Its words and cadences seem to have evolved for the purpose of conveying the experience of persecution, exclusion, and massacre, and at the same time redeeming it through humor and irony. There is nothing like meeting an old Yiddish-speaking friend from the past. The language itself is like a warm embrace. It is automatic membership in a club: no résumé, no interviews, no dues required. Those who know it but left it behind, perhaps embarrassed by their immigrant parents who remained stuck in a ghetto mentality and never learned to speak properly the language of the new country, may find themselves in middle or old age longing for what now seems a comfort zone of Yiddish-connected memories. Yiddish is like some metaphysical substratum to which I always have access.

My parents' lives were shaped by the great catastrophic events of our century: revolution and world war. My father grew up in the Pale of Settlement (a sort of reservation for Jews) between Odessa and Kiev, the son of the richest merchant in the village. His father owned a large store that sold miscellaneous items, including candles to the local churches. His business required travel outside the Pale of Settlement to St. Petersburg, and the czarist government granted him the right to travel, a rare privilege for a Jew. But the life of my father's family was hardly privileged—or it was "privileged" in a wholly unwelcome sense. He told me of a pogrom in which the Cossacks entered his father's store. One of them grabbed my grandfather, forced his head on the counter, drew a saber, and threatened to cut off his head. My father's stepmother went to her knees, begged for her husband's life, and bought it with whatever cash there was in the store. My father witnessed the scene. On another occasion, there had been a warning that the Cossacks were about to enter the village, and my father and his brother were sent up to the roof of their house, where they stayed for three days.

It's hard to measure the lifelong effect of such events on the consciousness, but it surely formed the abiding mistrust my father felt for Ivan Shtink, the goy. In America, where in his business as an insurance agent he dealt regularly and amicably with gentiles, he could never achieve the trust of friendship. "Scratch a goy," he said, "and at some point you'll find the anti-Semite." And he warned me against marrying one, because in a crisis anti-Semitism would rear its ugly head. My first wife was three-quarters Jewish, my second and present wife one-half Jewish. Does this count as defiance of parental authority or compromise?

The Russian Revolution may have emancipated the Jews, but it didn't liberate my father. The Bolshevik cavalry entered his village and its captain billeted himself and other officers in my grandfather's residence. The captain took a shine to my father, who was then nine-teen years old and invited him to join his cavalry, but my grandfather intervened and forbade it. He was an Orthodox Jew, and much as he disliked the czarist regime, he disliked the Bolsheviks even more. They may have officially emancipated the Jews, but this was less important than their atheism. The idea that his son would join a god-less movement appalled him, and he told my father that if he joined he would be disowned. My father solved his problem by emigrating to America. He fled in the night with a forged passport, and acquired a birth certificate in Germany on his way to America. (On the certifi-cate, which remains among the papers in my possession, is a photo of my father as a young man. It's as if he had sprung into life fully formed.) His first cousin Nathan, a wheeler-dealer who knew whom to bribe, paved the way to America. Cousin Nathan wound up a player in Philadelphia politics; his son is a district court judge who capitalizes on our family name by officiating at a mass marriage ceremony on Valentine's Day.

My mother came from Belz (a part of Bessarabia, now Moldova). She emigrated to America in 1924. In the teens and early twenties of the twentieth century, Bessarabia was a combat zone between Russia and Romania. Though she lived under Romanian rule for six years, my mother had grown up speaking Russian and had gone to Russian schools. Her father had left Belz for America in 1912. The small busi-ness he started there was collapsing, and he hoped that he would make enough money to return to his family and eventually arrange their passage to America. The First World War intervened, and it took him four years to return. Meanwhile, my mother's mother suffered kidney failure and died, leaving a sixteen-year-old girl (my mother) in charge of her younger brother and sister. (Two older brothers had already gone to America to join their father.) My mother speaks of these years as if she is still living them. She has been forever marked by the poverty and anxiety of the time. When she finally came to America with her younger brother and sister, her experience as a surrogate mother thrust her into the role of housekeeper for her father and her four siblings. She cooked the meals, washed the dishes and the clothes, and ironed her brothers' shirts while they gallivanted in the world. A bitterness about her lost youth lies barely beneath the surface of her existence even to this day.

My parents escaped the oppressions and squalor of the old country, but they would never overcome their attachment to it. Once in America they could not be expected to take easily to its new ways; indeed, they felt threatened by them. Life became a struggle for existence, as it had been in the old country. From the perspective of displacement in the New World, the old country was suffused with nostalgia, it acquired the glow of a lost Zion. Immigration was the kind of adventure that extinguished subsequent desire for adventure. My parents' preferred existence (and they were typical in this respect) was a kind of inertia, risk-taking being anathema to them.

My great-uncle on my mother's side, Isaac Goldenberg, founded one of those *landsmanshaftn* that sprang up in New York and other cities with large Jewish populations. Their purpose was to reunite immigrant Jews from the various shtetls from which they had originated. The Belzer Bessarabian Sick Benevolent Association revived the shtetl in the heart of New York. "Sick Benevolent": the first thought was mutual aid in illness and crisis. In a brief narrative of events leading to the establishment of the association, my great-uncle speaks of Belzer immigrants "pour[ing] our their bitter hearts about their loneliness and isolation among other *landsmanshaftn*" before their own *landsmanshaft* came into existence. Looking back after forty years of the association's existence, he observes with pride "one large family from Belz." "Family," "friends," "fraternity," "clinging," "ties" appear again and again in his speech. "Uprooted from their native soil, torn from their families and friends, clinging together, they joined hands and formed the nucleus of a fraternity bearing the name of their town,

Belz." To my surprise, he also speaks of members of societies prior to 1900 as wearing "on various occasions military uniforms with rich colors, golden epaulets and ribbons." My great-uncle and his brother, my grandfather, were not alone in trying to escape military service in Czarist Russia, and yet here is an account of a kind of patriotic atavism in which immigrants "perpetuate the name of the shtetl, the love for those left behind and of their abandoned fatherland by marching with their full regalia, with . . . infantry or cavalry uniform, just like at home. This was sort of a holy reminder of their birthplace and did help to unite each group." My grandparents' and parents' generations did not dress in the regalia of their oppressors, but my great-uncle's account of those who did is not only understanding, but admiring as well. I have never known such patriotic feeling in an America that never oppressed me. Maybe one needs the experience of exile and rupture to to know that feeling.

Writers speak of immigrant loneliness in the new country, my great-uncle speaks of it, but immigrants had an antidote: the solidarity of family and kinship and community, and in some instances a political movement. My mother, her three brothers, and her sister visited one another several times a week. *Visit* may not be the right word. My uncle Abe came every Sunday uninvited for breakfast. *Invited* implies formality and distance. You invite people outside your family, and he was family. My maternal grandfather (*zeide*) had suffered a stroke in his early fifties, which made him virtually deaf and impaired his speech. He lived with us and with my uncle at different times, as did my bachelor uncle. The apartments in which my parents, aunts, and uncles lived may have been separated by streets, but the separation was artificial. In their minds, they inhabited a continuous space.

Writing about his Brooklyn childhood a generation before mine, Alfred Kazin describes the "untiring solidarity" of his family: "Marriage was an institution people entered into—for all I could ever tell—only from immigrant loneliness, a need to be with one's own kind that mechanically resulted in the *family*. The *family* was a whole greater than all the individuals who made it up, yet made sense only in their untiring solidarity." Uncle Sam may have behaved badly, Cousin

Rose may have offended or acted inconsiderately, but family was family. Fallings-out did occur, and relatives did not speak to each other for years, but a falling-out never made for indifference. The grievances themselves were a kind of lasting bond. Though Uncle Abe did not speak to Uncle Sam for several years, they found themselves together at family events. A grudge was not expected to last forever, but honor had to be satisfied with an apology, if not an admission of fault. If an apology was not forthcoming, a third party would have to intervene, often after years had passed: *"Zei nit kein akshen"* (don't be stubborn like an ox.) At some public occasion the adversaries would somehow slide into reconciliation. Sometimes the reconciliation did not take place in life. I was twelve years old when a great-aunt, my grandfather's sister, whom I had never seen before, rose during the funeral service for my *zeide*, screamed out some Yiddish words which I didn't understand, and tore a piece of cloth from a garment she was wearing. Later mother told me that she was doing penance for not having made up with her brother before he died. (In memory it does not seem like penance but rather like a grab for attention.)

I have never heard my parents speak of loneliness. Frustration, disappointment, yes, but not loneliness and uncertainty–that existential condition that members of my generation share and admit to. We, not our parents, were lonely in America, uncertain about ourselves. Even now my ninety-nine-year-old mother knows her own mind with an unequivocal clarity that I am incapable of. My parents, for all their difficulties, limitations, and suffering, knew themselves or believed that they did. I have never known them to be insecure in their judgments. They were never confused about right and wrong. What gave the family certainty, Kazin tells us, was their purpose in life: "My mother and father worked in a rage to put us above their level: they married to make us possible. We were the only conceivable end to their striving; we were their America." And that was our burden. We would realize a life unavailable to them that they wanted for us. They knew what they wanted for us: achievement, success, prosperity, a family. Did we know what we wanted for ourselves? Could we want anything for ourselves that they did not want for us? If we were their America, what was our America? In devoting their lives to us, they were not sacrificing themselves. They were living through us, who in turn were living for them.

The Brooklyn where I grew up in the thirties and the forties was the home of the Brooklyn Dodgers, Coney Island, and the famous bridge, the accent unmistakable, the people eccentric, the whole atmosphere as fabulous as Texas. Or at least this was the Brooklyn of popular mythology. It leaves out its Jewish character. The great novelist of Brooklyn is Daniel Fuchs, who wrote a trilogy about life in Williamsburg, *Summer in Williamsburg, Homage to Blenholt,* and *Low Company.* Fuchs's Brooklyn is a generation older than mine, and what he captures is its un-Americanness. Unlike Texas with its wide open spaces, his Brooklyn was dense, airless, desperate, and oppressively intimate, rather like the Eastern European shtetl on a macrocosmic scale. This would be hyperbole for the Brooklyn of my childhood and adolescence, but Fuchs has caught its essential spirit. In upper Brownsville, where I lived, people sought the clearer *luft* of Eastern Parkway on a torrid summer night as if they were ritualistically repeating the flight from the old country.

We occupied a three-room apartment on the sixth (top) floor of the building. I slept in the living room on a couch that became a bed at night. It made me adaptable to almost any living situation. The doors of all the rooms in the apartment were open day and night. Occasionally I thought I heard the creaking of my parents' bed. *Privacy* was a word I can't remember hearing. I didn't know enough to desire my own privacy, so growing up I never thought that I had been deprived of it and had to do battle for it. I shared the life of my parents, scarcely knowing what was mine and what was theirs. As an only child and the sole object of my parents' attention, I absorbed all the affection and anxiety they had to offer. It was as if the family was a single identity and any claim for privacy was an act of rebellion and rejection.

I grew up believing that I was an only child because my mother had labored twenty-six hours to deliver me. It may also have been her perfectionism that decided her not to have any more children. She wanted to concentrate her energies on me; all her capacity for careful arranging, for anticipating consequences would suffer no distraction. All my life I have been the object of a child-raising conspiracy to make me into some ideal conception of a person and to protect me against danger. My mother worried that when I played ball I would perspire, catch cold, and get pneumonia. The possibility of illness required constant vigilance, existence being a daily battle against the threats of nature. My well-being and my appearance were their constant project. A suit was tailor-made to my unusual height, but it never fitted properly. Because mother worried so much about my comfort, everything I wore had a baggy look. My parents noticed every wrinkle in my clothes, every strand of hair that resisted or evaded the comb, and the scrutiny lasted into middle age. In my forties I grew a gray-white beard that I wore for nine years. Imagine, an aged son. My father said, "You look ten years older than you are. Shave the damn thing off." "None of your business." It *was* my father's business. Once he introduced me to an acquaintance as his grandfather. Mother said that she wanted to see my face before she died. Spitefully: "Call me when the time comes and I'll see what I can do." When father died I relented and made the gift. There was never a conflict between them where I was concerned. Every consideration, every affection, every anxiety, every misgiving would be redoubled. It never occurred to them that I might experience their united front as an obstacle, an oppression, as providing me with insufficient air to breathe—and loneliness.

Shadowed by two six-story apartment houses, our street ran on an incline, punctuated by manhole covers (sewers, we called them). Between the sewers we played punchball and stickball. My talent was for punchball. I could hit a "spaldeen" almost "two sewers" with my clenched fist and slap a ground ball between fielders for a base hit. My reflexes as a fielder were sharp; I could be counted on to catch the ball. My happiest memories of adolescence are the game-winning hits, the rally-stopping catches I made. My friends and I lived through the heroism and failures of the Brooklyn Dodgers. We grew up with Jackie Robinson, Pee Wee Reese, Dixie Walker, Ducky Wucky Medwick, Cookie Lavagetto, and Dolph Camilli. I preferred the reactionary

Daily News to the more liberal *New York Times* because the *News* provided the baseball averages of the players daily, while the *New York Times* reserved them for the sports section of the Sunday edition. At night I dreamed of making Pete Reiser–like catches against the centerfield wall or hitting a monster home run. My father took me occasionally to Ebbets Field and my mother allowed me to Scotch-tape the photos of my heroes on the hallway wall, since I did not have my own bedroom. But I felt their bemused remoteness from my enthusiasm. It was a part of America they had never really entered. Sports for me were a kind of spiritual autonomy from my parents.

Getting into fights was one sport my parents didn't approve of, and for a time in early childhood I was regularly beaten up by other kids without resisting. I had internalized my parents' distaste for violence of any kind. Fortunately, the black doorman of our apartment house, a witness to the scenes of my defeat, took pity on me. Crouching down to my height, he put up his dukes and showed me how to strike back. He may have forgotten to tell me that he was showing me how to *defend* myself, because I thought he was giving me license to strike first. I experienced the pleasures of beating up other kids. But I was not a natural-born fighter, and as I grew older I found myself at the losing end of most fights. I suffered my greatest humiliation when a kid solidly built and many inches shorter challenged me to a fight in the presence of other kids and with one punch in the abdomen knocked the wind out me, sending me to the ground. Street life in the thirties and forties in Brooklyn was, of course, a far cry from what it is now. Our weapons were our fists: no knives, no guns, at least not in my neighborhood. We formed a social and athletic club, but no gang. Once while walking on Eastern Parkway, I was suddenly surrounded by a group of gentile boys from another neighborhood. As far as I recall, I had done nothing to provoke them, but they were prepared to do me harm. Fear loosened my tongue, and I began to speak earnestly and rapidly. What had I done to provoke them? What were they trying to prove? I hinted that I had friends, older and stronger, who would seek them out if they hurt me. It was not so much what I said as the astonishing flow of language that came out of me. Looking bewildered, as if they had encountered a freak, they backed off, and I realized that I had a weapon: speech.

As I grew older, my athletic abilities declined. My arms were thin, my hands small (despite my height), my stamina deficient. In college, the basketball coach, observing my height, thought maybe he had a potential player on his team and asked me to dribble down the court and shoot, but my small hands could never grip the basketball and I shot it wildly over the backboard. The fencing coach, again impressed with my height and the length of my arms, put me to the test, which I failed. Though reading and writing would become my athleticism, I have never lost my passion for sports, now sublimated in hours before the television screen, watching basketball, football, baseball, and even golf.

During my childhood, my mother's family was close-knit. One of my earliest memories is of a regular Sunday visit from my uncle Abe, who would sit in our kitchen for an hour or two, drink a cup of tea accompanied by a generous portion of my mother's homebaked cake, and exchange gossip with my parents about family and friends. Once when I was ill, at about the age of ten, he came into my room and consoled me with the remark, "It could be worse, it could have happened to me." I always thought it odd that an uncle at least twenty years my senior would entertain me with a joking comment appropriate for a contemporary. Was it a mark of respect for me, a feeling that I could take it? This streak of sardonic humor informed a stoic pessimism. Life wasn't easy for him. He had twice lost a job, his older son an eye in a sports accident. But stoic pessimism doesn't quite describe him. He wept bitterly for his son, but his humor sustained him. He could always depend upon it.

There was bad blood between him and his older brother, Sam, who worked together as pressers in a shop in the garment center in New York. Abe complained that Sam was selfish and undependable. Instead of sharing work, he would leave the shop early and expect Abe to finish up. A handsome bachelor, Sam seemed always to have a date or a party to go to. Since Abe had a family and the compensation was for the pieces pressed (it was called piece work), Sam assumed without asking that Abe wouldn't mind the extra work. But he did mind, and he resented Sam's inconsiderateness. Abe had Sam's number, and his was the consensus view of the family. The family regarded him as a popinjay and ladies' man. My own view of him differed. In my early childhood he lived with us in our three-room apartment and shared the living room, which served as bedroom, with me. An only child, I thought of him as my brother (or, when in a Yiddishizing mood, my *brudele*). If my parents were the disciplinarians, Sam was a good-time Charlie, always taking me out for a treat.

A very late sleeper on weekends, he would occasionally ask me to wake him up. One morning he did not respond to my words or shaking. I had just seen a Chaplin movie in which Charlie, playing a police officer, knocks someone on the head with a billy club, and my uncle had bought me one, together with a police outfit. So I bopped him into screaming wakefulness. He laughed hilariously after recovering from his pain and never once reproached me. The episode became part of the family legend.

The quarrels and resentments between Abe and Sam were a persistent theme, my parents generally sympathizing with Abe. Sam was the black sheep, but he was my *brudele* and I his favorite nephew. He had the looks of a Hollywood leading man: not an irregular facial feature, a swarthy complexion, immaculately groomed. His clothes were purchased at the best shops, his taste impeccable. In his younger days he seemed like a free spirit, unlike his brothers and sisters, who were all saddled with obligations and whose demeanors expressed concern and anxiety. He lived with a married brother or a married sister, paid a nominal rent, and had all his needs attended to: meals when he didn't eat in restaurants, laundry washed and ironed, his bed made. When he lived with us, there were occasional flashes of resentment from my mother and father about his lack of consideration, but the resentment never threatened what seemed to be a deeply held feeling of obligation that my mother, a married sister, felt toward her unmarried brother. The unmarried state was the state of childhood, and children must be cared for.

His brother and his sister shared the responsibility. For several years at a time he lived with one or the other. With the addition of real children to the households, Sam's continued residency became untenable. He eventually found himself a room in the apartment of strangers. For the rest of his life, he lived among strangers, out in the mornings, home at night, eating in restaurants. As he grew older, the air of freedom he gave off in his youth disappeared. A sullen look of disappointment appeared on his face, which never left him. I try to imagine the dailiness of Sam's life. Waking up every morning to a present without prospects, he had no one to speak to, no friends to call. Yes, he had a family, but it was really no longer *his* family. And he did not have the resources of imagination.

My mother had a simple theory why he didn't marry. The women spoiled him and he believed that no woman was good enough for him. My aunt Anya once said that in the Catskills, where he vacationed, women carried mattresses on their backs to his room. The family cultivated his Don Juan legend with a mixture of disapproval and admiration. As I grew older, I began to suspect that what was supposed to happen in his room between him and a woman never happened, that it may have been the reason why he had remained a bachelor. Of course, I had no way of knowing, since he was of a generation of immigrants who never spoke of such things.

I suppose the statistical probability in a family of five siblings is that one of them will remain unmarried. This is pure supposition. For his sisters and brothers, his being unmarried was an *external* fact: a reflection of egoism, a refusal to accept responsibilities, a lack of consideration for others, in particular his family, who had to take care of him. My mother was sure that he would eventually rue his situation: "It's no joke being alone in the world." Of course, in his younger days he was not alone: he had his family. What my mother and her other siblings lacked was a capacity to imagine what went on inside his head, what made him what he was. I can't recall a single conversation in which my parents and aunts and uncles speculated about his motives or wondered aloud about what made him tick. It was his effect that they constantly remarked upon. Their generation lacked psychological imagination, including my bachelor *brudele* himself, whose taciturnity increased as he grew older. I suspect that he did not speak much to himself either. When he spoke it was to complain about not feeling well or not being treated right, but he never gave the impression of being in touch with his feelings. His devotion to appearances would not permit the tremors of self-doubt and anxiety to come to the surface.

It was strange having a *brudele* so different from me. My friends and I expressed every feeling we were ever conscious of having. Which is not to say that he never complained. Kvetching was the main activity of his generation, and he was good at it. For my uncle the source of the problem was elsewhere, never with himself. Was it pride that silenced confessions of weakness or fear or self-doubt? He never knew the pleasure of confession. Like Jean-Jacques Rousseau, I would "discover" myself in telling all, in letting it all hang out. I'm not sure that I learned anything real about myself in all the confessing I did. I suspect I was doing little more than venting anxiety, or perhaps I was playacting. As I grew older, it became harder for me to confess, and although my uncle's silence is still opaque to me, my memory of his demeanor provokes me to speculate about what it might conceal and to reflect about my own acquired inhibition to speak intimacies.

I am no longer sure that he was not in touch with his feelings. It may be that his feelings were so strong and so painful that he would not risk revealing them. He had shame, and I was shameless. I can no longer confess my deepest feelings to others, not because they are shameful in their eccentricity. More often than not they are the common coin of the emotional life, but the confession implies the claim of uniqueness, of something extraordinary, because it wants astonished attention, it wants to amaze. (Rousseau began his confessions saying that he was like no one else. And he was like no one else, not in what he confessed, but in the sheer torrent of his confession.) Since the auditor hears not the uniqueness but the common coin, the confession falls on deaf ears or is met by glazed eyes. If the confessor is not blind to his effect, he must hate both his auditor and himself for having confessed.

Let us imagine that my uncle had opened himself up, what would he have said? "I am alone and unloved" Not possible. "You don't love me, you don't care"? He might have wanted to make the accusation, but how can one speak to someone that way? You need the permutations of art to disguise and justify the expression of such feelings. Without art it was better to trade on the dignity of a pregnant silence—to suggest depths of feeling by concealing them. Of course, living alone without a family, with a minimal fare of experience, he must have had very little to report of interest to anyone. He was no John Marcher, of Henry James's *The Beast in the Jungle,* with a fantastic inner life to compensate for not having lived. How much of my uncle's pain, I wonder, came from the monotony of the "events" of his inner life?

Uncle Sam seemed to be waiting for something to happen. He must have lost the will to make things happen. He was a presser by trade, but I don't recall a single thing he did: a sport, a hobby, an object that he made, an interest that he acted upon. In retrospect, one might say he suffered from depression, but it didn't seem that way at the time. The problem was not with him. It was as if his very existence entitled him to someone, to something that would bring him happiness. As he waited, his resentment grew. Since his whole life was on a low flame, the intensity of his resentment was always well within bounds. It would never explode and make a loud sound. The effect of his resentment was in the look on his face, which communicated a sense of injury. Things did not come his way, and while he waited, age came upon him with a vengeance. He acquired a facial tumor that had to be operated on, and the surgeon's knife accidentally cut a nerve that destroyed the symmetry of his face. Therapy improved matters somewhat, but the once handsome and perfectly featured face had become a grotesque version of itself. (It reminded me of the episode in the film *Mondo Cane* in which the camera moves to Rudolph Valentino's birthplace and shoots the faces of men in the town who look like grotesques of Valentino, the camera performing the role of my uncle's surgeon.) My uncle lost most of his hair, his teeth were stained from tobacco, and perhaps neglect further demolished his looks. Vanity would not allow him to accept the change. He bought himself a hideous toupee and powdered his face. When I read *Death in Venice,* my uncle comes to mind in the figure of Gustav von Aschenbach during his final days.

Illness—a blood disease, kidney trouble, gallstones, and finally leukemia—overwhelmed him. Despite Uncle Sam's Don Juan reputation, I think of him now as a man without adventure. His egoism was sheer inertia. The movements in his life were the illnesses that traversed his body, and they challenged him as nothing else in life challenged him. He felt utterly alone and helpless, filled with complaint and grievance. Too proud to beg, in his misery he became fiercely resentful of his sisters, my mother and my aunt, who, as they said, had their own problems. They tried to help, but it wasn't enough. They would not, could not take him in and become his nurse. My mother found him impossible in the last years and although she felt for him, she resolutely refused to feel responsible or guilty: "I'll do what I can for him, but there are limits. He made his bed, lived the high life, thought of nobody but himself, and now . . ." She shook her head in despair.

He left the world with scarcely a trace. Yet he looms larger in my memory than do any of my other relatives. Something in the minimalism of his life was compelling: his resentments, his hermeticism, his taciturnity. The most minimal existence leaves its traces and spaces to be filled in. At the funeral of another uncle, years after Uncle Sam died, I was asked by the wife of a cousin whether I knew the cause of Uncle Sam's death. "I thought it was cancer," I said. She knew something I didn't know: "I heard the doctor warned against kissing him on the lips." "What does that mean?" "He had AIDS. I'm sure he had AIDS." I felt a shock, although I was not astonished. I had always suspected the possibility that he was homosexual. But the warning about kissing, if indeed there had been a warning, was hardly evidence. I decided to ask my mother, his elder sister, and she responded with outrage: "Wouldn't we have known? For years, we lived so close together. There would have been a friend, some indication. This kind of talk is scandalous, scandalous." Mother convinced me, but the real story is not whatever the truth may be, but the need we have to fill the empty spaces of someone else's life with a story.

• • •

When I left home for good in my mid-twenties, not extraordinary for my generation, I kept in regular phone communication with my parents. The expectation was that I would phone two or three times a week, and I rarely disappointed them. Most of our phone conversations would begin with their asking, "What's new with you?" "What's new with *you?*" "What should be new with us? We're old, you're young." I can hardly remember a time when the start of a conversation was not a variation of this exchange, and it immediately impoverished our conversation, because hard as I tried I could rarely produce the "something new" that was required of my youth. The failure to do so came to be judged as an absence of generosity in me, a stubborn refusal to give them what they wanted. As I grew older I would deliberately withhold news about my life as a kind of revenge upon their expectation.

If my parents did not understand my need for privacy, they protected me from the demands of the practical world. I was never assigned chores or required to work after school. I was expected to give myself completely to my studies. Something of a throwback to the Yeshiva *bocher,* I never learned to do anything with my hands. My parents secured me against distractions that would keep me from intellectual accomplishment. From time to time, they would leave our apartment for no other reason than providing me with the necessary quiet for my schoolwork. I thought it a normal part of family life.

I grew up in a state of anxiety that I would never fulfill the expectations of my parents and teachers. My sixth-grade teacher, the virago Miss Crassner, discovered me. I could express myself on paper and in class discussion and she placed me in the first row, though I was the tallest kid in class. The seating arrangements reflected your standing as a student. (Other teachers with more humane instincts assigned me to the last seat in the last row, so that the views of the shorter students would not be blocked.) Miss Crassner was a spindly spinster with a gaunt face that was saved from haggardness by the intensity of her expression. She had an eagle eye for mischief, and every infraction of discipline was swiftly punished by a demerit. Everyone behaved in her class. Her teaching sounded like a series of commands. Every week she graded your performance and your seat would change according to your grade relative to others. I alternated between the first and second seat in the first row. Occasionally after a relatively unimpressive week, I was placed in the third seat, but I can't recall having fallen any lower than that. Monday was the day of judgment, when my anxiety was at its peak. The anxiety has stayed with me. We were given quizzes, asked questions in class, required to write book reports. Sometimes I answered the question with confidence, at other times with uncertainty or with a shot in the dark, but always there was a wait for approval or disapproval. My life became a perpetual expectation of a grade. Graduation from elementary school was a great triumph. I received all the prizes, including a book with an inscription from Miss Crassner, *Dave Dawson and the Pacific Fleet.* Much would be expected from me.

Prizes came my way in junior high school and high school. In college I did well, but I competed there with students whose achievements were comparable to my own or who knew more or were more talented. In my mind, the sixth grade was my consummate achievement. But all my early successes were contaminated by a fear of failure. My thoughts did not travel smoothly through my sentences. A kind of static appeared in my speech. I would strain to complete a sentence as rapidly as possible for fear that the animating thought would break down and I would lose the attention of my audience. The rush to finish the sentence might mean a violation of idiom. It offended my sense of fastidiousness about language and made me miserable. My father's impatience played a role: "Come on, get to the point." The expression on his face was enough to get me to the point. I think writing became a recourse against my father's impatience. On paper I could bide my time before expressing myself. I could daydream between sentences, interrupt the act of writing and pursue some distraction, and no one would rebuke me. But inevitably my writing was affected by my father's impatience. Nothing I wrote gave much room to the distraction of ornament or to the pleasures of digression. My writing always had to make its point and make it quickly.

I resented my father for his impatience, particularly since he himself suffered from a similar affliction. Although the manner of his conversation always affected a certain confidence, I heard the same nervous apprehensiveness in his own speech: the hesitations, the occasional blurring of focus. I must confess that I have reenacted my father's impatience with my own son. I try to check it, but it is a compulsion that takes away my initiative.

I was given piano lessons, and my third and most memorable teacher was another version of Miss Crassner. Jewish children were given music lessons irrespective of whether they had talent or cared for music. Did the existence of Heifetz, Elman, Menuhin, and Horowitz imply that the Jews had a gene for music? Every Jewish mother in her heart of hearts hopes for a prodigy. I cared for music, but my fingers possessed limited talent. My teacher's name was Miss Davis, and she sported a pimple on the tip of her nose that seemed trained upon my fingers as I moved up and down the scales. It was a pimple of perfectionism. Rarely letting me complete a measure, she would find fault with my fingering, with my dynamics (my *piano* was too loud, my *forte* not loud enough), with my phrasing, but mostly with my tempo, which was erratic. I counted aloud at her insistence, but it made little difference, for I stretched or quickened the count to accommodate the varying difficulty of the piece. Miss Davis would bark *one,* two, three, four, *one,* two, three, four. She would keep the beat by tapping on my arm as I played, but to little avail. The result was that I never seemed able to play a piece through from beginning to end. She said I was musical but deficient in technique, and, so that I would not take comfort, added: "Without technique, being musical doesn't mean a thing."

Every year Miss Davis hosted a recital in her Riverside Drive apartment in which her students performed in the presence of their parents. Like Miss Crassner, she ranked her students, the least proficient playing first, the most accomplished last. To my surprise, one year she placed me next to last. My parents and I took the subway up from

Brooklyn. I was to perform several Bach preludes. I remember the hourlong subway ride up to Miss Davis's home as a state of continuous anxiety. We were supposed to perform from memory. When my turn came, I sat myself down on the piano bench, played three measures, and stopped. My fingers failed to remember the rest. There was a long pause and not a sound from the audience. Miss Davis urged me to try again. This time I collapsed after two measures. I got up, walked toward the audience, read the humiliation on the faces of my parents, sat down, and had to endure the successful performance of the last student.

The humiliation I read on my parents's faces was, of course, mine as well. It did not prove long-lasting, however, because piano playing never became inextricably part of my self-esteem. It was an ornament, a possible source of pleasure when I played well. But it wasn't where my self-esteem resided. Even sex, which in my youth provoked anxiety and made me vulnerable, didn't have the power to humiliate as did an affront to my intelligence. I eventually switched to another teacher, the concert pianist Vivian Rifkin, who allowed my liberties with tempo and phrasing, so that I could at least play a piece through from beginning to end. We don't need Freud to tell us that no one (if it can be helped) should be denied the satisfaction of completion.

The facts of life were not part of the school curriculum or my parents' teaching. Teachers and parents must have expected us to learn what we had to learn in the street, though they would have never approved of the instruction we received there. We learned the language of sex, "dirty words," before we knew to what they corresponded. I felt urges while awake and in my dreams when I was supposed to feel them, and left evidence on bedsheets. But I did not have the courage of some other kids on the block, who would grab at the breasts of girls in the wardrobe of the classroom or in alleyways and hallways. You don't have to be taught that you feel desire. You do have to learn what to do about it. The method of teaching in the street is apprenticeship, not book learning. There were boys who seemed to be born with the knowledge of what to do. They were tough and bold and usually poor students. In their early teens they were already beyond the stage of merely rubbing against and feeling up girls. They "scored" and told the less advanced students about it. Some of the stories they told were fiction, but there was also truth in the boasting. I envied the bold ones.

Experiencing sexual desire doesn't mean knowing the facts of life. I was in elementary school and had not yet made the connection between sex and legitimate procreation. It was the time of the Errol Flynn trial, when the actor was accused of statutory rape of an under-aged girl. It was lunchtime and I was walking home from school with a friend who lived in the same apartment house. His name was Bobby Burns, which was the name of his father as well, and he was Jewish. His father had been a journeyman prize fighter, and it was rumored that after his retirement from the ring, he had become a runner for Murder Incorporated. My uncle in fact had once witnessed a beating the senior Bobby Burns had received at the hands of what appeared to be a member of a rival gang. Bobby Junior was one of the tough boys, precocious with girls. We were talking about the Flynn case when he dismissed the fuss that was being made about the accusations: "Everybody does it, your parents do it." I was indignant: "Maybe your parents do it, mine don't." Sex was a dirty business; its place was in the street, not the home. Bobby laughed me off. On entering my apartment I immediately confronted my mother with what I had been told. I have a vivid memory of a moving tableau. Peeling carrots in the sink with her back turned to me, she said, "When two people love each other . . ." And I knew the worst.

I recently read a memoir by Elias Canetti, the Bulgarian Jewish Nobel laureate, who lived most of his adult life in England. I met him once in a café in Hampstead, where I lived for a year on a fellowship. He appeared to me as a man of distinction, fastidious in his manners and speech. I knew nothing of his work. He took an interest in me and presented me with a copy of his most famous book, *Crowds and Power*. In the memoir, he describes an incident similar to the one I have just recounted. He too returns from school with a companion, a poor student, but one of the bold ones with street smarts, who tells him the facts of life. Disbelieving and in a rage, Canetti confronts his mother, who, unlike mine, tells him that his companion is lying. A firm believer in her as truthteller, he vows revenge on his friend. The next day in class, his companion, asked to identify Rome on a map of Italy, points to Naples instead of Rome, but the teacher, who is distracted, does not notice the mistake. Canetti does and he stands up in class to point it out. For his mistake, the companion receives a demerit. Canetti's persecution of him continues for an extended period of time, and it ends only when the boy's mother confronts Canetti, who is made to feel remorseful. It is a dreadful story. Its villains are the Canettis, mother and son, liar and persecutor respectively. My story ends differently—or does it? My mother did not declare Bobby Burns to be a liar, but she composed a fiction about sex. Imagine how starved we would be if we could only enjoy it when we fell in love. Both Canetti's mother and mine tried through an understandable, but misguided, idealism to protect their bookish sons from the sordid life of the streets. My mother, fortunately, did not succeed. I came of age sexually, but this is a frequently told story that I have no interest in retelling.

My parents had a number of choices about where to send me for a Jewish education. I could have been sent to a Hebrew school to learn prayers for my bar mitzvah or to one of several Yiddish *shulehs* of different political orientations: Workmen's Circle (social democratic and anti-Communist), Bundist (socialist), Sholem Aleichem (a sort of nondescript liberalism), the International Workers Order (fellow-traveling Communist sympathizers with the Soviet revolution). I was sent to the last mentioned, the IWO.

The International Workers Order was a benevolent association of fraternal organizations based on ethnic identity: Hungarian, Slovak, Russian, Finnish, Italian, Polish, Ukrainian, Rumanian, Croatian, Greek, Czech, Spanish, Cuban, Puerto Rican, Mexican, and English-speaking sections, some with Negro membership. By far the largest organization was the Jewish People's Fraternal Order (JPFO) with a membership of thirty-five thousand out of a total of one-hundred thousand. The IWO had in fact emerged from a split within the Jewish socialist Workmen's Circle between the social democratic "right" and the Stalinist "left." (In the fifties, when President Eisenhower's attorney general, Herbert Brownell, composed a list of subversive Communist Front organizations, the IWO was given a place of honor.) The sections of the IWO were like *landsmanshaftn* of a whole people not confined to a single shtetl, a mutual aid society with a political agenda devoted to the cause of working-class emancipation. Jewish sweatshop labor was not yet an historical experience. The IWO looked to the Soviet Union as the vanguard of "progressive" forces in the world. My parents' decision to send me to an IWO *shuleh* was the product of my grandfather's accidental observation of a class taught in one of the *shulehs*. He liked the teacher and her way with her pupils. My parents were buying me and themselves into a whole worldview. For me the IWO was the JPFO: our solidarity with the other organizations was rhetorical.

In *shuleh*, we were taught two great lessons, the history of Jewish oppression and the struggles of resistance. The "history" carried us from the time of Moses in the desert to the Maccabees and Bar Kochba up to the pogroms that our own parents had lived through and finally to Jewish life in America. America, as it turned out, was not the land of plenty for its new immigrants; the streets were not paved with gold. We read selections from the work of the classics of Yiddish literature, Mendele Moicher Sforim, Sholem Aleichim, and I. L. Peretz. Peretz's "Bontche Shveig" is a classic story of the Jew as perennial victim and silent sufferer, who when entering heaven and being granted anything he might desire can think of nothing more to ask for than a fresh roll and butter. The angels hang their heads in shame that he has not demanded what is rightfully his. We were taught that the poor have a right to the fruits of the earth, heaven being only a metaphor. The Yiddish stories and poems we read by immigrant writers such as Abraham Reisin and Morris Rosenfeldt weren't merely exercises in reading, they were lessons in right action and right feeling. We experienced the exploited sweatshop worker's indignation and his hope for "a better world." If we ourselves had never experienced the

terrors of immigrant loneliness and poverty, we came to know them
intimately, partly through our reading of the stories and, of course,
partly through our families. I suspect that these stories satisfied the
adult reader in much the same way. They consoled him in his suffering, encouraged his indignation, and relieved him somewhat of his
bewilderment in the new country either by a nostalgic evocation of
the old country or an apocalyptic vision of an earthly paradise.

I suppose I qualify as a Depression baby, but growing up I did not
experience the Depression in any immediate way. My father's income
as an agent for the Metropolitan Life Insurance Company was modest, but it was reliable enough to provide a decent life. The Depression, of course, fed into our sense of grievance about "the system."
World War II was the momentous, inescapable reality of my early
adolescence, but like the rest of America on the home front, we
escaped its ravages. My father, in his early forties when America
entered the war, did not serve in the military. The war was an event
we heard and read about.

Years later (I was in my thirties), in reviewing an anthology of stories
and poems about life in America by immigrant Yiddish writers, I
recalled with an irritation I had not felt when I first read some of them
in childhood the persistent lament for a past that contained more sorrow than joy. A phrase from one of the stories resonated with my early
memories: "the faint sound of a Russian song, like smothered weeping." The American present for these writers was filled with "the insatiable regret of childless parents, the inconsolable Jew, victimized by
the landlord, the boss, the oppressive heat of the city, or an ungrateful
'assimilated' son." Injustice was indiscriminately everywhere in life: in
nature, human beings, the social system: in the sweeping phrase of one
of the poets, "the unjust practices of life." It was as if the humid heat of
the city, the ungrateful son, and the callous landlord had the same evil
root. As a child, I was absorbed by pathos, that particular admixture of
self-pity and the sense of injustice so strong in immigrant life.

Of course, one can't live by pathos alone. There was no misery that
couldn't be turned to humor and self-irony. I learned to recite a poem
entitled "Zibn Teg fun Voch" (Seven Days of the Week), each line con-

taining an affliction that had struck the unfortunate speaker on each of forty-eight days: a stomachache, a headache, a backache, a stuffed nose, a pain in the neck, a sore throat (I can't recall the whole catalog of ills) and a visit to one doctor after another. The speaker was a veritable Job. But on the forty-ninth day, he declares: *"Hob ich es in drerd un gei in die movies"* (I say to hell with it and go to the movies.) For every affliction I was required to display the requisite agony. I grabbed my head, my stomach, my back, and writhed in pain: the spectacle of suffering as Jewish comedy.

We were expected to memorize poems and to recite them at gatherings of parents and members of the oganization. I had an unusually sensitive ear for the diction and intonation of spoken Yiddish and an enthusiasm of delivery that made me a star declaimer of poems. My teachers picked me out for special occasions, and I was almost always chosen to perform last on the program—as the star turn, so to speak. My reputation for performance created anticipation in the audience. I recited the poems of Bialik, Feffer, Chashmal, and Suler, among others, mostly minor poets more notable for their sentiments than for the distinction of their verse. The one poet of real distinction was Chaim Nachman Bialik, who wrote in both Hebrew and Yiddish. I recited the Yiddish version of "Schite Shtudt" (City of Slaughter), which commemorates the Kishinev pogrom of 1903:

> From steel and iron, cold and hard and mute, carve out
>   a heart for yourself
> Come with me to the City of Slaughter, and see with
>   your own eyes
> Touch with your own hands, the fences, columns,
>   towers and walls
> The stones of the street, the darkened dry blood of your
>   brothers' heads and necks . . .

It is a powerful poem, and I still experience a shudder every time I recite it to myself. In my mind it represented the oppression and terror from which my parents fled when they came to America.

The history of Jewish oppression, we were taught, was linked to the struggles of the working class inspired by the great Jew Karl Marx. The Soviet Union was held up for us as the site of liberation for both Jews and workers. It was much later in my education elsewhere that I became aware of the irony that for the working class, the Jew was the very incarnation of the bourgeois, and that Marx himself had demonized the Jew. If I had to single out one event or item in our education that represents this irony most vividly, it would be the poem "Ich Bin a Yid," by Itzhik Feffer, the Soviet Jewish poet. Here are three of the many stanzas of the poem.

> The forty years in ancient times
> I suffered in the desert sand
> Gave me strength.
> I heard Bar Kochba's rebel cry
> At every turn through my ordeal.
> And more than gold did I possess
> The stubborn pride of my grandfather
> I am a Jew.
> . . . . . .
> I am not alone. My strength increases.
> The struggle is my daily bread.
> I praise the flame, I bring the storm
> That will destroy the hated brownshirt.
> My power is no longer uncertain,
> It shouts fiercely from the earth.
> Inspired by the blood of fallen heroes,
> I am a Jew.
> . . . . . .
> I am a Jew who drank from Stalin's cup of happiness.
> To those who wish to destroy Moscow
> I say death to them.
> I march together with the peoples of the east.
> The Russians are my brothers.
> I am a Jew.

And the poem concludes on a note of triumph:

So despite the hatred of our enemies
Who prepare graves for us,
I will prosper and rejoice
Under the red flag.
I will tend my vineyard
And be master of my fate,
I will yet dance on Hitler's grave.
I am a Jew!

This fairly literal translation of mine reveals the dreadful banality of the content of the poem, which in Yiddish has an impressive, almost prophetic cadence. Itzhik Feffer, the poet, knew how to rouse and move an audience. The Russian poet is practiced in shutting his eyes and intoning from memory to a large audience.

In the poem, Feffer both laments and celebrates Jewish suffering and struggle through the ages. He recalls Moses' wanderings in the desert, the Maccabean uprising against the Assyrian Greeks, Bar Kochba's against the Romans, the pogroms and the Nazi ravages, all the while singing the praises of Stalin and the Red Army. It is a poem of triumph over the Nazis who want to destroy him but whose deadly designs he will anticipate and subvert in his march under the red flag.

Feffer was the consummate synthesis of apparatchik and word-smith, soldier-poet of the Party. A volume of his poetry is titled *Roitarmeish* ("Of the Red Army"). The terrible, unwitting irony of the poem is in the last stanza. While Feffer focuses his bravado on the graves the Nazis are preparing for him and his fellow Jews, a grave is being prepared for him by his own god, the being from whose hand he has received, so he tells us, the cup of happiness. Shortly after he wrote the poem, Feffer was denounced and killed *under the red flag*. It is hard to believe that he could have been so naive as to believe what he wrote in his poem. As an apparatchik, he must have known the score. The poem then should be read as an exercise in propitiating the god who prepared to mete out the direst punishment for sins real or imagined. My mother still has a photo of me in white shirt and ducks standing next to Feffer after I had recited "Ich Bin a Yid" in his presence. I must have been twelve years old. Feffer was traveling in the United States during World War II on behalf of the Russian War Relief, raising money and creating goodwill, and he made a stop at the IWO summer camp where I went, first as a camper, then as a counselor. (I learned later, in Irving Howe's *The World of Our Fathers*, that in its early days the camp had thirty-six bungalows, each one named after one of the Soviet Socialist republics) I recited the poem with my clenched fist in the air. The poem embodied for me the spirit of protest and of defiance against unjust authority.

The children of my generation whose parents could afford to send them to summer camps learned horseback riding, archery, canoeing, tennis, riflery, and crafts. We did play softball, and we were taught square dances and the hora. As counselors we foxtrotted, lindyed, and rhumbaed at night. We became good dancers. For my cohort, summer camp was our political and Jewish education by other means. The only difference between our lives in the city and our lives in camp was the pastoral setting. It was a time of pageants about Jewish history and working-class struggle in which campers and their counselors marched and sang in the presence of visiting parents and dignitaries of the sponsoring organization. Whenever and wherever possible, we identified ourselves with oppressed people everywhere—even Indians, as our Native Americans were then called. I had a counselor, an elderly Jewish man (elderly in my fourteen-year-old eyes; he was probably no older than forty-five), tall, thin, with the angular features of a Hollywood Indian. He wore buckskin moccasins, fringe, and beads, and occasionally wore his hair in braids. He had lived among the Indians and in fact had given himself a Jewish-sounding Indian name: *Rukatavi Dixi*. He was the author of a book in Yiddish about his Indian experiences. I never read the book, so I cannot say how he managed to join an Indian tribe, but I and my fellow campers believed every Yiddish word of every story he told about his experiences. All I remember now was his way with snakes. He would crouch on a stone and observe them with a long keen look. Every Sunday, we marched to breakfast and saluted the flag with a defiant Indian salute. We were the Jewish Indians of Camp Kinderland, multicultural before the word ever existed.

Adjoining Kinderland was Lakeland, a camp for adult members of the JPFO and an ideal place for the parents of Kinderland campers to vacation while observing their children away from home. I had been a camper for a number of years and then a counselor for several more when I decided to work in the Lakeland dining room one summer. Shouldn't I have the experience of being a worker in a working-class camp? Moreover, there was the financial adventure of receiving tips. (Bourgeois appetites never die.) My performance as a waiter turned out to be a disaster. One time I exited from the kitchen, holding a fully stacked tray of dishes filled with food, only to see my parents entering the dining room unexpectedly. They had come on surprise visit from New York to see me. I promptly confirmed their long-standing suspicion of my dexterity and dropped the tray. My downfall, however, was the result of hubris. I prided myself on my memory, having successfully memorized reams of Yiddish poetry to recite. I would not use pencil and paper to take the breakfast egg orders. One morning the guests seated around one of the tables in my station ordered what seemed to be the whole gamut of preparations: hard and soft boiled, scrambled, poached, sunny side up and down. I walked into the kitchen and promptly forgot the exact orders. My solution was to fill the tray with an abundant supply of the variety of preparations. Arriving at the table, I remembered that one of the guests had ordered a soft-boiled egg, but didn't remember whether he had ordered one or two. Playing it safe, I gave him two and to my astonishment he exploded in a rage. He had ordered only one soft-boiled egg and in giving him two I showed myself to be careless and wasteful. Here was a working-class guest in a working-class camp chewing me out and I exploded in turn. What right did he have to speak to me in this manner? (What right did I have to speak back to him?) He complained to the management, and a meeting of the staff was held in which it was decided that I was not cut out to be a waiter. In a "bourgeois" camp I would have been promptly fired. The comrade manager transferred me to another job. I became a busboy.

My bar mitzvah was a secular affair, a dinner party in the living room of an uncle and aunt (they had the largest apartment in our family) where I delivered a Yiddish speech that I had written and recited Feffer's "Ich Bin a Yid." No rabbi, no rituals, no mention of God. If there was an invisible divine presence in the room, it was a curious compound of Moses, Bar Kochba, Judah Maccabee, Marx, and that strange honorary Jew, the anti-Semitic Stalin. Each of these historical characters was a revolutionary hero in our eyes, an embodiment of resistance to oppression and injustice. I only recently discovered that the Maccabees were fundamentalist religious fanatics, who resisted the very idea of assimilation into Assyrian Greek society. If they had found themselves among us, we would have repudiated them, expelled them from our ranks. They had been remade for our "revolutionary" purposes. Of course, we did not know then that Stalin was an anti-Semite. After all, he had solved the national question and had given Jews Birobidgan, their first homeland since their dispersion from Eretz Israel. One of the Yiddish songs we sang together was a celebration of this Yiddish Soviet Socialist Republic, "Hey Jan Kulie, Hey Jan Kulie." We learned later that Birobidgan was a joke, a place in the Siberian tundra to which Jews were sent in exile, not exactly a concentration camp, but certainly a scene of despair whose inhabitants drank themselves into a vodka stupor.

A bar mitzvah without God, but not without faith. Real atheism, a cool, thoroughgoing skepticism, may be possible for some individuals, but not for a community. We were not taught Hebrew, the sacred language, but we acquired a faith in the aspirations of our people. The scriptures, to the extent that we became familiar with them, served as metaphors for our struggles. It may have been a false faith, but what made it false was not that it was a faith. What made it false was that it concealed a tyranny. All secular faiths breed tyranny, for they grant to human beings (a Lenin, a Stalin, a Hitler, a Mao) powers that belong to the wisdom of God. Those who lost faith in God after the Holocaust (how could he have allowed it to happen?) have failed to see that the responsibility lies not with God, but with the usurpers: the men who would be God. I must have been fourteen or fifteen years old when I read the famous French writer Henri Barbusse's hagiography of Stalin, in which the Soviet leader appears as a sleepless leader who looks out from a window in the Kremlin day and night with a paternal concern for the welfare of his countrymen. Barbusse had literalized Orwell's metaphor of Big Brother with no sense of its sinister character. Or perhaps it's more accurate to say that he had transformed Stalin into an all-seeing, all-powerful, benevolent god. I was too young and too innocent not to be inspired by the image. I write as a nonbeliever with a certain envy for those who place their trust in a nonhuman transcendent god. They have hope for the future that I am incapable of.

Our Eden was not the Garden of Genesis, but Spain before the Inquisition. Among my mother's papers is a crumpled copy of an essay in Yiddish I wrote while not yet a teenager on the golden epoch of Jewish coexistence with the Arabs before the advent of Ferdinand and Isabella and the Grand Inquisitor Torquemada. Spain, we were taught, was free, democratic, and progressive. My essay is filled with pride in the achievements of my people. Although we never read the sea poems of Yehuda Halevi or the poetry of Moses ben Ezra or the philosophy of Rambam (Maimonides), they became our heroes. The Jews of Spain were the Sephardim, whose descendants, I was to learn later, regarded my people, the Ashkenazis, with condescension, if not contempt. We were being taught an ideal, not an actual history. The golden epoch in Spain was the model for a binational state in Israel, which our movement advocated. Our Zion, however, was not Israel, but the whole world of harmonious cultural diversity. We quarreled with Zionists about Israel as a solution to the Jewish problem, opposing internationalism to nationalism, working-class solidarity to tribal identity. We didn't discriminate among Zionists, even though there were left-wing Labor Zionists who shared our Marxist sympathies. Zionism for us was bourgeois and reactionary. "The Final Solution of the Jewish problem" made our quarrel with Zionism irrelevant. After the Holocaust, it was impossible not to support the Jewish state.

Was it cowardice that I never joined the Communist Party, or an inchoate sense that the fanatical discipline of the Party was not for me?

As a student in *mittleshule,* I was once reproached by one of my teachers for expressing Titoist sentiments. I never learned how I had deviated from the Party line, being too intimidated to ask, let alone challenge my teacher, since he possessed truth and wisdom. My teacher never thought to understand how and why I, only fourteen years old, had arrived at these sentiments. While I was at camp, a popular folksinger came through to entertain and recruit for the Party. Friends joined, I was tempted. Triangular desire: what my friends want I want, but did I really want to join the Party? My father didn't want me to join. Was he fearful for me, or did he have his doubts? Wouldn't it be perversity to join just to defy my father? I think the answer is yes to all these questions. Contradictory yeses perhaps, but I was filled with contradictions.

We knew nothing of "peer pressure" at the time, but now I know that I was experiencing it. Joining would not have been a fully voluntary act. (Is there a *fully* voluntary act?) If I had joined, I would have brought with me a heavy burden of anxiety, fear, doubt. I know now, given my temperamental revulsion from groupthink, mass enthusiasm, political self-righteousness, that membership in the Party would have been asphyxiating. But I did not know it then, and I carried a burden of guilt for not joining. I can't say that I was proven right, for the consequences of acting or failing to act do not redeem motives. I did miss out on the experience of *leaving* the Party.

Even now when my old childhood friends gather together on New Year's or Christmas, the guitar players and singers of songs produce "Hey Jan Kulie," as well as the Red Army songs and those of the Spanish Civil War that had been part of our Jewish education, and we join in and sing with a mixture of exuberance, nostalgia, and irony. Camp in every sense of the word.

Shuleh was after school, an hour or two, two or three days a week. Its three levels were elementary, middle, and the higher courses, and it lasted through high school. Who remembers exactly what he has learned in childhood and adolescence? What survives are the faces of teachers and classmates, the anxieties of classroom performance, scoldings and punishments, mischief. *Shuleh* could not compete for my ambitions with public school, where there was much more time spent, more to learn, greater rewards to be gained. We were tired and distracted after school, felt deprived of time in the streets that our friends who did not go to *shuleh* enjoyed. Not much could be expected of us by our teachers.

And yet . . . *shuleh* and the movement of which it was a part formed us, even shaped the kind of students we were in public school. We "knew" something about the world our classmates didn't know. In 1948, as a senior at Boys High, Brooklyn, I "knew" that America was responsible for the Cold War. I "knew" that the workers needed to organize against capitalist greed. I "knew" that Negroes had not yet achieved the emancipation that Lincoln had proclaimed, and I possessed a rhetoric to go with this knowledge. During the time of the Rosenberg trial, I "knew" that they were innocent, because Sacco and Vanzetti were innocent. Their innocence and their persecution were in a tradition of political martyrdom. Since their innocence was a given, we didn't have to examine the facts of the case. (Years later, when I reviewed a collection of essays by the literary critic Leslie Fiedler, I remarked on what I thought was the intellectual irresponsibility of an essay he wrote in which he decided their guilt on the basis of a close reading of their prison letters to each other. I no longer held a brief for the Rosenbergs, but I objected to a judgment based on the methods of literary criticism in a life-and-death matter and not on an examination of the evidence. I had come a long way from my ideological indifference to evidence.) I knew all this, but I also had acquired the cunning to moderate my views. So, in a debate staged in the school auditorium, I took the position that both America and the Soviet Union were jointly responsible for the Cold War. If I was a closet Red, my opponent in the debate (a classmate of Italian extraction) was a not-so-closet Fascist (he admired Mussolini) and of course hated Communism. In the audience was my math teacher, Alexander Koral, the chair of the department, who also hated Communism. After hearing me, he decided that I was a fellow traveler who had to be punished for my views. I had just been elected co-leader of Arista, the high school honor society. As the faculty advisor of the society, Mr. Koral disqualified me from the leadership. I had my first taste of McCarthyism. I later discovered that Mr. Koral's brother had been expelled from teaching in the school system by a Red-hunting committee of the State Legislature for membership in the Communist Party.

Here is a conundrum. My teacher was right about Communism, and I was wrong. But he, like many ferocious anti-Communists at the time, and for that matter our own, was possessed of an Inquisitor's passion to expose the sinner wherever he could be found. I was no more than a high school fellow traveler, but Mr. Koral saw the full enormity of Communism growing inside of me. He was a handsome man in his forties or early fifties (adolescent judgments of age are unreliable) with a rich head of gray hair, five o'clock shadow, and unsmiling eyes that focused intensely upon you through thickly lensed spectacles: a caricature of a prosecutor, or so I remember him. In the light of what I learned about Soviet Communism, should I revise my judgment of him? I am not a revisionist of the past, because revision confers an unearned authority on the present. I did not know then what I know now. There is no way that I, a youngster of seventeen, having been formed as I was formed, could know then what I know now. Of what was I guilty, sympathies based on ignorance? My teacher had betrayed whatever was true and right about his knowledge of Communism by his conduct. He played the Inquisitor against the Inquisition and displayed the excess and indiscriminateness of all Inquisitors.

My father would not allow the event to pass. He went to the school principal and demanded that I be restored as co-leader of Arista, threatening to go to the Board of Education, if necessary. The principal agreed to speak to Mr. Koral and the result was an absurd compromise. I would be made vice-leader. (Did he agree to the compromise because my title would contain the word *vice*?) My father and I were grateful to the principal, for it hadn't dawned on us that Mr. Koral had effectively won. I was punished, although the sentence had been commuted. But Mr. Koral did not experience victory. He

had been overruled by the principal, and the day following the decision to make me vice-leader, he gave me a lesson in democracy.
"Imagine what would have happened in the Soviet Union if you had
protested the decision I had made. You should be grateful you live in
a democracy." The Inquisitor wanted credit for a system that he had
compromised by his conduct.

Nineteen-forty-eight was the year that Henry Wallace ran against
Truman and Dewey for the presidency on the Progressive Party ticket.
It was a watershed year for liberals and fellow-traveling sympathizers
with the Soviet Union. I had grown up during the administrations of
FDR, whose New Deal was responsive to the needs of people suffering
from the Depression. America's alliance with the Soviet Union during
World War II and Roosevelt's apparent friendship with the avuncular
Stalin (he was "Uncle Joe" during the war) diluted any antagonism that
we felt toward American capitalism. Moreover, Roosevelt was viewed
as a traitor to his class. As Jews we regarded him with filial affection.
Didn't some of his enemies rename him Rosenfeldt? But now the war
was over, and the Cold War had begun. Truman, the accidental president, was betraying the Roosevelt legacy in his hostility toward the
Soviet Union, whereas Henry Wallace, in our view, was Roosevelt's
true heir. He got little more than a million votes, and yet the Wallace
movement was a galvanizing force for youth in America (or a portion
of it), a sort of foreshadowing of the counterculture of the sixties. My
friends and I joined the AYD (American Youth for Democracy), a
young people's organization for Wallace. For us, it was little more
than an extension of the Jewish Young Fraternalists, the youth organization of the Jewish People's Fraternal Order of the IWO. We were
now in a larger arena, part of a movement that might gain power in
America—or so we thought. We dismissed charges that Wallace was a
puppet of the Communist Party as Red-baiting reactionary propaganda, though it would, of course, not have been a scandal for us if it
were the case, for the Party, after all, was the vanguard of progressive
America.

I had a Trotskyite uncle (American-born), who knew the truth
about Stalin and the Soviet Union. (I refer to my uncle as a Trotskyite,

the derogatory term used by Stalinists, the word I have always used. A knowing friend of mine tells me that *Trotskyist* is the uninvidious term.) Trotsky was the heir apparent of Lenin. He was of Jewish origins, a man of extraordinary intellectual power and physical courage, and possessed of a revolutionary fervor that embraced the whole world. Stalin was content with socialism (his version of it) in one country; Trotsky stood for world revolution. Trotsky's Jewishness held no sway over my father and me. What mattered was that he was not a genuine revolutionary, but a traitor to the Soviet Union. Later, when I came to appreciate his integrity, I recoiled from its ferocity. He was no less a killer than Stalin, but it was idealism, not cynical opportunism as it was for Stalin, that motivated him. We argued with my uncle constantly, my father and I denying every accusation: no, the Soviet Union was not a police state; Stalin's associates Bukharin, Zinoviev, Kamenev, and others whom he purged were not forced to confess; rumors of officially sanctioned actions against Jews were fabrications of the bourgeois press. We conceded nothing, and my uncle would turn away from us in dismay, knowing as he did that every future quarrel would produce the same result.

But the moment of reckoning came, or rather a gradual and irreversible erosion of belief. My uncle's accusations had lodged within me as I tried to repel them and I found myself asking questions of my mentors in the "movement." The head of the youth organization, with his intimidatingly striated granite face, scoffed at the charges that the confessions of Stalin's associates were coerced and wouldn't even discuss them; the cultural director, whose mild manner invited questions and discussion, managed to deflect every bit of evidence that Jewish intellectuals and artists were being persecuted and killed. I would walk away troubled but not ready to abandon the cause. Because, I now realize, it was more than a cause, it was a way of life, a cohort of family and friends. If I abandoned it, what would I have left?

But the doubts did not disappear. They gnawed at my conscience, the same conscience that moved me to raise a fist when I recited Feffer's poem. I had an advantage over some of my friends for whom disillusionment with the cause was an Oedipal rebellion. Their parents remained irretrievably fixed in the postures of revolution they brought with them from Russia, so any challenge to the cause would be like family betrayal. For me it was different. Like father, like son. I had inherited my father's sense of justice, which always resisted fanaticism of belief. If he had rejected the god of his father, he was capable of rejecting the god of the revolution. "If you continue to take this line, you may as well leave my apartment," a fanatical friend responded to my father's persistent questioning about events in the land of the revolution. He and his wife were old friends of my parents, and his wife began to cry at the prospect of a break between them. My father smiled at his fierce friend and simply said, "I'm not leaving." The friendship was too deep and too long-standing to be destroyed by a political quarrel. Or at least that was my father's perspective. Of course, political quarrels do destroy not only friendships, but families as well. When Jesus said he came to set son against father, brother against brother, he gave expression to the claim of the higher truth, the greater cause. Part of my father's sense of justice was knowing when to stop. He instinctively knew that an idea to which you bow down is a tyrant. The ferocity of my father's friend, on behalf of a cause which would allow him to destroy a friendship of many years, told me that he was in the wrong and my father in the right.

Not that my father lacked for indignation against injustice. For the most part he was a cheerful man, gregarious and genial with a joke or two a day that he picked up on his rounds as an insurance agent. What provoked his anger and impatience was the misbehavior of the world. You were expected to keep a promise, to pay a debt, to be grateful for a gift, to arrive punctually for an appointment. When my father honked the horn of his car it meant that I was to appear at once. To dawdle implied a lack of consideration and respect, and I felt his irritation at a distance when I walked toward the car. I have reenacted my father's maddening and demanding punctuality with my kids when I, a divorced father, picked them up on weekends. They grew to hate the sound of my horn.

Lack of consideration, unfairness, indifference, insensitivity enraged my father. But given the ordinariness of his existence, the occasions were small (specks or mites under the aspect of eternity) and the disparity between occasion and response sometimes made for comedy. In our family certain events achieved legendary status. There was the afternoon that my father sat at the counter of a luncheonette, sipping ice cream soda (it was in the days when ice cream sodas were affordable, only a quarter). He sipped, he stirred, he sipped, he stirred. The soda, he thought, was unusually bubbly. Then he dug his spoon into the ice cream, scooped up a biteful, and put it in his mouth. Shocked by its taste and texture, he realized immediately that he had bitten into a piece of soap: "What's this?" The man behind the counter looked amused. The soap he had used to clean the surfaces of the counter had slipped into the open vat of ice cream and had camouflaged itself. "Not to worry," the amused soda jerk said, "think of it as a free colonic irrigation." My father, an insurance man with an insurance man's litigious nature, was not to be trifled with: "Wise guy. It will cost you." And on his return home, he phoned a lawyer, one of his clients, and set a suit in motion. The luncheonette or its insurance company turned it over to its nuisance department and settled the case for thirty-five dollars, more than a hundred times the price of the ice cream soda. Seventeen-fifty went to my father, seventeen-fifty to the lawyer. My father had received satisfaction. Of what? His honor restored? Assuming that he had been dishonored by the patronizing smile (a dubious assumption), he would have regained his honor only if the soda jerk had sympathized and apologized. Instead, the matter had been turned over to a department that declared him a nuisance. It was not a shining moment for him.

I was expected to be truthful. My father was my severest critic (he never neglected to point out a responsibility I had failed to discharge, an oversight, a mistake), but he always honored my candor and honesty. Or at least what he perceived to be my honesty. I've never thought of it as a particular virtue of mine, because I experienced it as a compulsion or as an anxiety about not coming clean—as if some clear-seeing ubiquitous power would find me out. Call it God or con-

science or superego. I called it none of these things. It meant that
even little falsehoods and deceits, however harmless, must be
exposed for what they are.

An absurd early childhood scene: I could not have been more than
five or six years old. My parents had invited good friends of theirs
over for tea and dessert. We (the five of us) were all seated around the
table in the kitchen (every activity–cooking, eating, socializing, quar-
reling–took place in the kitchen). One of the guests farted (it was not
clear whether it was the man or the woman) and they both turned
their gaze on me. They didn't have to say a word. A six-year-old is a
convenient scapegoat. Impulsively (what else is a six-year-old but
impulsive), I blurted out, "I didn't do it. You did it." My parents
laughed, the guests may have laughed (I don't recall). After the guests
left, my parents savored the scene. It was a triumph of mine that
would become part of the family lore. There was a double moral:
don't blame others for your actions and don't allow others to blame
you for their actions. The spark of indignation was already struck in
the six-year-old.

We are all born in indignation, screaming: some of us remain indignant all our lives. The infant screams because he is thrust into the
world without resources. Our belief in entitlement begins at birth as
the infantile sensation of being deprived. The infant has known the
complete comfort of the womb, and now, suddenly thrown into an
alien world, he demands his comfort as a right. The emotion that sus-
tains the demand is indignation. There are gifted ones, virtuosos with
hair-trigger tempers, who can blow up at a moment's notice. I am one
of them. A friend calls me the fiery lieutenant, after the absurd character in *Crime and Punishment* who heats up with every grievance, major
and minor. My father preceded me as the fiery lieutenant. His neck
must have run a fever, for he was, more times than it was good for him
or for those he confronted, hot under the collar. Like my father, I have
waged numerous battles on the telephone with indifferent reception-
ists, inattentive clerks, uncomprehending customer-relations special-
ists, my voice steadily rising in indignation at their stupidity and
callousness. My wife, whose self-possession I admire but cannot emu-

late, finds my indignation the least tolerable attribute of my personality. When anger doesn't work, I shift tactics. My favorite tactic is to ask the object of my outrage, "Imagine yourself in my position, how would you feel being treated in this way?" (This is the reverse of the victim's psychology of identifying himself with the enemy in order to anticipate the enemy's moves. My tactic requires the enemy to identify himself with the victim. And I do this on the assumption that we have all at one time or another been victims.) I almost always get a pause on the other end. He or she is considering, and though I may not have immediately overcome resistance, I hear a modification in the tone of response and sometimes a concession or a willingness to think about it. Indignation has turned into an appeal for compassion or an inducing of guilt. When practiced over a long time, indignation is not the pure emotion of outrage it purports to be.

I grew up apprenticed to my parents' vigilance about the behavior of others. Like them, I remember past grievances as if they were present events. Many mornings I lie awake, remembering some slight or offense or injury from the past. The balance of life lies as much in the settling of accounts, in the requital of grievances, as in the requital of love. My temper flares when people do not return calls, keep promises, or arrive on time for appointments—when, that is, they fall short of the ethical life. Without religion, my parents proved to me that the moral life could be a calling. They would have approved the saying of George Eliot, whom they never read, that of the trinity God, Immortality, and Duty, the belief in God and Immortality may have weakened or disappeared, but Duty remained and required the passionate devotion that people in the past had given to God and Immortality. In my mind there is a link between anger and the moral life. When I am not occupied with a particular task, my mind recalls grievances past and present. Sometimes an anger from the past wells up in me and I speak the anger to an empty room, guiltily hoping that I have not been observed.

The trouble with this kind of anger is that it is never satisfied. It remains confined to the room of one's mind. The word for it is resentment, which the philosopher Max Scheler characterized as an "evil secretion in a sealed vessel like prolonged impotence." The sense of injustice grows larger than the occasion for it. The resentful person holds grudges, which are impervious to the passage of time. Grudges are memory's bitterest fruits. My parents and I ate them daily and in some perverse way relished the taste. In my "maturity," I have been taught by mocking or exasperated friends, wife, and children to "cool it." I see in the mirror of their irony or exasperation the absurd disfigurements of my rage.

Is indignation a Jewish emotion? Jackie Mason does a funny routine in which he contrasts the behavior of Jew and gentile in a restaurant. The gentile enters the restaurant and quietly accepts his place at a table, the Jew walks in and complains about where he is placed. "Is this a table for a man like me?" Mason intones in a voice of mock indignation. Jews display a touchiness about their dignity even when they have not been affronted, a habit formed over centuries of indignities.

Without indignation we are acquiescent victims scarcely above the level of animals. Animals suffer predation, drought, and famine, and they fiercely attack and defend, but they don't possess the moral sense that indignation requires. The writers of Genesis understood this, when they represented the origins of morality as an act of disobedience, a protest against divine authority. Moral knowledge forces Adam and Eve out of paradise. And the history of mankind becomes an arbitrary exercise of power. God plays favorites. He likes Abel's gifts, not Cain's, and gives no reason. The result: the favorite dies and the survivor carries the burden of guilt for the rest of his life. God chooses Noah and Abraham, good men, but then commands Abraham to play the monster and sacrifice his son. He blesses the scoundrel Jacob, who steals his brother's birthright. He plagues the Egyptians, so that they will let his people go, and then with inexplicable duplicity hardens the Pharoah's heart to delay the liberation of the Israelites. The "logic" of God's behavior from the time of his creation of the world leads to Job, the hero of indignation. Why should Adam and Eve suffer because they want moral knowledge? Why should Cain's offerings be spurned? Why should Esau be made to suffer?

Why is Job afflicted with boils? Why, Dmitri Karamazov asks in *The Brothers Karamazov*, must innocent children suffer? Why did my uncle, vital, bright, productive, suffer a major stroke? Questions, questions and no answers. We are given the emotion of indignation because without it we would be no more than sheep. The root of indignation is the root of dignity. Dignity requires the capacity to be indignant. Aristotle defined man as a rational animal, but a good case could be made for him as an indignant one. Without indignation and the rebellion it breeds, one is not human.

This is the indignant man speaking, justifying himself. The emotion precedes the occasion for it. The indignant man always stands ready to complain or protest or grieve, because he "knows" or, better, feels in advance that his appetites will not be sated, his desires not satisfied, his expectations not met. How could they be, since the world does not exist for him? The style of indignation is excess, baroque excess. It is unstoppable speech, filled with repetition, subordinate clauses that recall episodes of injury, sentences and clauses introduced by moreovers, proving again and again the case against injustice. "Ideally," there is no closure to the indignant statements, because closure implies satisfaction, and the indignant person can never be satisfied, Consider the inordinate length of the speeches in in the Book of Job. Once Job's patience is exhausted and he breaks his silence, what issues from him is a torrent of feeling that the conspiracy of "comforters" cannot dam up. Job's indignation provokes a counterindignation in the comforters, and only God can put an end to their interminable rage. Indignation is finally unreadable; we hear its sound and pay decreasing attention to its words and meaning.

Indignation wants what it can never achieve, the transformation of the world into a state or condition of complete satisfaction. This is the meaning of the expulsion from paradise. Only the return to paradise will eliminate indignation. In Adam and Eve, God created dissatisfaction. After the expulsion, every event in life is arbitrary. A is born with talent, B has none. C is loved, D is rejected. Life is unfair. The deep question at the core of man's indignation is why he was created if his existence is to be a series of bafflements. Indignation is a protest against creation, a refusal to accept its terms. God has no one but himself to blame for the Jewish quarrel with him. He created not only the world, but also expectations that he has constantly disappointed. And he created the Jewish mind, for which an unquestioning faith is all but impossible.

When I was eighteen, in 1949, I got a summer job as a social director in an adult camp of the Workmen's Circle near Framingham, Massachusetts. My talent as a declaimer of Jewish poems and the modicum of acting ability I possessed impressed the camp director. The Workmen's Circle was not simply another organization, it was the enemy of the organization in which I had grown up: social democratic ("social fascist" in our lexicon of contempt) and anti-Soviet. It was the enemy of the working class disguising itself as its representative. The Workmen's Circle had several summer camps. One of them was located in New York State, across a lake from Camp Kinderland. Except for the time of the Peekskill riots over the appearance of Paul Robeson, campers from the opposing camps avoided each other like the plague. At the time of Robeson's concerts at Peekskill, I recall standing guard at the edge of our side of the lake, a baseball bat in hand, in anticipation of a possible assault by the "social fascists" from the opposite shore. What the two organizations had in common is what I possessed, Yiddish. I could recite Yiddish poems and act in Yiddish plays. What the Framingham Workmen's Circle camp did not know is where I had learned my Yiddish.

As it turned out, it was I who was exposed in a rather bizarre manner. The camp was host to an extraordinary Yiddish poet, an émigré from Poland who came with stories of executions of Jewish artists and intellectuals. He spoke in detail of the execution of Feffer, probably ordered by Stalin himself, and gave as the reason Feffer's celebration of the creation of the state of Israel in 1948. Zionism and rootless cosmopolitanism had become the code words in the denunciation of Jews by Soviet authorities, and Feffer among many others had become a victim. The Polish poet, Rubinstein was his name, spoke the most beautiful Yiddish I had ever heard. His Yiddish was rich in vocabulary, inventive in its phrasing, and always eloquent and impassioned. He told me Feffer's story, which I resisted in my inadequate Yiddish. This took place in the social hall where, unknown to me, the loudspeaker had been turned on. Our quarrel had been broadcast to the entire population of the camp. I had been exposed as a fellow traveler. The authorities did not fire me, as I expected, but I became an object of suspicion and could hardly wait for the summer to end.

We had been fortified against accusations about the Soviet Union by our mentors, who, whenever the issue was raised, told us not to worry about the Soviets. They could take care of themselves: "Worry about anti-Semitism in America." It never struck me and my comrades (we were addressed as *chaverim*) that for us anti-Semitism was an abstraction, something notional, not experienced. (The first time I heard the word *chaverim* was in elementary *shuleh*. I heard it as an insult, because the Yiddish word *verim,* which I knew, meant *worms.* My parents, much amused, set me right. I was to learn, however, that Stalin and his ilk treated their comrades as if they were worms.) How were we to find something we ourselves had rarely encountered? Anti-Semitism, we were taught, was an omnipresent evil, and had to be constantly fought—everywhere but in the Soviet Union where by definition it could not exist. For us the Soviet Union was an ideal rather than a reality. We were never taught what was happening there, but what was supposed to happen, and what was supposed to happen was real.

My doubts would take on giant proportions with the purge trials that were taking place in the fifties in all the Eastern European countries in the Soviet bloc. The targets of the trials were the general secretaries of the ruling Communist Parties in Romania, Bulgaria, Hungary, Czechoslovokia, and Poland. I was particularly disturbed by the trial of Rudolph Slansky, the Jewish general secretary of the Czech party, who was accused of treason. Among the charges against him were Titoism and Zionism. Later I learned that Zionism implied loyalty to a capitalist state in the Western imperialist bloc. ("Cosmopolitanism" was another charge. In Soviet discourse, the internationalism of Marxist philosophy had been transformed into loyalty to the Soviet Union.) Zionism had been anathema to my "progressive" Yiddishist formation. I suspect that Hebrew was low on the agenda of our education in *shule*, because of its double association with the Bible (the Book of the opiate of the people) and Zionism. To my surprise, the charge of Zionism against Slansky touched, what should I call it, my national pride. My father and I were troubled by something else. Assuming that Slansky and the general secretaries of the other Eastern European parties were guilty, what possible defense could be made of a movement which breeds leaders that systematically betray it? Having reached the pinnacle of power, what could their personal motives have been? Assuming, on the other hand, that they were not guilty, what one gets is Arthur Koestler's version of events in *Darkness at Noon:* innocent defendants confessing to crimes they did not commit because they were tortured or because they remained loyal to an idea that was travestied by those in power but that they would not betray even if it meant their death. Their very innocence had been corrupted by their devotion to the cause.

As for my father's latecoming to a perception of Stalinist corruption, he was old enough to have seen through the purge trials of Bukharin, Kamenev, and Zinoviev. Why didn't he and other decent people see this travesty of justice? Some did, but for most people more than one shock to the system (I mean a person's system) is needed. Bukharin, Zinoviev, and Kamenev, after all, had confessed. Why trust the deeply mistrusted bourgeois press that said the confessions were forced? Our own ambassador to the Soviet Union, Joseph E. Davies, had been present and vouched for the genuineness of the trials. Marx once said that history repeats itself, the first time as tragedy, the second as farce. The real puzzle is how others in the movement continued to believe as farce followed farce, and horror followed horror.

Two: Higher Education

IN THE FALL of 1949 I entered Columbia College. Unlike the city colleges, which accepted students entirely on the basis of their grades and test scores, Columbia College wanted a student body of diverse social and cultural backgrounds, meaning that it placed a limit on the number of New York Jews that it admitted. Highly competitive, though not as competitive as Harvard or Yale, Columbia was the place that ambitious, bright Jewish students from New York aspired to. (Brandeis University, founded in 1948, represented an effort to provide an alternative for the bright Jewish student who failed, for one reason or another, to gain entry into an Ivy League school like Columbia.) One might say that the mind-set of elite universities up to the time when the quota system ended was a kind of reactionary "multiculturalism" based on a system of negative, as opposed to affirmative, action for minority groups. We need to be reminded from time to time in the light of present-day multiculturalism that Jews contitute a minority group.

Columbia made me feel the insufficiency of my Brooklyn culture. In retrospect I think of the university as a WASP enclave in a Jewish city, charged with the intensities of the Jewish mind but divested of its parochialisms. The faces of many of the students were familiar, so we did not have to conceal who we were. We read and discussed Homer, Dante, Spinoza (not Maimonides), Goethe, and Dostoyevsky. There

47

was the expectation that we would become different from what we were, that our education would transform us.

Unlike many of my classmates, I did not move into the city. One third of the student population were commuters. The tuition at the time was six hundred dollars for the academic year. I had a New York State scholarship, which contributed $350, so that I or my parents could have afforded the rent for a room in a dormitory or a shared apartment with other students. My parents in fact offered their support in my junior year, but I must have preferred the comforts of home and my mother's wonderful home cooking. I commuted from Brooklyn to Columbia and lived out the contrasts on a daily basis. Manhattan was New York, the cosmopolitan city. Brooklyn was the shtetl or Pale of Settlement on a macrocosmic scale. I wanted to be transformed into a person who spoke with the eloquence of my most eloquent teachers and had read and grasped the ideas of the greatest minds. On the train back to Brooklyn from Columbia, I would mouth to myself phrases that I had heard for the first time that impressed me. But I remained emotionally dependent on friends and family. I devoted my mind to Columbia, but my feelings, my manners, my clothes belonged to Brooklyn. My baggy look amused a classmate who came from one of the expensive suburbs of New York, and he wondered aloud to a mutual friend of ours: "Why does he dress the way he does?" It was like asking why I walked or talked or felt the way I walked or talked or felt. I would not break my Brooklyn connections until the age twenty-nine, when I took a job as a college teacher, married, and completed my doctoral degree. Then again, I never really broke the connection, it went underground and reemerged from time to time. To break the connection would mean unmaking the Jew in me. Did I want to unmake the Jew or remake it by casting aside its association with Stalinism? The fact is that the Brooklyn world of my youth was a safe place where my friends and I could walk the street in full possession of them. No cossacks, no gangs of alien and hostile faces.

As a commuter, I was on the periphery of the college's social life. My participation in extracurricular activities was minimal: a brief stint on the debating team and a role as an idiot in a Ring Lardner play. (Directors at various times have cast me as Snout in *A Midsummer Night's Dream*, as Eeyore in *Winnie the Pooh,* and as Troubleall in *Bartholomew Fair.* All my performances were triumphs.) I had exhausted all my extracurricular ambitions in high school, where I was editor in chief of the school newspaper, vice-leader of Arista, a contributor to the literary magazine, captain of the debate team, and salutatorian. I would have loved to be part of the college's literary life, but was intimidated by the sophistication of the poems of Richard Howard and John Hollander. Their poems represented a culture of books in which they had grown up and that I was only beginning to acquire. My own prize-winning poetry in high school had never reached beyond pastiches of Sandburg's "Chicago," a chest-thumping bravado that came to embarrass me. If I were a real poet, I would, of course, not have been intimidated. I did not have the conviction and courage of my inspiration.

One effect of my education at Columbia was that it substantially altered my way of thinking and feeling about politics. My political conversion would have doubtless occurred if I had not been at Columbia, but it did occur there and in the presence of professors with the political experience and sophistication of Lionel Trilling, Fred Dupee, and Richard Hofstadter, among others. Here were teachers with an authority to overmatch my mentors in the movement. The early 1950s was the golden age of Columbia College. Its faculty consisted of Trilling, Dupee, Hofstadter, Jacques Barzun, Richard Chase, C. Wright Mills, and many others of great distinction. In high school only Mr. Koral challenged my politics, and I experienced his presence as entirely sinister. He was my persecutor, not my teacher. The anti-Stalinism of my teachers at Columbia was persuasive—not that it was programmatic in any sense. I read selections of philosophical writing and works of literature that had nothing to do with Marxism or the struggles of the Jewish people. Until I came to Columbia, my conception of philosophy was wholly derived from a vulgar book by Howard Selsam in which every major philosopher was reduced to oversimplified Marxist categories. There were ways of thinking and talking about the world and ideas that didn't require translation into the terms of oppression and struggle in which I had grown up. I read, not for the first time, *The Communist Manifesto,* but this time in a course with the historian Richard Hofstadter, who entered the class one morning and wrote on the blackboard: "The history of all societies present and previously existing is a history of class cooperation." I raised my hand to correct him. He had written cooperation rather than conflict by mistake. But it wasn't a mistake. "Don't classes cooperate as well as engage in conflict, and isn't cooperation the normal course of events? Could you have a viable society without cooperation?" Hofstadter didn't mean to insist on class cooperation. He was trying simply to teach us that there was more than one way of seeing reality.

My "conversion" did not come easily. Old habits, as they say, die hard. In my sophomore year I was interviewed for admission to an advanced seminar in the humanities; in answer to the question "What book have you read during the past year or two that has moved you?" I said *An American Tragedy.* Theodore Dreiser, a onetime member of the Communist Party, was part of the cultural baggage I had brought with me from the "progressive" movement. The interview was conducted by three professors, but dominated by an admirer of the late Henry James. It was then the fashion to oppose James, the writer of sensibility and high intelligence, to the crude energy and bad prose of Dreiser, a fashion with which I was not yet familiar. The Columbia English department was in the vanguard of Jamesians and my interrogator was one of them. He had a round face with an impenetrable expression and deep baritone voice that suggested power. He spoke in long, intimidatingly convoluted sentences in the manner of the late James, at once suggestive and opaque. After the interview he asked me to come to his office. Without preliminaries he told me in a voice no different from the one that spoke at the interview that I was serious and intelligent, but I might never experience "the higher triumphs of the imagination." Later I was able to translate this to mean that I had to give up Dreiser and embrace James, but at the moment, only nineteen years old, I was devastated. I returned home, went into the living room, lay down on the couch, and felt as if a boulder had entered my chest and rendered me immobile. I am sure that I got up that evening and went into the kitchen to eat (my mother and father would have insisted). I must have also left the house to run errands and do whatever I had to do during the week that followed, but the only thing I remember is that I lay on my bed for a week in the grip of a humiliation that would not relax its hold. The professor, I felt, had not passed a political judgment, he had judged my intelligence. Or rather the quality of my politics was the quality of my intelligence. In retrospect, the remark by the professor seems harsh and unjust to Dreiser, its harshness compounded by the fact that it was addressed to a nineteen-year-old. In *mittleshule,* I had been accused of harboring Titoist sentiments, now I was being judged for a failure to follow high literary fashion. The issue is not whether James merits the admiration accorded to him (I did become an admirer), but rather the imperiousness with which the professor asserted his authority. As a teacher I have always tried to exert authority modestly, to allow a student to speak his thoughts without fear of being judged stupid. A teacher must pass judgment, but he must also know when to hold back, so that the student can find his own voice. Whenever possible the teacher should persuade rather than judge.

It was Lionel Trilling who had the most decisive influence on my intellectual and political development at Columbia. Before encountering him, I was already unhappy with my ideological habits and increasingly aware of the grim realities of Stalinism but unable to find any real alternative in what seemed to me the vacuous conventional politics of the fifties. I was drawn to Trilling through what I thought was a quite independent interest in and love of literature. What I found to my surprise was the possibility of a dialectic between literature and politics that was to reform my whole way of thinking. His book *The Liberal Imagination* had an enormous impact on me when I first read it. What Trilling offered was not an escape into art, but art or literature as a paradoxical political activity, subversive of ideological rigidity, responsive in its imaginative capacities to the adversary. One of the book's deep attractions was that it did not foreclose the possibility of a radical position, though Trilling himself was not a radical.

He did not argue or polemicize, let alone evangelize—a characteristic of his conversation that I found at first unsettling, for I had been brought up on long, intense, exasperated argument. He was a formidably subtle polemicist, but without the manners of one. He proceeded both in his essays and his conversation through complicity. He would invoke the common experience, qualifying every bold assertion to retain the nuance and thus strengthen the assertion. The effect was a superb style, a fusion of baroque elegance and classical lucidity. I admired the long, sinewy sentences of his written prose, its careful modulations and equivocations. Rereading his essays, as I do from time to time, I find them old-fashioned, though when I first read them they were the newest fashion to me. His prose is a silvery gray, deliberate in its manner, a far cry from the nervous energy and quickness of contemporary American prose, not given to charged metaphor or careless enthusiasm. I can understand why critics hostile to him and not susceptible to the charm of his deliberateness might find the prose and the man it reflects pompous. For me, however, it represented an unfamiliar and worthwhile way of seeing the world. And even now I find the very pace of the prose a tonic, especially in the age of the sound bite, when everyone is in a rush to express an opinion in quick time.

As a teacher, he was persuasive without a trace of stridency. When a student misunderstood a text or betrayed a lack of critical tact, Trilling was able, through the example of his own *quick* perception of the real issue, to direct the student to the heart of the matter. His teaching was authoritative, but without the coercion of charismatic display that one often finds in brilliant teachers and critics. He never tried to dazzle his students. He had an unfailing civility, yet his standards were strict, unaffected by sentimentality. What was the secret of his strength? He had to an extraordinary degree the historical sense, a remarkable capacity to perceive a work simultaneously in its own historical context and in its different life in our own time. Never simply personal and subjective, he tried to represent our shared cultural experience. The public "we," which is prominent in his criticism, registered an assured conviction about the dominant features of contemporary life. Although the questions he asked in class did not presuppose a single correct answer, it soon became evident that the discussion had a dramatic intention and was expected to move toward a revelation. In the hesitations of his speech, one sensed a man waiting upon some new truth of life and literature. This dramatic quality marks both his written work and his teaching. He had the rare capacity to move his readers as well as instruct them. I recall having tears in my eyes after reading his wonderful essay on the letters of Keats, in which he epiphanizes, so to speak, the poet's heroic quality.

If I were forced to say what the essential theme of his work was, I would say that it was the historical life of the modern self. The theme is the subject of his last major work, *Sincerity and Authenticity,* and the motive of his persistent interest in Freud. It figures prominently in his magisterial study of Arnold and is the animating concern of his novel *The Middle of the Journey.* In a late essay, Trilling identified the ideal of a humanistic education as the shaping of the self, and accounted for its demise with an elegaic precision that characterized his work in the last years of his life. His immediate target was the counterculture of the sixties, for whom the shaped self was the repressed unliberated self.

The desire to fashion, to shape, a self and a life has all but gone from a contemporary culture whose emphasis, paradoxically enough, is so much one's self. If we ask why this has come about, the answer of course involves us in a giant labor of social history. But there is one reason that can be readily isolated and which, I think, explains much. It is this: If you set yourself to shaping a self, a life, you limit yourself to that self and that life. You preclude any other kind of self available to you. You close out other options, other possibilities that might have been yours. Such limitation, once acceptable, now goes against the cultural grain—it is almost as if the fluidity of the contemporary world demands an analogous limitlessness in our personal perspective. Any doctrine, that of the family, religion, the school, that does not sustain this increasingly felt need for a multiplicity of options and instead offers an ideal of a shaped self, a formed life, has the sign on it of a retrograde and depriving authority, which, it is felt, must be resisted.

The shaping of self was Trilling's subject, even his doctrine, and he implicitly recalls in the passage quoted above the Greek idea of a humanistic education as a *paideia,* a shaping and strengthening of the self, an address, in Matthew Arnold's words, to the desire for conduct and the instinct for beauty. It was one of Trilling's characteristic gifts that he could not only give classic expression to an idea—in this case his own ideal—but could explain with incomparable incisiveness and lucidity the conditions both of its vitality and its failure. And even when he acknowledged failure, one detected in the strength and clarity of his mind a faith in the possibility of renewal.

I said all this in a eulogy I wrote for *The Chronicle of Higher Education* on the occasion of his death. It is an idealization of his life and work and their effect on me. What I failed to note, for it came to me as a later realization, was how abstract Trilling's conception of the self was. Though he apparently conceives the self as a social being situated in "the family, religion, the school," he himself lived the life of an intellectual who cultivates an idea of selfhood at the expense of the solidarities of politics, religion, and community. As an academic, he was loyal to the institution in which he taught. As a professor of English he stood aloof from its professional organization, the Modern Languages Association, which represented in his mind all that was academically conventional and mediocre in literary studies. Alain Finkielkraut is illuminating on the subject: "The most common tack to take in a society bereft of common beliefs and collective heroism is to turn inward, value the self before all else, and most importantly, to carve out an individual niche." "The shaping of the self" becomes a way of distinguishing oneself through a work of intellect and imagination.

Hannah Arendt divided pre-Nazi German Jewry into pariahs and parvenus. Judith Shklar summarizes the distinction: "The parvenu is the assimilated Jew, a universal figure of ridicule and contempt. Pariahs are outcasts who develop an intense sense of personal honor and pride in their status as aliens. They do not deign to toady to a hostile majority." I don't know how just this striking division of German Jews is. Dichotomies simplify, leave things out, but they may also cast an unexpected light on what is complicated and obscure. I hestitate to apply the distinction to American Jewry, but there is something of the pariah disposition in the mental set of the Jewish intellectual who enjoys his status as an outsider and resists a communal way of life, even (or especially) a Jewish communal way of life. The Jew as outsider is a familiar trope, but as an outsider to his own community a less familiar one. It may well serve as a description of Hannah Arendt's provocative and contentious relationship to the American Jewish community. (*Eichmann in Jerusalem* is the work of a pariah.) *Pariah* is too strong a word to describe Trilling's position. There may even have been a touch of the parvenu in the success he made of his career. But his intellect had the aspect of an outsider to the philistine pieties of the general society, those of his own profession, and those of the American Jewish community.

As a Jew, Trilling was of a type different from what I was familiar with. There was no Yiddish in his intonation, no sign of the frictions and indignations that marked my own existence. Though he belonged to the company of New York intellectuals whose Jewishness was unmistakable, he seemed removed from them in the refinement of his personal style. In a review of a book on Trilling, I characterized the effect he had on my generation of New York Jewish students at Columbia in the forties and fifties.

[He] represented the possibility of entering into a world of letters and cultivation not to be found in the boroughs of New York where we grew up. It is easy retrospectively to take the view that we were all suffering from Jewish self-hatred, but the phrase doesn't accurately encompass the range of experiences of young Jewish intellectuals whose minds were being formed in the thirties, forties and fifties. I myself don't recall ever feeling ashamed of being Jewish; I even confess to its having been on occasion a source of pride. But I sensed in the books I read, in the teachers I encountered at Columbia another kind of air in which it was possible to breathe another kind of life, richer and more ample. Aspirations of this kind risk snobbery and self-falsification, but the risk does not discredit the aspiration. A number of Jewish intellectuals who freed themselves of their origins, rediscovered in later life pleasure and value in the early lives. That

Trilling was not one of them has to do with the particularities of temperament and experience.

He was a Jew of Ashkenazi origins, but Ashkenazi by way of his English-born father. The Yiddish burden of immigration did not weigh upon him as it weighed upon East European Jews—so he was not denying a past because he never possessed it.

And yet there was a residual Jewish sentiment that appeared from time to time in his work. In an essay on Wordsworth he posited a link between the poet and the rabbinical fathers of the *Pirke Aboth*: "My knowledge of the Jewish tradition is, I fear, all too slight to permit me to hope that I can develop this new hypothesis in any enlightening way. Yet there is one Jewish work of traditional importance which I happen to know with some intimacy, and it lends a certain color of accuracy to my notion. This is the work called *Pirke Aboth,* that is, the sayings, the *sententiae* of the [rabbinical] Fathers." In that work, Trilling finds a spirit comparable to the spirit of Wordworth's "sentiment of being." Wordsworth's antiheroic characters, such as the beggar in "Resolution and Independence," are cherished simply because they are alive. Against Byronic power, charisma, and willfulness, Trilling says Wordsworth, like the rabbinical fathers, affirms passive receptiveness to the experience of being alive:

> In that silence, while he hung
> Listening, a gentle shock of mild surprise
> Has carried far into his heart the voice
> Of Mountain torrents; or the visible scene
> Would enter unawares into his mind,
> With all its solemn imagery, its rocks,
> Its woods, and that uncertain heaven, received
> Into the bosom of the steady lake.

Did Trilling need the rabbinical fathers to say what he wanted to say about Wordsworth? Doesn't Christianity provide the poet with what he needs to embrace the humble and the elemental? I suspect that however tenuous the hold of Judaism may have been on him, Trilling wanted to find in his own disappearing tradition a resonance with what Wordsworth was offering him.

Yiddishkeit had a decreasing resonance for me, which from time to time would be revived in my encounters with childhood friends, with Saul Bellow, and with the Israeli writer Aharon Appelfeld. Bellow's culture, wit, and sensibility had easy commerce with the *Yiddishkeit* of his childhood and it was uncontaminated by Stalinism. He told me how Hannah Arendt, a German Jew, once spoke of Yiddish as a jargon, and he responded, "Do you mean my mother did not speak a language?" I was recently presented with an anthology of American Yiddish poetry and was surprised to discover how few of the remarkable poems collected in it were part of our education. We were taught poems of indignation and of the pathos of victimization and suffering. I don't know how much our teachers knew of the great achievement of Yiddish poetry in America, the work of A. Leyles, Jacob Glatshteyn, Moyshe Leib Halperin, and H. Leyvik, among others, but we, their students, never learned of them. When I left the movement and wrote an article in which I contrasted the achievement of American Jewish writing in English after World War II with Yiddish writing by immigrants in the first half of the century, I wrote in confident ignorance of their imaginative achievement. Rather than regretting my Yiddish education, I now only wish it might have been richer than it was. Most of my contemporaries went to Cheder to learn prayers for their bar mitzvah, after which hardly a trace remained of what they had learned. For all its poverty and distortions, however, my Yiddish education has remained an indelible part of me.

If *Yiddishkeit* remained lodged within me, however attenuated, Stalinism was increasingly in the forefront of my consciousness. I read Whitaker Chambers's *Witness* in a course in American history and was, to my surprise, unsettled by it. I'm not sure of how to write the next sentence. Though it didn't change my politics, against all expectation I found it profoundly moving. Or though I found it profoundly moving, it didn't change my politics. I'm not sure where the emphasis should be. Chambers represented in the world from which I came the worst sort of person: a renegade and lying informer. To give credence to anything he said was the political equivalent of sin. There was, of course, no question but that he was a renegade and an informer, but was he a liar? I had read Rousseau's *Confessions* in a humanities course, and Chambers's book gave off the same impression of a powerful and anguished sincerity. But sincerity is not necessarily truth-telling. Rousseau, I learned, had invented much of his past. Chambers had been a classmate of Trilling's and a friend of Meyer Schapiro, the great art historian at Columbia. What was I to make of all this? I wanted to fight the book, but found myself helpless before it.

In my early twenties, while in graduate school, I began publishing articles and reviews. One of my first reviews was of Isaac Bashevis Singer's *Satan in Goray,* a parable about the destructive consequences of messianic belief. Singer's subject was the false messiah Sabbatai Zevi, who in the seventeenth century promised salvation to the Jews in East Europe only to bring them catastrophe. The moral of Singer's work is that you can believe in the messiah, but you should dread his coming, for "death is the messiah." The sentence concludes Singer's early novel, *The Family Moskat.* The messiah is a figure of the radical transformation of the world, and we know the price that our century has paid when messiahs have appeared. All self-declared messiahs are false messiahs, the true messiah never comes. Singer invites the reader to translate religious messianism to secular utopianism, for instance, the Soviet "experiment." Against the messianists of whatever persuasion, he poses the patient "conservative" view that the messiah, always desired and expected, will never appear, and that after all may be a good thing. I had always associated *Yiddishkeit* with revolutionary feeling and utopian expectation. I. L. Peretz's "Bontche Shveig" was an exemplary challenge to the poor, Jew and gentile, to demand and possess what rightfully was theirs. But here was another Yiddish master who had rewritten Peretz's story in "Gimpel the Fool" in which the passivity of the hero is transfigured into an imaginative acceptance of the world as it is. Gimpel's "folly" is that of the artist. Singer's work is a caution against the destructive revolutionary will, and it is bred out of a Jewish instinct for survival.

He was relatively unknown when he published *Satan in Goray*. My uncle, the ex-Trotskyist, was director of the Lecture Bureau of the Jewish Welfare Board and Singer's booking agent for lectures and readings. He arranged for me to have lunch with him in the Tip Toe Inn, a vegetarian restaurant on the Upper West Side. Singer was perfectly happy to cultivate his reviewers. He played the innocent. Did I know Mr. Malamud? (Mr. Malamud! One writer referring to another writer?) People said that there was a resemblance between his work and Malamud's. What did I think of Malamud's work? (I didn't ask why he hadn't bothered to read Malamud and satisfy his curiosity.) He was grateful for Bellow's translation of "Gimpel the Fool." Why were the Jews getting mixed up in the civil rights movement? Didn't they have trouble enough of their own? (Our conversation took place in the late fifties.) So this was the practical result of Singer's antimessianism, or was he putting me on? Singer played the faux naïf. I sensed a smart, unsentimental, and whimsical intelligence behind his *kleinshtetldik* manner. Although the remarks about the civil rights movement were unacceptable, they were strangely refreshing in what would now be heard as political incorrectness. His was a Yiddish voice antithetic to the voices of my Yiddish education. And he wrote for the *Jewish Daily Forward,* the "social fascist" rival of the *Morning Freiheit,* the Yiddish fellow-traveling Communist newspaper that my parents read. Years later I began to contribute to other enemy journals such as *Midstream, The New Leader,* and *Partisan Review*–for the longest time with a residual feeling of guilt.

As my ties to the movement were dissolving, I experienced a complicating event that was hardly unique to me. The year was 1954, a year after my graduation from Columbia, and I was still living with my parents. My mother and I were having lunch when the phone rang. My mother answered the phone. The voice at the other end asked to speak to me, and when she told the man to wait, he hung up. Several minutes later there was a knock on the door, my mother asked who it was and the response was "The FBI."

Two very WASPish, courteous, well-dressed men sat with me at the kitchen table and asked about the organizations I belonged to, the summer camp I attended, the people I knew. Though I was frightened, an instinct undisturbed by my fear told me not to give out information that they did not already know. McCarthyism had entered the family kitchen. When I mentioned a name, it was from the masthead of stationary which I knew from what they were telling me they already had in their possession. Hard as they tried to elicit information, I cooperated in telling them only what they already knew. The climax of the interview was a question about an article I wrote at the age of seventeen for a literary Yiddish magazine. (It might have been the first and the last time that my published work reached a high circle of government.) It seemed very strange when the clipped WASP voices read back to me translated phrases from the Yiddish. They were interested in one phrase in particular in which I pleaded for a "better and more beautiful world." "What did I mean?" they asked with professional sternness. I don't remember exactly how I answered. As they took notes, I must have said something like this: "a world in which people were free to speak their minds and in which they were free from poverty." The interview ended with the arrival of my father, who quickly sized up the situation and with great "social skill" (developed over the years as an insurance agent) struck up a pleasant conversation about a totally unrelated subject. When the agents left, it suddenly struck me that I might have let drop a name not on the masthead of the familiar stationery. I experienced a sickening feeling of guilt and told my father, who suggested that we immediately visit the man I had named to warn him. We did, and to my relief (though it did not completely dissolve the feeling of guilt), he told us not to worry: he was already known to the authorities. "You know," he added, "you don't have to speak to the FBI. They can't force you to say anything."

Recently, I requested and received the FBI dossier on me under the Freedom of Information Act. The agent making the report describes me as "as exceptionally nervous" during the interview and speaks of my insistence that my interests were educational and cultural, not political. I didn't betray anyone, but I was protecting myself by being "cooperative," the agent's word. What I should have said, but didn't have the presence of mind to say: I have a right to my politics, whatever they are, without being hounded by investigators. The case was closed because of "insufficient information"–about what? It was decided that I did not present a "danger to national security." The episode was chilling and, I then thought, sinister. At the time, I questioned my disillusionment with the "movement." I am revolted by recent efforts to rehabilitate McCarthyism as a genuine response, whatever its excesses, to the danger of Communism in America. A federal agency that could permit itself to assume that I might constitute a danger to national security on the evidence that they possessed and devote time and money to frighten me is either sinister or stupid– or both.

I did not serve in the Korean War, the war of my generation. My allergies, which would later blossom into asthma, kept me out. Lacking patriotism for the war, I had no qualms about not serving. The medical examination for the draft had its hilarious moments. We were lined up on a factory belt of doctors assigned to examine our various parts. In one segment of the line, conscripts were lying down one after another. It turned out that someone had fainted at the head of the line and in the spirit of obedience we all followed suit. We were rehearsing for the discipline of army life. Instructions were posted about how we were to approach a doctor, the information we were to provide and so on. I had carelessly read the instructions for the proctologist, and instead of giving him information before the exam, I turned around, bent over and spread my cheeks. The doctor, who had been staring at a form that he was to fill out, looked up expecting me to speak only to be confronted by my rear end. He became apoplectic with rage, as if I had deliberately insulted him. It was a good thing that the army rejected me. In the war, I would have probably marched in the wrong direction. My friends from the movement who served were found out and suffered the indignities of political persecution. One of them was awakened during the middle of the night and interrogated about his political activities, others were assigned permanently to the lavatories.

I am recalling my past without the benefit of notes, and there is a strong temptation to construct a shapely narrative of disillusionment, to present a moment of crisis and of decisive change. In an earlier version of this memoir, I described political changes that I had undergone that corresponded in my memory to changes that had taken place in my family. In my memory those changes had occurred earlier than the time in which I actually experienced them. I discovered this to be the case while going through my mother's papers after she had been moved to a nursing home. She is something of a magpie. Among the items saved and neatly packed away was virtually every letter I had written–from Virginia, where I studied for a year; from Paris, where I spent several years on fellowships; from Chicago, where I taught. The letters show that I held on to certain ideological pieties after I had in recollection given them up. In one letter of 1954 I reproach my father for suspecting that North Korea had started the Korean War. I cringe when I read the letter, filled as it is with the comfortable self-righteous language of fellow-traveling Stalinism. The earlier date that I gave for my "conversion" is self-serving, for it tells a story more gratifying to me. I mention this as a caution to the reader about the unreliability of memory and its bearing on other events that I describe in these pages. I'm not sure how I would defend myself if some person involved or familiar with events recounted here would challenge my version of them. Writing often takes a shape that may not always correspond to precisely what happened. The refractions of memory become part of the story.

Although college life is, or at least was, the culture of books, it is also the time for friendships, which may or may not last a lifetime. My college friendships were few and intense, and have not lasted a lifetime. My closest friend in college was Larry, a passionate character with a moon face and an owl-like look, who might have been the model for Holden Caulfield. *Catcher in the Rye,* the book of the moment, was Larry's bible. His father, who had died shortly before his arrival at Columbia, had been a prominent press agent for Hollywood stars. Larry was my first connection with glamour: third degree of separation. But authenticity, not glamour, was his shtick. He had a nose for phoniness, and my friendship with him fortified my defenses again the sophistications of some of my classmates. We had nothing but scorn for pretension, though I envied certain pretenders without ever admitting it. We cultivated our own sense of superiority.

Authenticity had been in the air ever since Jean-Paul Sartre had fabricated it as the main doctrine of existentialism. Sartre was reacting with his own pretensions against those of French academic culture. Authenticity was already in the ethos of American life, although it didn't always go by that name. Sartre got his inspiration from American writers, Hemingway and Faulkner, as well as from a French-speaking Genevan, Jean-Jacques Rousseau, and of course the inauthentic Heidegger. Authenticity came back to America packaged as a prestigious philosophical formulation. Salinger gave it its artful, half-articulate, very American form. Authenticity was feeling rather than verbal expression, though of course you needed words to express it. Larry found phoniness everywhere: in politics, speech, dress, relationships. He was a hippie before the fact, a rebel whose cause was the exposure of hypocrisy, pretension, and injustice. He suffered from a case of petit mal, a mild form of epilepsy, which would manifest itself periodically in a roll of the eyes, a signal to me that he was blanking out and that I should be silent. He would stare ahead, conscious that he was losing consciousness. I would sit with him and wait several minutes for the event to pass. He had medication to control it, but he could not eliminate entirely its symptoms.

His main contribution to my development was that he triggered a late Oedipal rebellion against my parents. I had been the good son for too long, and Larry, with his precocious sensitivity to all forms of oppression, however subtle, however apparently benign, pointed his finger at my parents. One evening when he was a guest at our table, he suddenly turned on my parents, accusing them of trying to manage my life. If I wasn't going to rebel, he would rebel for me. My parents never imagined that a terrible influence would come into my life when I entered college. After all, I had survived the influences of the street during my early adolescence and remained a good son.

Soon after my graduation from college, our friendship (David and

Jonathan in its intensity) began to fade, for reasons that I can no longer recall. I went to graduate school at the University of Virginia, Larry to law school at Columbia, where he received his degree. He then moved to California and, as I heard from a mutual friend, suffered a nervous breakdown. His days were spent in motels watching television. I wondered how he supported himself. I lost touch with him. All recollection of the reasons for our breakup faded, and I would be seized at times with feelings of guilt and a terrible sense of loss. Many years passed, and then out of the blue a letter came from Larry addressed to me and my parents, announcing that he was about to be married. He had had a hard time holding a job. He was now a social worker, anxiously hoping that he would be able to keep the job. The hope was in the happiness that he had met someone with whom he could share a life. To my parents' astonishment, he remembered them as wonderful people. It was like an acknowledgment that his rebellion had failed.

Do all rebellions fail? I suppose it depends on how you measure success or failure. Rebellions often result in wrecked lives for the rebels, but they leave something in their wake, whether for good or ill. I was never a fan of the sixties counterculture and its war against convention, hypocrisy, and injustice, not because I have an affection for hypocrisy and injustice (convention is not such a bad thing), but because I discerned in the self-righteousness of the rebels' hypocrisy and injustice as well. Larry was not a hypocrite, nor was he particularly self-righteous, but his passion for the genuine was insatiable, illusory, and ultimately self-destructive.

If my parents disapproved of Larry, they were enamored of David, whose friendship with me lasted through college into graduate school and beyond. Our education gave us a language for expressing our friendship. He called me Jean-Jacques. I was a confessor, in the Rousseau tradition, a speaker of intimacies. I wore my heart on my sleeve. He was Alyosha, after the character in *The Brothers Karamazov*. For all of us who knew him, he was the light toward which we all came to confess ourselves—not our sins, because we were all secularists to the core, but our anxieties. Alyosha assured us, but he never sought reassurance from us. He invited our confidences, but his reserve was absolute. Seated at a table in a diner or café, he would bend his giant frame toward you in an attitude of reception, smoking endless cigarettes, and invite your confidences with the most sympathetic and intelligent eyes.

It is hard to describe David's gift, the special aura he emanated. I was not alone in feeling that I was in the presence of someone extraordinary. He and his family had emigrated from Vienna in the early days of the Nazi takeover of the city, where his father had been a member of the Communist Party. A lawyer and intellectual, his father was forced to take menial jobs in order to survive and as a consequence experienced a terrible decline in spirit and health. David's most vivid memory was the visit from the Gestapo to his home; his father had escaped shortly before the arrival of the Germans and he and his mother had remained behind, expecting to follow him in a few months. The memory of the grim-faced Gestapo officers was indelible. David was the only person of my generation whom I knew who had encountered Evil, and it seemed to have given him a wisdom and compassion unavailable to his contemporaries. He was old before his time, without the slightest trace of childhood in his bearing.

We met in public spaces. I can't recall a time either during my college days or after that I ever visited him where he lived. He made no invitations, and when others uninvited knocked on his door, he would not let them in, suggesting instead that they go out to a café–as if there were something shameful behind the door or some vast disarray that he wanted no one to see. But its effect was, strangely, to enhance him in my eyes. He projected a mystery to which I would never have access, whereas I had emptied myself out to him and there was nothing more to be known.

He was the only saint I knew. After graduation, he and I briefly maintained our connection, but drifted apart as I formed other relationships and married. David married, had children, divorced, remained single, and virtually disappeared from view. I could never learn anything about him, except for the external facts of his life. I heard that he had become a teacher in a small college, a great teacher much loved by his students. One of them, whom I met at a party long after she had graduated, spoke adoringly of him. She said his great gift was to elicit something of value from the garbled expression of his students. I thought to myself: he had found a profession for his Alyosha gift. Years later, I encountered him by chance in the city. He was aging rapidly and those remarkable eyes of his had undergone a change: they seemed inward-looking, furtive and defensive—as if they were about to be put in the unaccustomed role of confessor. In a moment of rare candor, he told a mutual friend that he had grown to hate his Alyosha role. He eluded every effort I made to get in touch with him. I think he detested Jean-Jacques as much as he came to detest his role. Jean-Jacques must have been like a torrent of water engulfing Alyosha. Here was a case of giving and receiving, not mutual and reciprocal, but a division of labor: one the giver, the other the receiver. But who was the giver and who the receiver? I poured myself out so that he did not have to show himself. I cherished him for his generosity in hearing me out and worried about my selfishness in not giving him a chance, but I know now that he didn't want the chance, indeed dreaded it, because of God knows what he harbored. He must have feared the Jean-Jacques in himself.

We were more alike than different. He and I were only children. Think of all the possibilities in the phrase: children but nothing else, a rhyme for *lonely children,* a partial pun: owned by our parents. The only child more than most knows the need for friends. They are the brothers and sisters others grow up with. Without a brother or sister one has only one's parents. But what of the friendship between two only children where the need is illimitable—like two imperial powers confronting each other? For all my geniality toward the world, my acceptance of or desire to accept people for what they are (a friend speaks of me as nonjudgmental, a strange thing for a critic to be), I am, down deep, a resister, a loner, someone who believes that the best part of life is being alone, uncompromised by the temptation to ingratiate.

Dostoyevsky had once played Jean-Jacques to Turgenev. (Does it make sense to speak of Dostoyevsky playing any role other than himself?) But Turgenev was no Alyosha, and he retreated in embarrassment when Dostoyevsky confessed some horrible sin or crime he had committed (had he violated a child or simply fantasized it?). Humiliated by Turgenev's response, Dostoyevsky exclaimed that however much he thought himself despicable, he found Turgenev even more so! Only a saint can endure the friendship of a Jean-Jacques or a Dostoyevsky. But don't believe in saints, because their inner lives must be impossibly composed of the emotions of sympathy, generosity, kindness, selflessness, and forgiveness: emotions that in their greatest intensity can be sustained only at the greatest cost, if at all.

Larry and David were very different in appearance and temperament. Larry's round face was a register of changing moods, delight, anger, dejection; he shuffled when he walked as if in readiness to catch a forward pass or a high fly ball (an American male walk). I remember his sliding down an iron railing and surprising a professor (a very distinguished one) coming toward him by calling out his first name. David, by contrast, had a massively square face, benign but rarely changing in its expression. He walked and talked with a gravity beyond his years. And he was nothing but courteous in my parents' presence. Larry was quintessentially American, David European. But I was drawn to both of them, I think, for similar reasons. They represented or at least created the illusion of offering a place I could express my deepest feelings and be most myself. I'm not sure that *illusion* is the right word for it, for it disparages what I felt. It is the presumption of the "wisdom" of maturity to pass judgment on the "innocence" of youth.

I have never recovered from the pathos of lost friendships, though I know that friendship has its phases and that only a few survive them. There is the unconscious friendship of childhood play in the sandbox. At some point in childhood, the child speaks the word and refers to the playmate as a friend. But fully conscious friendship begins in adolescence. Among males, its site is usually the sports field. The unfortunate ones are those without athletic ability or inclination. They become the loners, friendless and introspective—if they have the gift, artists and scholars. Adolescent friendship is in the swagger, sometimes in sympathy with the swagger of others, sometimes in confrontation. What matters is who is taller, stronger, more agile, more skillful in hitting, throwing, passing, catching, dunking. Friends wrestle, box—mostly wrestle. D. H. Lawrence's instinct was perfect in having Gerald and Birkin wrestle in *Women in Love*. When I was fourteen or fifteen I wrestled my best friend to the floor in the hallway of our apartment house and we beat each other's head against the floor. We used to thump each other's arms to see who could hurt each other more. The freedom we had to hit each other was a mark of friendship. It was horseplay always verging on something more dangerous.

Early adolescence is friendship of the bodies, later of the emotions. Both the bodies and the emotions change, and friends grow apart as they age. I broke with my childhood friends for reasons that may be different from what I remember. I remember a quarrel with my best friend at the age of seventeen that made me feel that there was more rivalry than affection between us. (He was great with girls, I was the better student.) Another friend came to seem cardboard stiff, a habit foisted on me by my mother's friendship with his mother. The friendship with still another "best friend" eroded because of a discovery he made that our friendship excluded a host of friends of mine that he had never met and didn't know I had. He found this out at a going-away party my parents gave me before my departure to France on a Fulbright. My friend arrived and found himself among people he had never met. It was as if he had discovered me to be someone he did not know. In my behavior to others, he saw me in a light different from anything he had experienced with me. And he was deeply jealous. Months later, he wrote to tell me this, pushed, I suppose, by his therapist; the friendship never recovered.

Triangular jealousy, the bane of lovers, is also the bane of friendship. One evening three of us, all friends, went out to dinner. I drove both friends back to their respective homes. After driving one friend back, the other friend and I stood next to the car and we spoke to each other for some time. He had something to tell me: a problem in his family that troubled him. I was the sympathetic ear. We noticed that the other friend whom I had just let off stood at the window of his apartment, and though his features were not discernible in the dark, I could almost feel his jealousy for have been excluded from the intimacy of the conversation down below as something palpable. What was he thinking? Were we talking about him? Or were we displaying a connection between us in which he had no place? We had in effect disburdened ourselves of his presence. We should have been considerate enough to drive away, but my friend, fully conscious of what was occurring, smiled with a faintly sadistic delight and continued talking, and I was complicit.

What remains of adolescence are the weekly card games, the tennis dates, the golf outings, and the silliness that goes with them: making oneself the butt of comedy, giving a friend the freedom of abuse. Those who have the gift of silliness into their fiftieth or even sixtieth year (I have it) have stayed young. I'm told by people that my attitude is young, and I say, lapping up the compliment, "because I'm immature." In adulthood, we grow into the rituals of marriage, adult responsibility, professional duties. The need for the intimacy of friendship gets buried or absorbed by the spouse. The dinner parties, the collective outings with other couples are exercises in sheer gregariousness: they have little to do with friendship. Who are friends in the relationships of couples: the men, the women, the men and women? Rarely all together. Scales fall from the eyes of anyone who has lived through a divorce (I have). In the divorce, friendship becomes a matter of loyalty—at least for those going through the divorce. The friends are forced to choose. "How can you remain a friend after the way he behaved?" The discrimination of friendship means support, and those who refuse to make the discrimination are seen as traitors. But the divorce may have an effect apart from the demands made by the warring couple. It can demystify the friendship. The husband or the wife discovers how little liked he or she was by "close" friends. It was one or the other, not both, who carried the friendship. Divorce betrays the hidden failures in all the relationships of the couple.

Remarriage creates new problems: each of the spouses late in life has to plug into relationships with people he or she would not care to know by themselves. My second and present wife resisted what seemed to her any demand that she reenact the patterns of my former life with friends. Young couples have the advantage of forming new relationships together. It took me a long time to see the justice of her view. If friendship becomes an obligation like family or a necessitous passion like love, it compromises its very principle—which is the freedom to choose. We don't inherit our friends, we choose them.

We all have met people with a "talent for friendship." They turn out to be smiling Jacks or Jills who bathe in the water of geniality. For the time you're with them, you may feel singled out; they have discerned your unique charm, your intelligence, your capacity for friendship, but then their attention slides to others and if you are present you observe that others receive exactly the same response. There is no alteration in their smiles or rapt attention. The "talent for friendship" is talent without discrimination. You begin to suspect—or at least I do—that they lack the capacity for friendship. Like fish in an aquarium, they slide against other fish for the momentary pleasure of contact. Neither adolescents nor the very old have this "talent," which comes with "maturity."All politicians must have it.

I grew up as an only child in a family that had brought a sense of familial solidarity from the old country. Parents, grandparents (if they were still alive), uncles, aunts, and cousins could always be counted on. But the sense of familial solidarity doesn't thrive in the soil of America. As the children of the second generation grow up, they move away, sometimes thousands of miles, to the other end of the continent. As an academic beginning a career, I was at the mercy of the national geography. I had to move to where the job was. I have a vivid memory of the distress on the faces of my parents at the prospect of an offer from the University of California at Berkeley. My triumph would be their loss—and perhaps mine as well. To their relief I did not receive the offer. When I received an offer from the University of Chicago they consoled themselves with the fact that Chicago was less than half the distance of Berkeley from New York. When my daughter went out to California to join her future husband, I had something of the same feeling of loss that my parents experienced, but it was attenuated: I was, after all, American-born. Instead of family, we have friends, who interest us more than family, perhaps, because they have been freely chosen. We share similar interests, feel a temperamental affinity for them. But friendship lacks the blood tie, the bonds formed in the earliest time of one's life, the deep sense of obligation of family.

As I grow older, friendship becomes harder. Boredom? An acquaintance (not a friend) once told me that his pleasure in old friends has diminished. They have become so predictable to him, he to them. That is part of the explanation, but the reasons may go deeper: changes in the cells. Why do we change as we grow older, why do we become more difficult with ourselves and with each other? We become more what we are and as a consequence less available to one another. We lose our eagerness for the reciprocal modifications of friendship. There may be a partial remedy for this in cross-generational friendship. Older persons have younger friends to keep young, younger ones older to become wise. I think of my friendship with Daniel Aaron, who in his eighties grows younger as I grow older. Eternal friendship, the utopia of the classic friendship essay, is an oxymoron, for it assumes that we are cast in marble or that we change in relation to each other like the harmonies of a string quartet. In relationships people are always pulling against each other. Early friendship, formed in the street and in school, is like youthful passion: incautious, transgressive in its intimacies. Young friends confess to each other without reserve and assume that they know themselves and have understood each other perfectly. They act under the illusion that they have formed a perfect bond. It was the illusion I inhabited. I had to learn that like everything else in life, friendship lives in the pathos of contingency and uncertainty, the contingency and uncertainty of just being alive.

Three: Innocent Abroad

AS LONG AS I can remember, I wanted to be a writer. I had an expressive talent, the question was what to express. My adolescent poems were political and moral speeches, my fiction barely disguised confessions of loneliness and sexual longing. In college I began to learn the language of criticism. I would become a critic and a teacher of literature. Leslie Fiedler, ten or fifteen years my senior, provides a cynic's account of the progress of Jews of East European descent in the American academy.

> The New York academics . . . represent the latest form of status striving among descendants of East European immigrants. In the first generation, there was a simplehearted drive to found fortunes in woolens, ladies' underwear, junk—no matter; in the second, an impulse to enter the (still financially rewarding) respectability of the public professions, law and medicine; in the third, an urge to find a place in publishing and the universities, to become writers and intellectuals. In my own generation, there are notorious cases of men with no taste (much less any love) for literature becoming critics out of sheer bafflement. Never have so many natural operators and minor Machiavellians pushed so eagerly and with less reason into the academy. The old tragedy of the poet forced into manufacturing paper

bags becomes the new comedy of the proto-tycoon lecturing on the imagery of Wallace Stevens.

As a man of taste who loves literature, Fiedler exempts himself from this story. He does not mention the non-Jewish members of the academy without taste or love of literature. There is both truth and hyperbole in Fiedler's portrait of the New York academic. In my own case, I came from a family that did not seek a fortune. My father was content to make a modest living and live a decent life. He did not fill my mind with thoughts of making a fortune. The financial satisfactions of the law or medicine or business were available in the academy when I entered it, but I never sought them. A graduate fellowship came to no more than twelve hundred dollars. My first full-time job paid thirty-five hundred dollars. I recall a conversation with a friend in the late fifties, a fellow graduate student, in which we agreed we would have achieved success if by the end of our careers we would be earning twenty-five thousand dollars a year. Academic life had its pleasures, its freedom from the tyranny of the workaday clock, but it was also laborious, with little of the melodrama that Fiedler attributes to it.

As a graduate student at the University of Virginia in the early fifties, I learned to drink hard liquor, learned that gin goes with tonic, not water (unless you were an upper-class Englishman), that rocks meant ice cubes, that cocktail did not describe the plumage of a barnyard bird. I felt a palpable wariness, if not mistrust, of my presence, and did not know why until I was told by a fellow graduate student at a party as it began to develop an alcoholic haze that people here didn't "cotton to hotshots from New York." Though still quite naive, I didn't have to be told that the student was speaking code and what the code meant. My experience of a contrast between Brooklyn and Columbia was pure illusion. What marked me as an intellectual from New York was no different from what marked me as a Brooklyn Jew in the eyes of these drawling yahoos, as I saw them from the perspective of my own New York provinciality. (Years later, during a stay at a research institute in North Carolina, I met the southern wife of a southern university professor, who completely disarmed me when she said with great charm: "Don't think we are stupid because we speak slowly.") I left the party furious and sober, vowing to myself to get out of Virginia as fast as I could. I got my M.A. in one year, record time.

The department of English had fallen on hard times. Professor D. delivered his opening lecture on the Victorian period from notes on yellowed paper in which he referred to the last war, meaning the first World War. "I wrote the lecture twenty years ago and haven't changed my mind." His firm convictions were undoubtedly bolstered by twenty years of hard drinking. Professor S. in another course referred to a "triumvirate" of novels (a student reminded him that the word was *trilogy*) and to an episode in a novel in which an "orgy" took place, pronouncing the *g* as a hard consonant (the same gutsy student corrected the pronunciation). He was abashed but appealingly grateful. In a course on Chaucer, the professor, the brother of a Nobel laureate in chemistry, summarized his introductory lecture on the period in which the poet wrote with the sentence: "Those middle ages were great." Every last one of them, I muttered under my breath. The same professor, whose "reputation" had been made by a study of the definite article, would make occasional forays into the history of the English language. He told us a story about the petrified genitive. Possession in Old English was indicated by the compounding of two nouns, for example, motherland. The apostrophe had come into the language late in its history, but compound nouns had survived in modern English. The professor went round the seminar table asking for other examples. I was the last to be called and could think only of *A Midsummer Night's Dream* (an example that contained both the older and the newer forms). Wrong, the professor said, the title of the play was *A Midsummer's Night's Dream.* Anyone with half an ear would know that *Midsummer's* would ruin the music of the title. I resisted for a while and then out of embarrassment for the professor conceded to him. But he knew that I was not convinced and insisted that I go to his office, extract his Shakespeare, and look up the title of the play. He added excitement to the episode by throwing a quarter on the table as a wager. But I had already conceded. He insisted and I went to his office, proved him wrong in the presence of the class, and refused to take the quarter. He never forgave me. The academy has its share of fecklessness, stupidity, and ignorance, though rarely does it take such blatant forms. I had arrived at a bad time for a department in a great university.

The subject of my M.A. thesis was John Donne's conception of evil as expressed in his holy sonnets and sermons. Could there be a more goyish subject: the fall, original sin, grace? I never thought that what I was doing was anything unnatural. I was a Jewish scholar defining myself through the Christian tradition, an English-speaking American who happened to be Jewish in the process of becoming a scholar of English literature, one of many. Even now there seems nothing unnatural in it, though everywhere around me in the culture there are cautionary signs about how different we all are in our group identities. Beware of the "hegemonic," we are now warned. Don't allow the dominant group to define your identity. To my mind, Donne was a study in mental anguish, a doubt-ridden genius who believed in his God, but thought himself damned.

> Batter my heart, three-personed God; for you
> As yet but knock, breathe, shine, and seek to mend.
> That I may rise and stand, o'erthrow me, and bend
> Your force to break, blow, burn, and make me new.
> I like an usurped town, to another due,
> Labor to admit you, but O, to no end!
> Reason your viceroy in me, me should defend,
> But is captived, and proves weak or untrue.
> Yet dearly I love you, and would be loved fain,
> But am betrothed unto your enemy.
> Divorce me, untie and break that knot again;
> Take me to you, imprison me, for I,
> Except you enthrall me, never shall be free,
> Nor ever chaste, except you ravish me.

How different from the Jew who has the chutzpah to wonder about God's justice. Speaking of the misery of Jewish life, Sholem Aleichem has one of his characters say: "Apparently, if He wants it that way, that's the way it ought to be. Can't you see? If it should have been different, it would have been. And yet what would have been wrong to have it different?" I had enough anxiety in my life to identify myself with Donne's anxiety, but I also enjoyed the ingenuity and subtlety of his casuistry. His was a mind that tested my own. Scholarship permitted me to live in another tradition, another culture. It was a passport (a way of entry), then an identity card (a permission to stay), and finally naturalization papers (citizenship). I did not experience the process as the unmaking or the remaking of me, though doubtless I was being remade in significant ways.

When they entered the faculties of universities in large numbers, Jews took it for granted that they were laying claim to a tradition that was as much theirs as the gentiles'. There was perhaps a difference in tone in the way certain Jewish scholars and critics approached texts, less reverent and more critical. I am thinking of Leslie Fiedler, who made a career of critical chutzpah, as in his then, but no longer, notorious essay on homoeroticism in Mark Twain's novel, "Come on the Raft, Huck Honey." It is risky to make generalizations about the Jewish presence in the academy. The temptation and desire to blend in was also strong among the pioneers. A joke went the rounds about the hard-of-hearing Harry Levin, the first Jewish professor in the Harvard English department: he was deaf on one ear, the joke went, the ear that heard Levine. What is the case, however, is that Jewish scholars did not approach literature as a special-interest group. Great literature was a world literature. As secularists and universalists, they did not promote ethnic studies. That would occur decades later with blacks, Hispanics, and feminists (an idiosyncratic ethnicity) declaring their disaffection from the universal claims of literature.

Jewish scholars of my generation were on the cusp of full acceptance into the academy. In the natural and social sciences, acceptance came earlier, because qualifications for entry depended less on style and manners than it did in the humanities. A graduate student several years ahead of me applied for a position at the University of Delaware only to be rejected after an interview because his accent wasn't quite right. The letter of rejection acknowledged that he had distinguished himself in the interview (he was a remarkably gifted student), but teaching English literature was also a matter of teaching it in the right accent. My New York Jewish schoolmate gave excessive weight to his consonants and there was more than a soupçon of *k* to his pronunciation of the participial *ing*. My professor at the University of Virginia had pronounced "orgy" with a hard *g,* a case of flagrant ignorance, but *he* had a Southern accent. It was still possible in the fifties for the chairman of a search committee to admit to the discrimination. No doubt the chairman thought himself to be exercising discrimination as in the distinguishing of quality, and not bigotry. The judgment of the chairman may have been based as much on antipathy toward New York as toward Jews.

New York vs. America: how different America is in this respect from most European countries. Paris, the great city of France, is France; London, England; Rome, Italy; Berlin, Germany. New York is not America. America is elsewhere. Outside of other great cities, one finds the provinces. But there are no provinces in America. Main Street is everywhere, but not in New York, which is the capital of the Immigrant Nation, the entry place into America, but not America. In my time as a New Yorker from Brooklyn, New York was or felt like a Jewish city. Now it is at least equally black and Hispanic—and countless other ethnic groups, a heterogeneity worthy of Whitman's country. It is a city of new blood, energy, and violence, and it is a city of intellect and the arts. Hannah Arendt once remarked that coming from Berlin and Paris to New York, she experienced no culture shock. It was for her as if these great cities constituted a sui generis territory of their own.

I had experienced the difference between New York and the rest of America on a hitchhike with a friend, Ray Stollerman, across the country when I was nineteen. We had odd encounters: a beer-drinking driver; a not-so-slightly insane driver through the Mojave Desert who spoke into the gear shift as if he were communicating to other automobiles; a gay hustler who invoked the great tradition of homosexuality (Beethoven, Whitman, Leonardo, Michelangelo, and the chief of police in Pittsburgh). Then there was the hod mason and his son; as it turned out, the hod mason was an admirer of both Henry Wallace, the champion of "progressive" America, the darling of Communists and their fellow travelers, and Charles Lindbergh, American hero, American Firster, the admirer of Nazi Germany. This would be an impossible combination in New York and the Northeast, but in the Midwest, both Wallace and Lindbergh spoke to a populism we knew nothing about. On the way back from California we hitched a twenty-six-hundred-mile ride to Canton, Ohio, with two boys slightly younger than us who, we soon learned, had never encountered Jews before. While driving at night in the Black Hills of Dakota, they found out that we were Jewish. Rabbits were drawn to the headlights of the car only to be crushed, an occasional bison appeared on the side of the road. The boys from Ohio greeted the news that we were Jewish with an ominous silence and then proceeded to speak to us in an absurd accent of their own construction, which obviously was meant to be Jewish. We were in no position to get out of the car. That night, together in a motel, we had it out in a session that proved to be cathartic. They were no anti-Semites, their reaction to the news that we were Jewish was an instinctive xenophobia. We became friendly in the course of the trip. When we arrived in Canton, Ohio, we were treated for the first time in our parochial lives to sausages in a town diner. Our hosts were astonished. "You've never had sausages?" My reply: "Have you ever eaten lox?" "What's lox?" It was a meeting between innocence and innocence.

It did not strike students of literature of my generation, as it did a later generation, that the literature we were studying (Chaucer, Shakespeare, Milton, Donne, Dickens, Eliot) was a source of bigotry against us. We did not feel that our Jewish identity was threatened by Chaucer's "The Prioress's Tale" or *The Merchant of Venice* or *Oliver Twist*. As a New Yorker from Brooklyn, I never felt that my Jewish identity was under threat. For me, anti-Semitism (for all the indignation that I was taught to muster against it) was notional rather than experienced. I crossed the picket line protesting the showing of Alec Guinness's portrayal of Fagin in *Oliver Twist*, the first picket line I had ever crossed. My loyalty to art was greater than whatever tribal feeling

I had. This may be putting it too grandly. It seemed foolish to me that a showing of *Oliver Twist* in the Park Avenue Cinema would incite anti-Semitic feeling, let alone pogroms. I recently saw a production of *The Merchant of Venice* in which Shylock was played as a nasty, farcical Jew from the shtetl. I had my reservations about the production. Should a post-Holocaust representation of Shylock not take advantage of the pathos in Shylock's most famous speech? "I am a Jew. Hath not a Jew eyes? Hath not a Jew hands, organs, dimensions, senses, affections, passions? Fed with the same food, hurt with the same weapons, subject to the same diseases, healed by the same means, warmed and cooled by the same winter and summer as a Christian is? If you prick us, do we not bleed? If you tickle us, do we not laugh? If you poison us, do we not die? And if you wrong us, shall we not revenge? If we are like you in the rest, we will resemble you in that . . ." Perhaps the director resisted what he thought might be too easy a path to take. In any event, the performance did not affect my sense of my own identity, and I was unoffended by the enthusiastic applause. There was no sense of scandal.

And yet when I now glance at my old Neilson and Hill edition of Shakespeare, I wonder how we could have not protested sentences like the following from the editors' introduction to the play: "The penalty that [Shylock] renounce his religion appears to us today as wanton cruelty, but to Shakespeare's contemporaries it probably did not seem so. Critics have, indeed, suggested that they would regard it as an act of charity to admit Shylock to the benefits of sacraments. However that may be, it is impossible to accuse Shakespeare, who made of Shylock so intensely human a figure, of anti-Semitism." It is not clear how the second sentence follows from the first and what view the editors take of the Christian "charity" of the unnamed critics they cite. But "impossible to accuse?" I have no desire to accuse Shakespeare. Should we, however, excuse the Christian editors of a 1942 edition of the plays who instruct their readers in the matter of what constitutes or does not constitute anti-Semitism? Shylock, the Jew, is evil in his Jewishness. His humanity subtracts nothing from this fact.

Bardolatry as well as insensitivity to anti-Semitism explains the editorial comment.

But how can we not excuse these editors when Jewish scholars of my generation offered little in the way of protest against the anti-Semitism of the great modern writers: James, Wharton, Eliot, Pound, Lawrence, Hemingway, Wyndham Lewis (the roll of dishonor is very long)? And even now I cannot summon a sense of outrage when I encounter or reencounter anti-Semitism in the work of these and other writers. My failure to do so now may have to do with an allergy to political correctness, the habit of imposing contemporary standards of decency on works of imagination, irrespective of time and place. But then, it may also reflect a sense of the limitations of my own Jewish identity (Ashkenazi, parochial and lacking in a richer culture). Did these writers know something about the world I came from that I didn't know? Was there a trace of Jewish self-contempt in my lack of affection for nasalized, high-pitched Yiddishized English and my desire to educate whatever traces were present out of my own speech? I did not think that I was betraying my Jewish identity in educating myself as a scholar of English literature, but neither did I have a desire to assert it.

In recent years, I have come to appreciate Joyce as a rare exception among the great modern writers in his representation of the Jew. In teaching and writing about Joyce's *Ulysses* for many years, I have puzzled over the significance of Leopold Bloom as the hero of a work by an Irish modernist writer. Like me, Bloom is without religion, a completely secularized Jew of the diaspora. He and his family have gone further than I away from Judaism (his father was a convert to Christianity). If anti-Semitism had not reared its ugly head, Bloom's Jewishness might have faded into nothingness. Early in the book, he tries to ignore or propitiate the anti-Semites; he wants only to be accepted. But he is given a second chance when the anti-Semitic Citizen (Joyce's version of Homer's Cyclops) attacks him, denying him his right to citizenship in Ireland. To his surprise, he discovers his own tradition in Spinoza, Marx, Moses Mendelsohn, and the Jewish Jesus of

the Enlightenment. Willy-nilly, he becomes the protagonist of civilization, asserting universal values against chauvinism and bigotry, love
against hate, justice against violence, civilization against barbarism.
But he does so with an awkwardness that provokes the scorn of critics,
who foolishly expect self-possession and sustained eloquence from
Bloom. "But it's no use, says [Bloom]. Force, hatred, history, all that.
That's not life for men and women, insult and hatred. And everyone
knows that it is the very opposite of that that is life." Alf, a barfly, asks,
"What?" And Bloom lamely replies, "Love . . . I mean the opposite of
hatred." Have these critics ever confronted the Citizen? Do they know
what it is to have your breath taken away?

Joyce sympathizes with Jewish suffering: "Their full slow eyes
belied the words, the gestures eager and unoffending, but knew the
rancours massed about them and knew then their zeal was vain. Vain
patience to heap and hoard. Time would surely scatter all. A hoard
heaped by the roadside, plundered and passing on. Their eyes knew
the years of wandering and, patient, knew the dishonours of the flesh."
He saw in the Christian persecution of the Jew the Egyptian oppression of the Israelite, the Roman of the Greek, the English of the Irish.
In each case he must have identified himself as an Irish artist-pariah
with the Jew as pariah. Stephen Dedalus makes the right response to
Mr. Deasy, the anti-Semitic headmaster in the school in which Stephen
teaches, when he condemns the Jews for having sinned against the
light. Stephen replies: "Who has not sinned against the light?"

Sartre was criticized for his failure to honor the Jewish tradition
when he wrote that the Jew was a construction of anti-Semitism. Without it, he argued, the Jew would disappear into humanity—as if there
would be nothing positive left in the wake of the end of anti-Semitism.
Joyce seems to parallel Sartre, but he comes to another conclusion: in
the face of anti-Semitism, the Jew *is* humanity. Simone Weil criticized
the racialism of chosenness in Biblical Judaism; George Steiner concludes his novel *The Portage to San Cristobal* with a speech that he
invents for Hitler who claims to have gotten the idea of Aryan superiority from the Chosen People. But the Jews in their long historical
experience of suffering and persecution have been chosen in a quite

different sense. In the diaspora the Jew is a rebuke to xenophobic barbarism. Jewishness, not as chosenness and self-congratulation, but as the gesture outward, the embrace of the other, common ground, universalism. I would like to think that Bloom's Jewish universalism is my own. Why should Jews, the most tribal of peoples, have become universalists? Perhaps to escape the opprobrium of tribal existence and to satisfy the desire for a larger life. We should not forget, however, that the Jews are a nomadic tribe without roots. Eretz Israel was a relatively brief interlude in their history. Nomads before and nomads after, one hears in their universalism a tribal inflection; they adapt themselves everywhere and with a certain discomfort.

Unlike other oppressed peoples, who have internalized their oppressors' view of them, Jews do not have a sense of inferiority. Or whatever social or physical inferiority they may feel is compensated for by a sense of intellectual or spiritual distinction. They have the Book or, for secular Jews, a thousand books. Excluded from full participation in the life of most societies, they have been acknowledged for their gifts even by their persecutors, who granted them positions in trade and commerce. Jews have not had to be taught ethnic pride, it came to them as a birthright. Even their pariah status has been in a sense a mark of success. Could it be that the perceived superiority of Jews provoked the Nazis to reduce them to garbage, that mere persecution or killing was not enough?

I returned to Columbia University to continue graduate work toward a doctorate. Graduate school is a sort of blur in my memory. The graduate-student population at the university was large, the faculty remote. I had the advantage of having been an undergraduate there and had access to professors with whom I had already studied. But there were few opportunities for intellectual engagement in lecture courses, in which the students in attendance were passive receptacles of information that might be useful when they took their comprehensive examination. One year I attended somewhat erratically the course in the Renaissance as preparation for the exam. The subject of one of the classes was Machiavelli, and the professor read out a Machiavellian passage and asked the students who they thought the author might be. I sensed that the answer would be unexpected. If not, why would the question be asked? The answer I assumed would be a writer whose reputation was as remote as possible from the cynical Machiavellian note struck in the passage. I said, "Jefferson," the right response, to the surprise of the professor, who may have been disappointed that he himself was not the agent of surprise. I did not take the exam and returned the following year to the course in the Renaissance and to the class on Machiavelli. The professor repeated the performance, and again I said, "Jefferson." His response showed no sign that he remembered my answer the previous year. The students were ciphers, their presence in class simply an occasion for a repeat performance.

The already famous Barzun-Trilling seminar in cultural history was a welcome exception to the rather dreary course offerings in graduate school. The year I took it Barzun conducted it alone, since Trilling was on leave. It was a memorable experience. Each member of the seminar was required to present a paper, which he was made to feel represented the state of his critical intelligence and his mastery of language. We were all enlisted in the activity of criticizing one another's paper, but the suspense in the discussion was in the anticipation of Barzun's magisterial judgment, which was incisive, merciless, or generous, depending of course on the quality of the paper. The discussions tested not only your intelligence, but your character as well, your capacity to accept criticism. I was one of the fortunate ones. Barzun admired my work and became my strong supporter, and he helped make me a better critic and writer.

The comprehensive exam for the doctorate, the chance to show the faculty what had been learned during your time in graduate school, was an absurdity. In less than three hours, the candidate was required to display knowledge about four historical periods of English literature. The questions often seemed random and capricious, offering no chance to think through an issue. The questioners were cold and matter-of-fact, impatient with what you knew, but patient with your ignorance. If you did not know the answer, as your discomfort increased, the questioner would insist upon his question. "And then what happens in Book I of *The Faerie Queen*?" the professor specializing in the Renaissance asked me. "You don't remember? Are you sure you don't remember?" The examiners had little interest in your capacity for interpretation. What was tested was your ability to remember detail. Those with sangfroid and well-functioning memories for fact thrived and received marks of distinction. Often they were not heard from again in the profession.

The anxiety leading up to the exam was excruciating. There was the story of the young man who, in answer to the first question, opened his mouth and threw up, the assembled scholars around the table recoiling in horror. The exam was canceled and rescheduled for another time. The examiners uncharacteristically dealt kindly with the student the next time around. And there was the story of the middle-aged man who was greeted by an examiner with the question: "Mr. C., is it for this life or the next?" Professorial cruelty was part of the initiation in the profession. Of course, not all professors were cruel, and on occasion there was a brave show of kindness. The head of the department, Majorie Nicholson, once rebuked the selfsame specialist in the Renaissance for his high-handed way with a student: "Professor V., you have already demonstrated your scholarship, will you allow the student to demonstrate his?" It gave me little pleasure that I did well on the exam. In my own conduct as a professor, I have tried to obey the spirit of the chairman's question. The life of a graduate student is hard enough, a time of self-doubt and continuous anxiety about one's capacity and worth, that professorial kindness is the least that one can provide the student. All that the professor has to do is remember his own time as a graduate student.

In my fourth year in graduate school, I was given a reprieve and traveled to Europe for the first time, on a Fulbright scholarship to Paris. It was Barzun who urged me to apply for the scholarship and provided the necessary support. I was twenty-five years old, the year was 1956. Jet travel was not yet the fashion, so along with other Fulbrights I spent five or six days on the French ocean liner *La Liberté*.

Apart from a bout of seasickness, I experienced the crossing as pleasant and uneventful. When we arrived in Paris, the Fulbright commission put us up in the various *maisons* of the Cité Universitaire for ten days, so that we could find our bearings before looking for places to live. My first appearance in a café was a comic catastrophe: I ordered a sandwich *dommage,* instead of *fromage* (cheese), to the general hilarity of the waiter and the customers who overheard me. Did the waiter hear *dommage* (damage or pity) or *d'hommage* (homage)? I never found out. I was not prepared for French plumbing: Turkish squatters in cafés and no toilet paper in the bathrooms of the *cité.* Newspapers substituted for toilet paper, and the newspapers varied from *maison* to *maison* according to the politics of the residents. The conservative *Figaro* graced the Maison des États-Unis, where I was staying. Other houses featured the Communist *L'Humanité* or the leftist *Libération.* Wouldn't it have been more fitting if each house had the newspaper of the opposing camp, given the function it performed? Everywhere you turned in Paris, you were confronted by politics; there was no escaping it.

I found a room in the apartment of Madame Bloch in Barbes Rochechuart, a mixed neighborhood of Jews and Arabs. One afternoon I decided to visit the Louvre for the first time. I am impatient with maps and depend upon directions from pedestrians, so I stopped a small elderly man and asked in broken French for directions. He scrutinized my face and, recognizing a landsman, said with a faint smile: *"red Yiddish"* (speak Yiddish). I would have this experience again in foreign places. The old man led me on to the bus he was taking and we spoke to each other in Yiddish. When I asked him what he did, he answered with a question (a Jewish habit): *"Vos macht a Yid? A shneider."* (What does a Jew do? I'm a tailor.) It turned out that he was a concentration camp survivor. We parted before I could learn more about him. My stay with Madame Bloch lasted only a month. She was the solicitous Jewish mother who would have prevented me from experiencing student life in Paris. True to form, she was hurt and I felt guilty, but I steeled myself and moved into a small hotel in the Latin Quarter.

Nineteen-fifty-six was an eventful year. The Soviet Union sent troops into Hungary to put down a revolution against its rule. Nikita Khrushchev, the general secretary of the Soviet Communist Party, denounced Stalin in a report to a Communist Party congress. The story went the rounds that when a delegate at the congress shouted out a question about where he stood during the dark period of Stalin's rule, he responded by asking who had posed the question. When no one responded, he said, "That is where I was." My project for the Fulbright scholarship was a study of the novels of Émile Zola, but my real course of study would be the intellectual and political life of Paris, which for the year I was there revolved around the events in the Soviet Union and Hungary.

While in Paris, I performed the ritual of reading Henry Miller's *Tropic of Cancer*. Miller was obsessed with the Jewish presence in Montparnasse in the twenties:

> Borowski . . . puts on that he is a Pole, but he is not of course. He is a Jew, Borowski, and his father was a philatelist. In fact, almost all Montparnasse is Jewish, or half-Jewish, which is worse. There's Carl and Paula, and Cronstadt and Boris, and Tania and Sylvester, and Moldorf and Lucille. All except Fillmore. Henry Jordan Oswald turned out to be a Jew also. Nichols is a Jew. Even Van Norden and Cherie are Jewish. Frances Blake is a Jew, or a Jewess. Titus is a Jew. The Jews then are snowing me under. I am writing this for my friend Carl, whose father is a Jew. All this is important to understand. Of them all the loveliest Jew is Tania, and for her sake I too would become a Jew. Besides, who hates the Jews more than a Jew?

Albert Memmi speaks of Miller as philo-Semitic. Philo-Semites evidently share with anti-Semites the same obsession with Jews. I chose not to be offended. Miller was exercising his freedom of speech. Away from America he felt free to express his prejudices, just as he felt free to screw anyone he pleased. Jew, Jew, Jew, Jew, Miller can't stop saying it. It's the lechery of prejudice.

If the Jew was the center of Miller's Parisian consciousness, the

Negro (not yet a black or an African-American) was the center of mine in 1956. My year was spent mostly in the Tournon, a café across the street from the Luxembourg Gardens. Despite its unsavory recent history (the *patronne* had collaborated with the German occupiers and had her head shaven after the liberation of Paris), the café became a meeting place for Marxists and Negro artists and intellectuals. Its most famous personality was Richard Wright; the novelists Chester Himes and William Gardner Smith and the cartoonist Oliver Harrington were also regular visitors. Occasionally the conductor Dean Dixon visited from Sweden, where he directed the Stockholm symphony orchestra. And before my time, Ralph Ellison came to the café briefly and disastrously. Himes accused him of being in the pay of the CIA, a knife was drawn, and a fight broke out between them. Ellison never visited the café again. Politics, politics, politics was the main staple of conversation in the café. Conversation is not quite the right word. The talk was hard, tough, quick, and often hilarious.

There was a young, tall, and handsome Negro, whom I shall call Dean, a Marxist and mathematician, who had studied at the University of Chicago and whose deep and resonant voice had the inflection of authority. Smart, quick, and fluent, he said bold things and drove them hard so they became bolder and bolder. Insensitive to nuance, he knew how to embarrass the sensitive mind. His speech was punctuated by the laughter of self-appreciation. What he appreciated was the virility and flair of his own intelligence. There was always an urgency in his argument, and its motive was the defeat of his opponent. I had grown up in an atmosphere of acrimonious debate, but the force and bravado of debate in the café were new to me.

It also took a while for me to get used to the manners of the café regulars. One night, Hilail and I, two Jews from New York, were seated at a table with William Gardner Smith. Dean, his wife, and Oliver Harrington were seated at another table. Smith seemed vaguely annoyed with our presence. Though he was never openly rude, there was a special freedom that he enjoyed in the café, a superiority to social obligation. The café paid him court, and he felt his presence as grace to be conferred. Dean must have sensed his annoyance, and he waved

Smith over. Smith resisted for only a moment, but then got up without excusing himself and went over to Dean's table, evidently relieved. Hilail and I felt hurt, but as I learned, it wasn't an unprecedented action. The café gave you the right to be bored and to act upon it.

Over in the corner sat two Scandinavian girls, observing Dean, Smith, and Harrington with undisguised admiration. It struck me that these three constituted a kind of aristocracy. The café had inverted the American hierarchy. Black was the privileged, the more exciting, the more commanding color. And at the moment, I was conscious of what I had simply taken for granted: I was a white American. What made the American Negro so attractive to Europeans? Sympathy for the oppressed? That's hard to believe, given the history of European prejudices and given the way the French treat their Arab underclass. Perhaps it was their unthreatening exoticism. The Negroes in Paris were artists, writers, scientists by profession, the most articulate and sensitive of their race. If they could not quite lay claim to representing it (in their most conscientious moments they suffered from the knowledge that they had run away from the struggle), they could nonetheless speak powerfully for it. And they could reinforce the notorious anti-American prejudices of the Europeans, in particular those of the French. By contrast, white American expatriates seemed tedious and, of course, *colorless*. Their problems and preoccupations were private. They belonged on the analyst's couch. It was among the Negroes that one found the socially significant forms of intelligence.

I had grown up in a movement that preached equality between blacks and whites and had identified the struggles of Jews with black struggles against oppression. One of my most memorable adolescent experiences was shaking Paul Robeson's hand after a concert he had given at Madison Square Garden. The impressiveness of his figure, the radiance of his eyes and smile, the strength of his grip made me feel that I was in the presence of greatness. I had occasional hostile encounters with blacks. Boys High, which I attended between 1946 and '49, was equally divided between blacks and whites. When I entered a classroom one morning, a door swung hard into my body. "Watch what you're doin'," I exclaimed in annoyance. The black student who had opened the door walked brusquely passed me. I sat down at my desk in pain. He soon returned with a threatening look on his face: "You called me a nigger." "No, I didn't, I don't use such language." "You called me a nigger, and I'm goin' wait for you after school." I managed to avoid him when classes were out. Other minor episodes indelibly registered in my memory, but they never got translated into conscious racist sentiments. I remained a committed supporter of the liberation of Negroes in American society. Robeson trumped any racial incident I might have experienced. The effect of my politics was to repress the consciousness of any disagreeable prejudices I might have. I didn't want to be conscious of the differences between black and white, as I didn't want to be conscious of the differences between Jew and gentile—except in the positive sense. We all compose the rich diversity of humanity, my education trumpeted. The Café Tournon forced disagreeable sentiments into consciousness. An outsider, an observer, a white American, I was marginal to the life of the café. Of course, I was a Jewish white American, and I recall a conversation in which Dean half-jokingly made an exception of Jews when he spoke disparagingly of white Americans. He was willing to think of us as honorary blacks, a far cry from the black anti-Semitism that was to emerge in America in the decades that followed.

The main character in the Tournon was Richard Wright, the world-famous writer about Negro experience in America, and more recently about Africa, where he had witnessed the emergence of black power. He had also become a friend of Jean-Paul Sartre and Simone de Beauvoir. (They had offered him a coeditorship of their magazine *Les Temps Modernes*, which he had refused.) Wright had been living in Paris for many years by the time I had arrived. When he left the States his departure was lamented by liberals. He would hold forth in the café about the role he was expected to play.

You know why, do you know why, hee hee hee, they didn't want me to leave—because I bother them. *I* was their conscience. I was a gad-fly, hee hee hee. Well, the hell, I got tired of it, sick and tired of it. I just didn't see a way out. On the one hand, I didn't want some stupid jerk of a party boss telling me how to write and think. On the other hand, I couldn't stomach the job of goading the liberals on to good works and salvation. You know, this may shock you, but I don't really care about America any more. Frankly, it's a tedious subject. It's the black in Africa who excites me, because that's where the new power lies. It's not enough to be aware of misery and persecution, to raise a voice of indignation. Man, how should I put it, you want to feel in the misery the power to negate itself. And that's what I feel in Africa.

His talk had a hilarious quality that would never survive the writing down. And this was the great disappointment. For if you had read his first novel *Black Boy*–the autobiographical one–with the picture of the young writer on the jacket and kept the book in mind, you would form an image of a sensitive and intense young man who wounds easily but fights back bravely. You would expect him to be silent, attentive, speaking occasionally in eloquent and poignant golden bass tones. Wright was so different from this expectation, disappointed it so completely, that it took a while to adjust to the real man, to see the real qualities beneath the buffoon.

In a way, the cartoonist Ollie Harrington was closer to the imagined Richard Wright than Wright himself. Where Harrington was calm and self-possessed, Wright combined hilarity and indignation. Wright said he hated politics, yet he had more to do with it than anyone else in the café. (He spoke of politics as organized hate. Hilail remarked, "So you hate hate." "Hee hee hee–you got me there, you sonovabitch.") Harrington never seemed to hate, though he had a cool satiric eye about everything.

One night Wright got into an argument with a Sudanese student at the Sorbonne, a son of a tribal chief, about black nationalism. The student was elegant in dress and speech. He wore a dark suit, a starched white shirt slightly worn about the collar, and a solid black tie, exquisitely knotted. His eyes were very small, but marvelously expressive: contemptuous, cruel, ironical. His French was choice: precise and certain rather than musical. His hands continually gestured in a way that gave every turn of phrase force and verve. His name was Ahmed. Neither Ahmed nor Wright spoke each other's language well (they moved back and forth between French and English), but they managed to make themselves understood. Wright had recently published *Black Power*, a book based on his trip to Africa. In arguing with Ahmed, he stressed the ethnic-tribal character of African life against Ahmed's insistence on Stalin's analysis of "the national question." A student of long standing in Paris, Ahmed was a thoroughgoing Marxist. Wright scoffed at his Marxism. "You've been away from Africa so long, you've forgotten where you come from." Ahmed responded with equal scorn. "Tell me, how much time did you spend in Africa, three months? And you think you can explain life in Africa? My God!" A role reversal. The disillusioned American (Western) Negro asserts the special ethos of Africa and makes himself its spokesman. The Westernized African black applies to his continent the principles of a Western ideology. I knew nothing about Africa, but my sympathies were with Wright. Here was Wright respecting the traditions of Africa while the Sudanese was colonizing it with a doctrine learned abroad. Besides, there was a humanism in Wright's way of arguing, that was missing from the Sudanese's.

There were other surprises in store for me. I met in the café a writer from Haiti named Jacques Alexis, very sophisticated and very much the Francophile. He affirmed the superiority of French culture to all other cultures. French culture, he declared, was universal culture. I may have replied that French poetry did not hold a candle to English poetry. Was there the equal of Shakespeare in French literature? But what astonished me was that I was hearing this from a black writer from a former French colony. I should not have been astonished. After all, the Enlightenment had its origins in France and was the revolutionary philosophy that promised the emancipation of mankind. That the Enlightenment could be a vehicle for imperialism and oppression was another matter. Conrad's *Heart of Darkness* had not yet delivered its message. Many years later there was a small notice in the *New York Times* that Jacques Alexis, had been discovered and killed by the notorious Tonton Macoute. He had been general secretary of the underground Communist Party in Haiti.

The café was a magnet that drew me every night. It tested my political convictions. The American who thinks that he has exorcised Marxism from his soul may find himself once more performing this ritual in Paris, for he encounters black and white disaffected exiles from American capitalism, Marxist advocates of oppressed colonials, and French working-class consciousness. In the late forties and early fifties, American Communism had been inflated by McCarthyism, but it was marginal to American life. In France, of course, the Communist Party was an immense political reality. It was the major party of the working class with what seemed at the time a real chance to achieve power. What its leaders said and how the Party acted meant a great deal. A friend, a Moroccan Jewish student who supported the Party, surprised me when I asked him whether he thought that the Party could be trusted if it came to power. How different would it be from the Soviet Party? Would the democratic traditions of France make much difference? He said: "Thank God for the Communist Party . . . out of power." He meant that the party did represent the interests of the working class, for which he was grateful, but woe to France if it ever achieved power. I recall a short Jewish man from Chicago who came to the café occasionally and whose coming was always an event. He had a lame arm and a brutal view of things. He was a *dur*–a Stalin and Rakosi man (Rakosi was the Soviet-supported premier of Hungary at the time of the Hungarian revolution). One day, he arrived with a copy of the *International Herald Tribune* and "proof" that the Hungarian uprising was the work of middle-class reactionaries in the pay of the CIA. "Look," he said, pointing at a photo on page 1 of the *Tribune*, "the demonstrators are all well dressed, counterrevolutionaries, all of them."

Orwell once characterized the euphemism as the naming of things "without calling up mental pictures of them." And he offered the example of some comfortable English professor defending Russian totalitarianism: "He cannot say outright 'I believe in killing your opponents when you can get good result by doing so.' " Maybe not the English professor, but certainly this little man. He was slow of speech, but the swift of speech were no match for him. There was a ferocious confidence in his slowness. He set the pace. No action on behalf of the revolution was unjustified, its enemies had to be eliminated. Khrushchev had betrayed the revolution. Dean, whose tolerance for revolutionary justice was generous, would laugh a little guiltily when the man from Chicago spoke. He was not prepared to go that far. The man from Chicago had rid himself of all moral encumbrance; for him, "reality," historical reality, was ultimate truth. I had gone to Paris to study French literature at the Sorbonne, but my real education took place in the café. I discovered in the man from Chicago the revolutionary cruelty concealed in the sentimental rhetoric about a better world.

My conversational French improved rapidly as I was forced to argue my "reactionary" views with acquaintances on the French left. They made allowances for my good nature and what they took to be my American naïveté. I was made to feel like an innocent abroad. But I stuck to my guns. In the light of what occurred during the past century, the sophistry of the Parisians with whom I quarreled appears at best as blindness and at worst as cynicism and corruption.

The beauty of Paris was not lost on me. It is the most pleasurably walkable of cities. When Sartre visited New York, he was struck by the sharp contrasts offered to the eye as you walk across Manhattan from Eighth Avenue to First. Paris is full of surprises as you turn down from one street to the next, but they are not so much surprises of contrast as of variation. Cafés, hotels, florists, *patisseries, boulangeries, boucheries,* museums are everywhere to be found; the pleasures of Paris are dispersed throughout the heart of the city. Even the buildings that are by themselves not beautiful contribute to the gestalt of the city which has the coherence of a work of art.

I was never really a tourist, concentrating attention on the sights of the city. Before we were married, I traveled with my first wife through France on trains, scribbling away at my dissertation, hardly noticing the scenes through which we were passing. In my correspondence with parents and friends, I rarely reported back what I had seen. Of course I visited Notre Dame, Sainte-Chapelle, the Cluny Museum, Les Invalides, the Louvre and L'Orangerie. I spent many hours in the Jewish quarter of the Marais and on Île St. Louis. I was among the first to consume an ice cream soda at the recently opened drugstore on the Champs Élysées. An occasional *flaneur*, I observed the walkers and idlers on the boulevards and spent hours on the terraces of cafés, sizing up the wonderfully slender and crisp young women walking by. In New York you have the sense of a mass of people crowding the sidewalks; in Paris, despite the human density on the streets, people appear in their individuality, in their distinctiveness. If I was occasionally the *flaneur*, I was mostly turned inward, preoccupied with the themes of whatever I was writing, with the politics and debates of the moment. I regret what I missed seeing because of my incorrigible inwardness. Can I, an atheist apparently indifferent to religious taboos, blame it on "our" tribal hostility to graven images? There's a stereotype that Jews don't have a visual sense (consoling at times to me) that doesn't square with the brilliant Jewish artists of the New York School and critics like Clement Greenberg and Harold Rosenberg who have influenced and formed our understanding of modern art. Are these artists and critics exceptions to what is the case, or disproof of a stereotype?

One night—no, it was in the wee hours of the morning (the café had just closed)—an American Jewish student of the Talmud, who was spending a year in Paris, and I left together to return to our respective hotels. He suffered from a crippling disease of the nervous system, which registered both in his walk and his speech. We had been discussing some serious subject in philosophy. I was tired and could not summon the energy required to attend to his difficult impaired speech. I looked up at the dark Paris sky and pointed to the full moon. My companion paused with a laugh that was a reproach: "You, you know what it says in the *Pirke Aboth*—it says says says that he who spends the whole night studying the Bible and then lifts his eyes to observe the beauty of the dawn, better that he had never been born." (Later I consulted the *Pirke Aboth* and found that my companion had freely paraphrased the original, but was faithful to its spirit.) I think now that my companion said more than he knew. We yeshiva *bochers* (you don't need to attend a yeshiva to be one) have been under the curse of the Talmud. We don't look up at the moon or the dawn, but burrow ourselves in books and moral dilemmas. I repressed a rejoinder. If you are looking at the moon and can only think about what you have read, of the letter or essay you have to write, better that you not be born. The episode came back to me years later when I met a young academic who with his gentile wife and child was held hostage in the notorious hijacking in Entebbe. "The worst of it, you know, is what I learned about myself" he said. "While my wife was consoling our daughter and not only our daughter but other passengers as well, all I could think of was that I would never finish my book on Milton."

In the summer of 1959 I took a walk with a friend on the rue Tournon up from the Odéon toward the Luxembourg Gardens, and we found ourselves across the street from the café Tournon. I was reluctant to cross over, for a year before I had published an account of my days in the café with Richard Wright and the other Negro expatriates. I had caught Wright's hilarious manner, but, as my brief account of him in these pages shows, my sympathies were with him. I had changed the names and the article was in a relatively obscure journal, but you can't tell, I told my companion: Wright and the others might still be in place, so they might have read or heard about the article, might find something objectionable in it, it would be awkward to encounter them. My companion was incredulous and goaded me to make the crossing. "Okay, I'll cross over, walk quickly past the terrace, and look in," I said. Past the terrace and safe, I thought—then, incredibly, that voice out of the past: "So you're back." It was Richard Wright, seated on the terrace. In my determination to peer into the café, I had missed him. "Come over here," he commanded, and we went over and sat at his table. "So you did me in in an article in a Trotskyist magazine." He hadn't read the article, someone had misinformed him. "No, Dick, the article appeared in a Zionist journal, and you're the hero." He was enjoying my discomfort and laughed in that familiar hilarious way of his, as if to say I was forgiven. He probably didn't believe me, but he had been my hero in '56, a man not to be reduced to any of the roles others wished to assign him: black victim, Marxist, anti-Marxist, expatriate. He embodied an instinct in my own being for autonomy.

Brooklyn had protected me from the experience of anti-Semitism. Virginia presented a mild case, compared to the shocks I was to receive in Paris. There were two instances, one worse than the other, both humiliating. In the first instance, I was unmarried and had started up with a charming and high-strung French girl. We had been out a number of times. On the third or fourth meeting, we walked along the Left Bank of the Seine. I don't recall whether we were headed toward my place or hers. No matter. A couple walked by us on her side and she spoke the words *"Les Israelites."* Just the words, *"Les Israelites,"* and I turned and saw a look of disgust on her face. Shock, but I said nothing. We continued walking and I brooded. Should I speak, should I strike out? But we continued to walk silently. Did my unbroken silence signal to her that I was one of them? I have always looked Jewish in the eyes of others. She obviously did not see me as Jewish, perhaps because I was American and not a native or immigrant French speaker. She would not know the identifying American signs. Some time later I began a relationship with a woman somewhat older than I, who had been a cabaret singer and knew the world. When I boasted to her about my accent in French, *"Je n'ai pas un accent américain,"* she responded with glee: *"Pas de tout, tu as un accent juif New Yorkais."* The anti-Semitic woman who was my companion missed the accent completely. When we reached the apartment, I knew I had two courses. I could leave her at the door, denounce her, and walk away. Or I could take my revenge by sleeping with her and then telling her, "I am a Jew." If I slept with her, she wouldn't have to be told. The evidence would all be there. This would become a stanza in Feffer's poem beyond the reach of his imagination. I decided on the second course. In the bedroom my efforts became a struggle, which she successfully resisted. The sexual anxiety I sensed in her from the very beginning exploded to the surface. She wanted, she didn't want, she wanted, she didn't want. I did not get my revenge, I did not condemn her. I had, to my shame, left her in ignorance of who I was.

On another visit to Paris with wife and children, in the early seventies, I befriended the concierge of the house in which we lived. Only an American with his casual egalitarian notions would think of befriending a concierge. But there I was helping him move furniture in his apartment and he was helping me with I don't recall what. We became chummy and eventually achieved the intimacy of exchanging political opinions. One afternoon, a corpulent, well-dressed, mustachioed tenant of the house descended the staircase while the concierge and I were conversing in the hall. The concierge lowered his voice and whispered, *"Un Rothschild."* Its significance didn't register on me at once, because *Rothschild* has the same charge and resonance in France as *Rockefeller* in America. Later in my apartment he told me about his political experiences: how he had been a member of the Communist Party and demonstrated with the students in the sixties, but then parted ways because the students had gotten out of hand and were bent only on creating chaos. He had also left the Party, having become completely disillusioned with all politicians. *"Vous savez, il faut jeter tous les politiciens dans le Seine. La France a besoin d'un homme fort."* (You know, we should throw all the politicians in the Seine. What France needs is a strong man.) "A Hitler?" I said with an irony that would surely check him. *"Je vais vous dire quelque chose. Je n'ai jamais aimé Hitler, mais il a fait une chose qui est bien; il a brulé les juifs."* (I'll tell you something. I never liked Hitler, but he did one good thing. He gassed the Jews.) Again I found myself completely speechless and walked him to the door to get rid of him. All the indignation I had been taught came to nothing. I had not said a word, I had not struck a blow. When the shock wore off, a feeling of humiliation welled up inside of me. Where was my courage?

For days I could not rid myself of the feeling. I sought out friends and, like the ancient mariner, told them again and again of the incident. I wanted them to judge me and to forgive me. Each one of them reassured me that my failure was understandable, that probably none of them would have acted differently. I did not believe them, convinced that they wanted to relieve me of the burden of guilt. But I think now that they were probably right. Mine was the "normal" response. And the puzzle is why. Why did the fiery lieutenant, always ready to do battle over some injustice, fail utterly to act up? I was always prepared to tell someone off for bad behavior. The feeling of injustice would overwhelm the intimidation of authority so that my behavior at times had the appearance of courage. Yet here was a lowly concierge and I could not speak a word. What could he do to me? Would he strike me? I did not pride myself on physical courage. But that did not explain my failure to speak out against the girl who sneered at *"Les Israelites."* What was it in the nature of the events that froze me? Could it have been a sense of shame at identifying myself with the object of their contempt? By declaring myself, I would be saying that I was one of them. I hate to think that it was a form of escape from my identity, not conscious and premeditated, but instinctive, the form of escape that sometimes goes by the name of passing. I would have demonstrated with others against anti-Semitic incidents, whatever their origin. But here were instances in which I had been directly singled out and my soul shriveled at the prospect. I don't know that I have explained these events. But this is the closest I have come to understanding my shame. As if to compensate for my failure, the police arrived at the concierge's apartment a week later to haul him off to prison for beating his wife.

I sometimes wonder how the Orthodox Jew or the Hasid or the committed Yiddishist would have responded. Would he have spoken out with the confidence in who or what he was? Would the memory of Moses, Judah Maccabee, and Bar Kochba have inspired the right instinctive response? What makes Jews like me a hard case is that we no longer have access to these instinctive responses. We constantly reflect upon and question who we are. We are so divided in ourselves, so much objects of our own irony, that when confronted with the enemy we are without resources. And what would I do now, if incidents like the ones I have described recurred? Would I say or do the right thing? A friend of mine says he is sure, knowing me, that I would not repeat the silence. I hope not. But whatever I would do now or in the future does not alter the facts of the past and of what they say about me. If I behaved differently now, it would be because I have thought my way to a right response, not because the right response is instinctive in me, when the right response should be instinctive.

When I recovered from my feeling of shame, I began to reflect upon the fact that a man of the left (a former member of the Communist Party) was such a virulent anti-Semite. I asked my *gauchiste* (formerly Communist) friends about it. How prevalent was anti-Semitic sentiment on the left? What happens after the revolution when the exploited come to power? The defining moment of modern anti-Semitism in France was the Dreyfus case, in which the defenders of Dreyfus and his anti-Semitic persecutors divided the country between left and right. But anti-Semitism was hardly confined to the right. Was it endemic to the country as a whole? Marcel Ophuls, in his great film *The Sorrow and the Pity*, revealed how extensive the support for Petain, the collaborator with the Nazis, was during World War II. My leftist friends, mostly Jews, agreed that there was a problem to which they had no solution. Because the left has inherited the Enlightenment embrace of all humanity we tend to forget the exception that great figures of the Enlightenment like Voltaire and Marx have made of the Jews. For Marx the Jew was a bourgeois demon. There are hatreds deeper than politics, or perhaps it is more accurate to say that there is a politics of hatred deeper than the politics of left and right.

Four: Teacher in America

UNLIKE THE CURRENT crop of graduate students in the academy, my cohort of candidates for the Ph.D. did not have to acquire their degrees before beginning full-time teaching at the college level. I started out as a part-time instructor at City College in 1955, three years into my graduate study, age twenty-five. On my first day as a teacher, I rode the elevator in the building of the Bernard Baruch School of Business, tears of anxiety in my eyes. There is little to distinguish the anxiety of the new teacher from the anxiety of the serious student. I entered the classroom, went to the table at the front of the class, opened my briefcase, removed my notes, placed them on the table, sat down, looked into the faces of students, and began to speak rapidly and enthusiastically. As in a nightmare, the students appeared puzzled, as if the rush of words was completely unintelligible to them. I checked myself: "Is this English 101?" Hilarity. "No, it's Math 201." Or was it Italian? I had entered the classroom early without carefully noting the room number and started speaking eagerly before the appropriate instructor had arrived. The nightmare had turned into farce. The day of judgment was postponed. There must be a circle of hell or heaven for schlemiels. When I arrived in the room assigned to me, reeling from my debut as college instructor, I could not resist telling the class about my mistake. They laughed, it broke the ice.

Some time later I read Bernard Malamud's *A New Life,* in which the protagonist, Seymour Levin, arrives like an immigrant from New York on the West Coast (the state is Oregon) and begins his teaching career by addressing his students with an enthusiasm like mine and receives a response from the students that seems to have been infected by his enthusiasm. Smiles of pleasure and amusement are on every face. And then at the end of the class he realizes the secret of his success. His fly was open. Only a Jewish writer about a Jewish protagonist would have written this scene. When I began teaching at the University of Chicago in the early sixties, I noticed a smile of intense pleasure on the face of a young man seated in the back of the room. After class (it was his first class), he came up to me and asked whether I came from Brooklyn. He too was from Brooklyn and heard in the intonation of my voice a landsman. Homesick in Chicago, he felt at home in my presence. And I thought he had been impressed by my brilliance.

I was returning home one evening from a class that I was teaching at City College. The class had been devoted to *Hamlet.* I was not yet comfortable in my role as teacher, too dependent on the approval of the class. My enthusiasm for the subject generally carried me through the class and sometimes even infected the students. On this particular evening I had caught fire in my lecture, the sentences spontaneously formed themselves. My voice was as resonant as when I recited Yiddish poems to an adoring audience. But then I observed a smirk from what had been an inexpressive face in the corner of the room, a smirk that issued in a half-repressed sound. The smirk filtered through the pervasive restlessness of the class. Why the smirk? Did he find what I said unintelligible? Had my eloquence (I felt I was eloquent) embarrassed him? Had I taken the wrong tone? Was he, was the class expecting something more down to earth?

I was feeling vulnerable as I walked down the steps into the subway dungeon on Fourteen Street. I decided to forget about it, it wasn't worth the trouble. I started walking slowly toward the opposite end of the platform when I suddenly noticed two familiar old men—acquaintances of my father—whom I had not seen for years. It had been so long that for the moment I was hard put to remember who they were or how I felt about them. But it came to me that one of them, Cooper, was a simple and generous soul. He didn't have the same trouble remembering me, for he gave a shout of delight and surprise. I responded in a friendly way, a little embarrassed by his warmth. There was so much pleasure in his greeting and so little in mine. It wasn't simply my present disquiet about the class I had taught. The old man belonged to the past from which I had moved away, and it was as if the warmth in his greeting was an assumption that the old tie from the past still existed. He and his friend were in fact coming from a meeting of the IWO. I had been long in their minds the smart boy who would grow up and be *somebody,* a credit to the movement. I had never really shown political gifts, so the obvious "organizational" path was closed to me. But intellectual and rhetorical gifts I had in abundance. And when the old man learned I was teaching in a college "and so young," he seemed pleased and justified in his expectations.

And so I was greeted with confidences that I did not welcome—not about the organization, but about the old man's daughters. I had liked the older daughter. She was like her father: warm, open, glad, with a slight dark streak of melancholy in the gladness, simple, not beautiful, about whom one said that she was "very nice." She was married to someone admirable and deserving of her. The old man was wound up. My presence seemed to stir something in him. His friend looked on sympathetically. The old man began to talk about his younger daughter: "You remember Irene, of course." Oh, I remembered Irene, whom I had never liked as much as Emmie, but she was certainly more interesting. She was tough and self-confident. And I learned that she had done an extraordinary thing. While spending a summer in South America she had met a student who was deeply involved in the revolutionary movement of his country, fallen in love with him, and, after a brief renunciation on behalf of her family, had gone off with him, perhaps never to see her family again. I was not surprised, knowing her temper as a whiny complaining kid who was never satisfied. The older daughter had always been preferred. She was softer, more tractable than Irene, but Irene was destined to do some bold thing. The old man obviously had not yet gotten over it: "When I went to see her off, I was silent. I didn't dare talk because if I opened my mouth, I would have given out a cry. But now I'm more or less adjusted. Right after she left it was terrible." In practical matters he was very sensible. "Parents are selfish," he said. "After all, if she is going to be happy, why should I stop her? But a man is no more than a man, and you don't want to let go what has given you pleasure for so long." He smiled in his peculiarly penetrating way, confident in the truth and yet simultaneously seeking assent. It came back to me that he had alway been sententious; he spoke a wisdom learned from hardship, *Yiddishkeit,* and the movement.

I listened, half absorbed, to what the old man was saying. I was embarrassed by the silence that followed; I was sympathetic but distant from the story, and felt my expression of sympathy was weak. The old man, however, did not perceive it. He extracted a piece of paper from the inside pocket of his jacket. "Irene sent me this letter. Here, read it." Sharing neither the joy nor the sorrow of his situation, I did not want the responsibility of the confidence. But of course I could not refuse, so I read: "Dear family, I love you and miss you very much. You don't realize how much a family means until you have been away. M.'s folks are very nice to me—I live with his sister and brother-in-law. We plan to get married as soon as he gets his degree and that should be in a few weeks. If you, daddy, only knew him, you would realize how wonderful he is and you would understand why I must be with him. . . . The political situation has eased up somewhat . . ." And then the letter proceeded to read like a code. There was mention of a certain friend who was in involved in "certain activities," who had been freed after two years in prison. Of course the new government was to be mistrusted, for the political situation was very volatile. The letter was filled with "they say," "they" being those who had fought and were still fighting the good fight. There were, to be sure, some unpleasant ambiguities in the efforts of the *they*—alliances with antagonistic groups depending on the circumstances. But this she managed to gloss over "because the differences between A and B were 'artificial' and one had only to be consistent in principle, not necessarily in tactics."

I read the letter quickly and returned it with a nod. Having tucked the letter back into his pocket, the old man asked me whether I was keeping company with anyone yet. The question gave me a slight shock. Given the man's age and his paternal interest, the tactlessness could be forgiven. No, it wasn't the tactlessness. Nor was it that the question was so "bourgeois." In private and family matters, the movement and this generation in particular were not radical. There would have been more obvious reason for the annoyance I felt if the old man had suddenly asked me about my present political attitudes. And yet the question annoyed me deeply. I tried to wave it aside, but now there was a new urgency in the old man's voice. "Listen, Irene has a friend, her very best friend. She spent three days with us before Irene left for South America. She's a wonderful girl, attractive, lively, intelligent—a very good person. Why don't you meet her?"

There it was! Implied in the first question was the presumption that I still shared his commitment to the cause. He was absolute in his sense of possession. The early bond was sacred, and nothing but an act of desecration could break it. I had no taste for desecration. My mind and heart were simply elsewhere, but how to tell him? Oh, I couldn't deny the affection I still felt for him. I respected his pride in the way he had adjusted to the possibility that he would rarely or never see his younger daughter again. The pride of self-sacrifice was among the old man's chief pleasures. For a moment I experienced the thrill of sympathy. The old man's manner sprang from a tacit belief in me. What if I told him outright that the belief in me was unjustified, that I no longer believed in the old way of thinking. I doubt whether he would have understood me: why I had changed, where I was going. I found myself envying his simplicity and certainty, which seemed to justify his view of the world. There was such clarity and directness in his feelings and actions. How different things were for me. I suddenly felt lonely and guilty—as if I had betrayed the old man. I also felt grateful that my father had not been so committed to the movement and that I could accept the change that I experienced without having to cope with the old man. How terribly difficult it would be for his children to make the kind of change I made, how total their feeling of disloyalty would be.

The old man's train was coming into the station. I shook his hand and told him politely that I would take him up on the girl as soon as I had the time. The anxiety about my encounter with the old man had displaced the anxiety about my teaching. I was doomed to perpetual anxiety.

I wrote a story about this encounter and sent it to the Zionist magazine *Midstream,* then edited by the inimitable Shlomo Katz, one of the great underappreciated characters in New York literary life. Katz found the matter of the story interesting and "intricate," but not quite successful as a story. He wondered, however, whether the "two familiar old men" whom the hero of the story meets in the subway were not perhaps members of the "Olgopol Benevolent Society." They were not; rather they were members of the Jewish People's Fraternal Order of the IWO. But Katz apparently recognized in my family name a landsman from Olgopol, the town in the Ukraine from which my father came. I was soon to learn that Katz was of a poor family of scholars and that his older brother had tutored my father's brother. The exchange of letters began a lively friendship, which ended with his death.

I sent him essays and reviews, and his replies were like nothing I had ever received from other editors with whom I corresponded, indeed, like nothing I had ever received from anyone. He published virtually everything I sent him, but he never minced words about what he thought of my work. "Got your review and of course I loved it as I do everything you write. Whether I quite understand it, I am not sure. I mean, I understand it, a certain way, but am far from sure it is the way you intended it to be." And then he accused me of Cabbalism and *gimitrias.* With my parochial "progressive" education, I was not sure what he meant. I had never heard of *gimitrias.* So he gave me an example from a lecture by the critic Leslie Fiedler.

"Somewhere toward the end" Katz wrote, "he says more or less the following: In *Henderson the Rain King* Bellow on the surface writes of Eugene Henderson. But the initials, E. H. are really those of Ernest Hemingway, and Hemingway admired a certain actor—I forget his name at the moment, considering I had four whiskies and three beers—

and that actor excelled in playing the hero in Cooper's *The Last of the Mohicans*, ergo, Bellow really harks back to the American Indian as his 'archetypal hero.' But at this rate, well, the world becomes completely impossible. Every broomstick becomes a phallic symbol and every bucket of slops a female symbol. When I read Fiedler's above gem, I said to myself, okay, let's look at it this way: Leslie is really Loeb, and Loeb (Loeb and Leopold) murdered the boy Frank (get it? Frank–innocent) therefore Fiedler wrote the book named *The End of Innocence*. Or, Leslie is Loeb, and Loeb is Judah (Judah Leib–the lion is a symbol of the tribe of Judah) and the Biblical Judah was a melancholy maniac of sorts and he 'departed from his brothers' as the Good Book tells us. This accounts for the fact that Leslie-Loeb Fiedler left his intellectual brothers and departed all the way to hell and gone to Montana. *Nu*, Gene, I ask you, does this make sense?" But Katz didn't stop there: he recounted a cabalistic Yiddish Ukrainian song about a shiksa who goes to a tailor to have her dress fixed and is taken to be the prophet Elijah by the cabalist tailor because when she says "tut" he hears *tallis* and *tefillin*.

The moral was clear. Even critics should learn to call a spade a spade. But to make his point, Katz showed his own genius for Talmudic exposition, parodying and loving it. He taught me before it became fashionable in literary theory the Jewish roots of criticism. Even someone like me who had never looked into the Talmud had the Talmud inside me. Katz would then conclude with a baring of the soul: "So you see, I feel bad, because–because it's cold and dreary and raining outside, and because I just passed another crucial birthday, and because I look out of the window and I see a tremendous traffic jam, and because MacArthur died–one of my favorite generals, a real general in the classic mold–and when the *malach hamoves* starts picking off great generals, I begin to feel personally threatened, for, after all, I am a bit of a general myself, and then there is that ill-defined little pain which I can't quite locate, and you know what that could mean–a real Breakdown . . ." His was a soul always in a state of anxiety and depression. More than anyone I have ever known, he lived the comedy of Jewish suffering. Every pain had its corresponding joke, its appropriate witticism.

And he lacked discretion in his relationships with contributors. He had asked me to review Cynthia Ozick's first novel, *Trust*. Ozick was a contributor to *Midstream* and was already showing in her reviews the quality that would make her one of our most distinguished writers. But the novel was a disaster—or so I thought. Heavily influenced in its manner by the late Henry James, it proved tough going, its rewards and pleasures few. There were virtuoso passages, such as an extended erotic scene, that displayed her talent, but they were far and few between. And I said as much in my review. Like a protective father, Katz wrote back to say that he thought it would be unnecessarily hurtful to Cynthia to publish the review. As I remember, he framed it as a question: didn't I think so? He was, in other words, leaving it up to me. After all, it was her first novel, a little compassion was called for. How could I not agree? Between justice and mercy, you always choose mercy.

Several weeks passed and I received a letter from Ozick, whom I had never met. She had run into Shlomo in front of the puma cage in Central Park and asked him when the review of her book would appear. Shlomo told her a review had been submitted, it was a harsh review, and Eugene Goodheart was its author. She was writing because she had always read my pieces in *Midstream* with interest and she would like to know what I thought of her book. I exploded. Here was Katz trying to protect her from my review and without asking my permission disclosed the fact that I had "flayed her alive." I wrote immediately to him expressing bewilderment and indignation that he would be so indiscreet as to give out my name. A week or so later I received another letter from Ozick, castigating me for using her letter to force Katz to publish a review he did not wish to publish. Katz evidently had chastised her for her indiscretion. Now she became the object of my anger. Did she know that Shlomo and I were old friends and that I had agreed that the review not be published? Who was she to write to me in the manner in which she had written, etc., etc.? A third letter, crumpled and stained, arrived from her shortly afterward. She apologized for the condition of the letter. Her daughter had dipped it into sour cream and she didn't have the time to retype it. Her father had always cautioned her about her haste in drawing conclusions. Shlomo had confirmed my version of events, so she was writing to apologize for her precipitous behavior. She thought it would be nice if sometime we could meet and we could have a friendly talk. I accepted the apology and decided to publish the review elsewhere.

I met Cynthia for the first time more than twenty years later, at the fiftieth-anniversary celebration of *Partisan Review*. She was already famous and comfortable in her fame. My review had appeared years ago and was reprinted as the only negative review of a work by her in Harold Bloom's volume on her in the Chelsea series on writers. As it turned out, she had read the review only several weeks before our meeting (more than twenty years after its first publication!) and she regarded the whole episode with amusement. We were characters in a story created by Shlomo Katz.

Katz was a modern Job with a chronic grievance against life itself. On the door of his office he tacked a dartboard, which represented life. Woe to anyone who opened that door without warning. In his reviews of books, he would indulge a bilious whimsy, sometimes under the pseudonym Shunra, the Hebrew word for cat and a half pun on the word for black tooth: he had darkly stained and malformed teeth. The novelist Wallace Markfield, a friend with whom he had a falling-out, had published a novel based on the short life of the gifted writer Isaac Rosenfeld. The title of the novel was *To an Early Grave*. The letter accompanying the review copy sent to Katz read: "Wallace Markfield sends you *To an Early Grave* with his compliments." It was an irresistible opportunity. Katz's review began: "What have I done to Markfield that he should want to send me to an early grave?" And the rest of the review was a complaint about the course of their friendship. What he did not say in the review was that Markfield had once offered to buy a story that Katz had written for its idea (the takeover of New York by gangster adolescents), because although the idea was brilliant, Markfield thought Katz's execution inadequate. Katz had been deeply offended. Markfield appreciated his imaginative gift, but perceived what was the case: that Katz did not possess the discipline of an artist. He was always anxious and depressed, always overwhelmed with emotion and without the patience for developing his ideas.

Anxiety is a universal emotion to which Jews are particularly disposed, Albert Memmi tells us. I am not a virtuoso of the emotion like Katz, but I have had an abundance of it all my life, in particular performance anxiety. Was it masochism that drove me to perform in my adolescence and to teach and lecture in adulthood? I jump ahead a decade. If my teaching debut was farce, my greatest academic triumph was a disaster. At the age of forty-two, I had been invited by the poet Theodore Weiss, a former colleague of mine at Bard College who had become a member of the Princeton faculty, to deliver the prestigious Christian Gauss lectures at Princeton. He saw a promise in me that the rest of the world had not yet seen. I was a last-minute substitute for a distinguished sociologist who had suddenly taken ill. Imagine my exhiliration, my apprehension. Minutes after receiving the call, I sat down to prepare the lectures. I read and wrote and read and wrote for several weeks and remember very little else about the time. Everything apart from preparation was on hold. Which meant that wife and children were consigned to the periphery of existence, something that my wife would remember as typical of me when she took her revenge. I remember a dinner party I contrived for the purpose of submitting my guests to a trial run of the first lecture. My poor friends had to listen for their supper.

The first lecture went fairly well. However, there was present a scholar of my topic: Marx and utopianism. During the question period, he rose, hand in pocket, to deliver a counterlecture, the point of which was that I had misleadingly conflated two distinct periods in Marx's career. He may well have been right (I am not a scholar of Marx and Marxism): my talk was a distillation of my reading of Marx and the animus born out of my experience of the Marxist dream of social transformation. The scholarship of the scholar had little to do with the gist of my argument It was one of those typical displays of "learning" that gives the academy a bad name. The point is not to illuminate a subject or to solve a real problem. There is in fact no point—except to show off the erudition of the speaker.

The first lecture was only the prelude to the disaster which took place a week later. I drove down to Princeton with a friend of mine, who accompanied me to Weiss's home, where I would spend the night. The topic of the second lecture was the politics of the imagination, with a special emphasis on surrealism. We chatted over drinks for about an hour. A dinner at the faculty club would precede the lecture. During the hour at the home of my friend, I got up once or twice from my chair to go to the hall near the entrance where I had left my briefcase. I extracted my lecture, reread several passages and made last-minute revisions. The dinner went so pleasantly that I virtually forgot my anxiety.

I arrived at the lecture hall in a mild alcoholic haze and sat down at the table, waiting to be introduced. The introduction was short, since I had already spoken the week before. I got up, opened my briefcase, and was shocked into complete sobriety: the lecture was missing. The discovery took place in the presence of the audience, so there was no concealing it. If one can imagine silence on a graph that represents it as zero, the silence of the audience was a minus quantity. Where had it gone? I looked out into the audience, searching for my host. I found him, and we drove back to his house and searched everywhere. No lecture. I drove back to the hall; the audience had remained in what seemed to me the same state of appalled silence. It was as if they had been frozen and suspended in time, waiting for someone—me, I suppose—to release them. The chairman of the occasion looked at me with compassion: "What do you want to do? Perhaps you want some time to jot down an outline from which you can speak." I began to jot down phrases. Then I spoke. The friend who had accompanied me from Boston told me later that I had spoken well, but I knew my mind was elsewhere, incredulously wondering where I had put the lecture. I broke off after ten minutes and said that I could not continue. Then the friend who had accompanied me spoke from the audience: "Your lecture will arrive in ten minutes." He got up, walked out of the hall, and returned in less than ten minutes with the lecture in hand. The solution to the mystery: when we had arrived at the home of the host, my friend and I had both placed our briefcases, virtual replicas of each other, in the darkened hallway. I had removed the lecture to revise it and had returned it to *his* briefcase, not mine. During my ordeal at the lecture hall, the solution had suddenly come to my friend.

I gave the lecture, which was followed by a question and discussion period that was animated and interesting, though half the audience had already disappeared. Someone told me afterward that he was convinced I had staged the event, since the subject was surrealism. (Nabakov has an episode in *Pnin* in which a character about to give a lecture reaches into the inside pocket of his jacket only to find someone else's lecture, which he then proceeds to deliver. I had not read *Pnin,* so I claim originality for my performance. Moreover, I think my reality easily surpasses Nabakov's imagination in *Pnin* for inventiveness.) I speak lightly and ironically of the event now because of the passage of time. The fact is that it triggered a year of nightmares. The event itself was a nightmare that for most people is never actualized. At times, I even wonder whether I did not dream it.

There is in the event a rebuke to the anxiety that led me to remove the lecture from my briefcase and make those last-minute revisions. I wanted to protect myself against the risks of exposing myself to an audience, to reduce the chances of vulnerability and failure. Nemesis punished my presumption by making me careless. Too much care leads to carelessness.

Joyce's story "The Dead" has always been one of my favorite stories. I first read it as a senior in college and was moved to tears by its ending. With Gabriel Conroy, the story's protagonist, I felt shattered by his wife Gretta's revelation of her love affair with Michael Furey. It took some growing up for me to realize that the real story was about a sensitive young man's insecurities (in my senior year he seemed pretty old to me). I have come to identify with Gabriel's presence at the annual family Christmas party and especially with his apprehensiveness before he has to deliver his speech. He has done it countless times before, but for him it is always the first time. Joyce is superb with the detail of anxiety: the longing gaze out the window at the Wellington monument, fringed with snow, as if the gaze itself were an escape, the fidgeting with the utensils and the tablecloth before the speech. The party swirls about him, but he is anxiously inside his head enjoying none of its pleasures. And then the speech, a tissue of clichés meant to ingratiate an audience easier to satisfy than he in his anxiety imagines. It all amounts to a scene in one of the circles of hell, though I won't exaggerate and say one of the lower circles. One of the memorable things Fred Dupee, my professor at Columbia, said was that it was a story about every sensitive professor who lacks confidence in himself.

In 1958, when I began teaching full time, there were jobs aplenty, though to be sure at low salaries. My first full-time teaching position was in a small "progressive" college in upstate New York, Bard College. I was appointed at the age of twenty-seven, before I had even passed my preliminary examination for the doctorate. The dissertation would eventually be written during the summers and the winter field periods of the four years that I spent at Bard. I was interviewed for the position and hired because the chairman of the department had read my article on Richard Wright. A writer himself, he liked the energy of the piece–a writer's judgment, not that of an academic. Bard was a remarkable institution, almost an anomaly in the system of American universities and colleges at the time. Sarah Lawrence and Bennington were comparable, but since they were women's colleges, they lacked (except for the liasons between male faculty and students) the erotic excitement of Bard. The writers who taught at Bard–Saul Bellow, Mary McCarthy, Ralph Ellison, Theodore Weiss, William Humphrey, Dorothy Van Ghent, among others–reflected by contrast the poverty of imagination of other university and college administrators at the time, most of whom would never consider hiring them because they lacked Ph.D's.

In the fifties Bard was already the sixties. The students had the hippie look that in a decade would be widespread: strategically torn jeans, T-shirts, unkempt hair. They strode the walks with the confidence of ownership. Bellow, who taught at Bard several years before my arrival, told me of a time shortly after he had published *The Adven-*

tures of Augie March and had won the National Book Award when a student notorious for his chutzpah approached with the "admiring" remark: "So Saul, I see that you're hot shit." As Bellow said to me, "So this was my student's acknowledgment of my having arrived. I had enough and quit."

Before it became widespread practice, Bard students formally evaluated their teachers. On the last day of the course, there was a knock on the door. A representative of the student committee would enter the room with a packet of evaluation forms and the instructor understood that he had to leave the class. I had been hired the same year as Ralph Ellison. Ellison evidently did not know the custom and when the student appeared at his door, he refused him entrance. "You evaluate the course and I resign." The students gave way to Ellison, already the author of *Invisible Man,* but not before a meeting with the student committee in which the students tried to explain themselves. I was not alone on the faculty in the sentiment that the students had no business evaluating us. A new hire beginning his career, who was I not to go along? I couldn't afford Ellison's defiance. And I have continued to hold until now, at the virtual end of my teaching career, a conviction weakened by the habit of aquiescence that student evaluations are something of a presumption. And yet I suspect there was a connection between the openness of Bard to academically uncredentialed talents of poets and novelists and the freewheeling behavior of the students. The whole institution was a question mark about entitlement.

How different from my Columbia education. At Columbia we knew how to keep a distance from our our professors. Part of our education was a four-year course in manners. To learn how to talk and write about books is like learning how to use a knife and fork at the dinner table. I was often nervous in the presence of professors, fearful that I would not speak well, that I would say the wrong thing, that I would give my anxiety away. To be a student was to be on trial, and the matter to be adjudicated your intelligence and industry. There was no final judgment, no closure to the process. Every grade was a provisional verdict, acquittal came with graduation. But even then, if you remained in school as an academic, the trial became a condition of your working life. Academics, I'm convinced, are perpetual adolescents, because they have never left school.

Going to Bard after the experience of the neo-Victorian decorum of Columbia was something of culture shock. Relations between teacher and students were free and easy, though not so easy for me, unprepared as I was for it, vulnerable in my youth, being less than a decade apart from my students in age. I had to show my faculty identification card to the librarian on my first visit to the college library to demonstrate that I was not a student. The main outcome of my vulnerability was marriage to a student, my first marriage.

At Bard I became friends with Saul Bellow, who lived nearby in a house that is part of the setting of *Herzog,* which he was writing during my time at the college. He would visit my wife and me from time to time to read from it with the pleasure and amusement of discovery, as if surprised by what he had put on paper. Then in his forties, he was a handsome man with a head that tilted slightly in a quizzical manner, a broad smile, and an infectious laugh. He told me that after his first novel, *The Dangling Man,* had been published, a Hollywood agent, seeing his photo on the book jacket, approached and asked him not whether he would be interested in having the novel turned into a film, but whether he had ever thought of a movie career for himself. Bellow's conversation had the wit and felicity of his written prose, but he was not voluble. He spoke only when he had something to say and listened with amused eyes as if expecting pleasure in someone else's conversation. He listened—not a common gift among intellectuals, writers, and academics. It took me a while to be at ease with him, partly because of his reputation, but also because I felt that in his attentiveness to what was said there was an expectation that I speak well and interestingly. He told and loved to hear jokes, and Yiddish expressions came easily to him.

He is now in his eighties. After years of not having seen each other, we find ourselves in the same city and have lunch together from time to time. His command of Yiddish still impresses me. There isn't a Yiddish expression I recall that he doesn't know, and then he trumps me with an expression I never heard before. I have always felt with him that I was in the presence of someone remarkable. And he has a most remarkable achievement to his credit: he brought modern Jewish literature into the mainstream of American and world literature. *The Adventures of Augie March,* published in 1953, began what came to be known as "the breakthrough." "I am American, Chicago born," Augie declares at the opening of the novel. No mention of being a Jew—and yet the idiom and tone of the novel are inflected with Jewishness. Katherine Anne Porter recognized this when she complained that Bellow had corrupted the language. In reviewing an anthology of American Jewish writing, I tried to characterize Bellow's achievement in *Augie March.* A chapter on one of Bellow's favorite characters, Einhorn, begins with an attempt to link him with the great men of the past. Tongue in cheek, but not frivolously, the narrator asks: "What would Caesar suffer in this case? What would Machiavelli advise or Ulysses do? What would Einhorn think?" And after exploring Einhorn's thoughts and feelings, he confesses his insufficiency in presenting his hero: "But when you believed you had tracked Einhorn through his acts and doings and were about to capture him, you found yourself not in the center of the labyrinth but on a wide boulevard." There are of course no boulevards in the shtetl. This was Bellow's achievement: to take the Jew off the side streets and put him on the boulevard of the imagination. To achieve this, the Jewish writer had to pass through the immigrant stage, to overcome his hysteria and hunger and fear of the new country and his blindness in it. But he also had to bring the culture of his immigrant father and mother along with him in some way. He had to write without embarrassment about who he was. And of course he had to have the genius to do it.

How different Bellow was in the grace and knowledge with which he accepted his Jewishness from Trilling, with whom he had never gotten along, perhaps because of this very difference. Trilling had an aversion to Jewish schmaltz and in particular, the schmaltziest of his fellow New York intellectuals, Alfred Kazin. He thought the protagonist of *A Walker in the City* was a shmoe. Bellow was not schmaltzy, but he was Jewish without embarrassment. I suspect that Trilling found *Yiddishkeit* (which Bellow enjoyed) something of an embarrassment. In the rare times when Jewishness entered Trilling's writings, as in his essay on Wordworth and the rabbis, it was the Jewishness of the Hebrew tradition, of which he had scant knowledge, but which had a dignity lacking in Yiddish. In Wordsworth he found affinities with the *Pirke Aboth*. When a close friend of mine, also a student of his, married a gentile, Trilling congratulated him on marrying outside his faith. The Jewish tradition benefited from being interwoven with another tradition. Or did he mean that it would benefit from being dissolved into something else? He once told me that he had misgivings about filling the faculty of Columbia's department of English with too many New York Jews, because they would only reinforce the neuroticism of its Jewish students. I should have protested, but I did not. I have never taken sides between them, but my friendship with Bellow made me see the price Trilling paid for his Jamesian sophistication.

The atmosphere of the literature division at Bard was literary, not academically professional as it was in most places. The college was also a station for intellectuals of distinction to come and lecture to a responsive audience. I recall in particular Erich Heller's splendid lecture on Nietzsche in which he became a transparent medium for all that was wonderful and alive in Nietzsche's thought. Heller received the kind of standing ovation that follows a virtuoso performance in a concert hall. And then there were the several visits of Hannah Arendt, whose husband, Heinrich Bleucher, taught at Bard. The most memorable talk was about the Hungarian Revolution of '56. She was an evangelist of the message of the revolution, for its spontaneous expression of the will of the people. As a fierce critic of totalitarianism (both its Nazi and Bolshevik varieties), she was careful to distinguish kinds of Revolution. Like the American revolution, the Hungarian in her view was a harbinger of democracy. If it had succeeded, which it did not, it would have avoided the fate of the French and Russian revolutions and their reigns of terror. I asked a question after the lecture that aroused her interest, so I was introduced to her. I would see her occasionally over the years. She was of course a controversial figure. Her book *Eichmann in Jerusalem* had created a firestorm. Even her friends (not all friends) in the *Partisan Review* circle were divided about the merits and morality of the book. After her death, the revelation of her involvement with the philosopher and Nazi collaborator Martin Heidegger, her teacher and lover, created another firestorm. What is not very well known is the genuine interest that she took in the intellectual and personal development of young people. Childless and maternal, she was a nurturer in her teaching and in the advice she gave. The last time I saw her, I was going through my divorce. She had asked me to meet her at her dentist's office, and we rode in a cab together to her apartment. In her apartment, she asked with compassion the philosophical question, *"Muss es sein?"* (Must it be?)

Bard was a way station for me on to bigger and better things—or so I thought at the time. To leave Bard for another job in a college or university, I had to complete my dissertation on D. H. Lawrence. I came to Lawrence through my interest in Thomas Hardy. In writing an essay on Hardy for the Barzun seminar, I came across Lawrence's remarkable essay on him (and everything else that came into Lawrence's mind by association), in which he identified what I loved the most in Hardy and had not yet found the words to identify, his explosive suddennesses:

> It is urged against Thomas Hardy's characters that they do unreasonable things—quite, quite unreasonable things. . . . This is quite true, and the charge is amusing. These people of Wessex are always bursting suddenly out of bud and taking wild flight into flower, always shooting out of a tight convention, a tight, hidebound cabbage state into something quite madly personal. . . . [They] explode out of the convention. They are people each with a real, vital, potential self, even the apparently wishy-washy heroines of the earlier books, and this self suddenly bursts the shell of manner and convention and commonplace opinion, and acts independently, absurdly, without self-knowledge or acquiescence.

Of course, this explosiveness was everywhere in Lawrence's own work; what I found in Hardy was even more powerfully present in Lawrence, and so he became my subject. I did not think of myself in the hidebound cabbage state of convention, but my inner life was filled with an anxious sense of obligation to parents and career. Lawrence's passion (sexual, creative, even religious) was an irresistible subject. Like other readers, I marveled at his sexual imagination (it was out of reach of my own anxious sexuality), and didn't know what to make of it. It was hard to figure out the positions of the bodies in the passion making (*love* was a word that had given out for Lawrence). The bodies of his characters seemed to exist in an indeterminate space. Much later, in thinking and teaching and writing about Lawrence, I saw that Lawrence's sexual mysticism was the product of an anxious torment of his own. Lawrence astonished, and there were things that you could learn from him about the inviolability of the person, the seriousness of relationships, but there were also things to be resisted and avoided: such as his anarchic strain, his ambivalent fascination with fascism, and his anti-Semitism, to which I paid little attention at the time I wrote my dissertation. Though I did not become a Lawrentian, I wrote about him with admiration and skepticism. The rational and skeptical part of my intelligence sensed excess and danger in all that explosiveness. Good for the imagination, but risky for life. The dissertation became a book, one of a number written against the prevailing orthodoxy of the time (as expressed by F. R. Leavis) that Lawrence's intelligence and vitality were all that was needed for the good life. I had written several drafts of the dissertation before Trilling found it acceptable and even admirable. The University of Chicago Press would publish it. I could now move on from Bard. In 1962 Bellow joined the faculty of the University of Chicago. He and Trilling mentioned my name to someone in the department of English at the university; I was interviewed for a job on the faculty, received an offer, and accepted it.

When my wife and I arrived in Chicago, we were taken up by Norman Maclean and his wife while we looked for an apartment. Their generosity extended beyond the accommodations they provided us in their very large apartment to the large amounts of bourbon we all consumed in the late afternoon. For weeks I lived in an alcoholic haze that loosened my tongue and made me giddy. I had begun to learn how to drink at the University of Virginia, but had never achieved the level of consumption that I achieved at the Macleans'. At Bard I was still very much the novice. One evening at the home of Gore Vidal (he had invited the literature faculty back to his mansion on the banks of the Hudson River for drinks after he had delivered a lecture), I asked for gin. "Gin and . . . ?" Vidal waited for me to complete my request. "And water," I said, only because he expected me to say something. Vidal looked at me as if he couldn't decide whether I was innocent or terribly sophisticated.

Maclean, a professor of English at the University of Chicago, had a great reputation as a teacher but had published very little. In retirement, years later, he would become famous for a short novel, *A River Runs Through It,* a work that remembered his youth in Montana, his family, the tragic death of his brother, and the almost religious art of fly-fishing. He was a laconic man, a character out of a Hemingway story, in whose pregnant silences one suspected disappointments that would never be spoken. He derived a certain pleasure from reminding me that I was from the urban East: "Goodheart, have you ever seen a cow?" Was this another way of telling me that I was "a hotshot from New York"? Chicago was not the West, but neither was it New York, and I never got over the feeling that I was a displaced person. Maclean made me feel like a New York provincial. He was one of many professors who had fallen under the spell of the neo-Aristotelian literary scholar R. S. Crane and the philosopher Richard McKeon, whom an unfriendly colleague had wittily characterized as the greatest man in the world within a radius of twenty blocks. The role of discipleship didn't fit Maclean. In retirement he became his own man.

The social ethos of Bard contrasted with that of Columbia. Columbia was neo-Victorian in its manners, hippie Bard had no manners. But intellectually Bard was a suburb of Columbia. Sixty or seventy miles from New York, Bard faculty, a number of them Columbia Ph.D.'s and moonlighting or ex-instructors at the university, commuted back and forth from Bard to Manhattan on weekends. Like Columbia, the University of Chicago was one of the great universities of the world, but how different my intellectual experience of it. Though the university was dedicated to the great ideas and great books of Western civilization, it seemed to have little to do with the politics and culture that were inextricably entwined with my education at Columbia. In his brilliant send-up of American advertising culture, *The Mechanical Bride* (1951), Marshall McLuhan features a photograph of Mortimer Adler, one of the gurus of the great ideas program at the University of Chicago, and his associates, framing a display of great ideas on cards alphabetically arranged ("angel," "animal," "aristocracy," "art" all the way to "war," "wealth," and "will": x, y, and z apparently don't qualify for greatness) as if they were tombstones in a cemetery of ideas.

In joining the faculty of the University of Chicago in the early sixties, I entered a world strangely reminiscent of the world of my adolescence. For several decades, a philosophical and literary theory, neo-Aristotelianism, was the guiding philosophy of the university. Its leading lights were Robert Hutchins, the president of the university, McKeon and R. S. Crane. Like the medieval scholastics before them, they took Aristotle–"the master of those who know," in Dante's memorable phrase–and gave their doctrine a democratic inflection by honoring a pluralism of ideas and literary forms. In theory pluralistic, but in spirit authoritarian. When I arrived the Aristotelians had lost some of their cachet, but their presence was still very strong, particularly in the undergraduate college. They ran the college, and although they called themselves pluralists, they acted more like absolutists. The core courses, the heart of an undergraduate education, were supervised at a staff meeting in which untenured instructors and assistant professors were required to take the objective tests that they would then give their students. Oedipus left Corinth because *a, b, c,* or *d.* Interpretive cruxes about which one could disagree were turned into objective questions in which there were correct and incorrect answers. The veterans of the course, trained in the neo-Aristotelian method, decided whether the answers were right or wrong.

When I protested that it was not clear whether the answer was *a* or *b,* or that another answer was possible (it was, after all, a matter of interpretation), I was rebuked for having failed to master the text. I exploded in a rage: "What is this, a Communist cell?" A younger member of the faculty, whose tenure had been longer than mine, cautioned me about the dangers of further outbursts. He told me that the professor who had rebuked me had once been a member of the Communist Party. He had obviously transferred the habit of groupthink from Marxism to Aristotelianism. Even in the classroom I was aware of a party line. In the first graduate course I taught, a student challenged me for having violated a critical taboo, according to the course in literary method, which every graduate student was obliged to take. I replied by confessing that, having been educated elsewhere, I had never taken the course, and that perhaps unfortunately for the class, the students would have to endure my ignorance. I detected a certain pleasure the students took in my reply. My classroom was the place where they could say the unsayable. The university was more serious about educating its students than any university in the country. They received an extraordinary education simply by virtue of the many great books they were required to read. And they were very bright and serious. (My most memorable student was Leon Botstein, the current president of Bard College and a man of many talents.) Many years later my own son would attend the university with my support. But for me, at the time, the Aristotelian party line was oppressive. I couldn't escape the feeling that there was something provincial and midwestern about Chicago and its great university: a case of New York snobbery perhaps.

The university had its share of extracurricular excitements for me. I attended a meeting of the Hillel Foundation in which distinguished members of the faculty who had survived the Nazi death camps spoke of their experiences. (To its credit, the university was hospitable to the some of the most distinguished European scholars, in most instances refugees from Nazism, among them Hannah Arendt, Paul Tillich, Bruno Bettelheim, and Hans Morgenthau.) In attendance at the Hillel meeting were Bruno Bettelheim, Hans Morgenthau, and a professor of law, Hans Zeisel. It turned out to be an extraordinary event in a way that the organizers did not intend. My recollection of it after many years is imperfect. What I remember was the explosion that occurred. Not a terrorist bomb, but Bettelheim's prideful declaration that he had managed to escape the death camps in the early thirties because he was not a parochial Jew. As a universalist, he had connections throughout the world and therefore access to people who could help him escape. He also knew the enemy mind in a way that enabled him to anticipate its moves. It was not only the content of the declaration, but its tone (superior and confidently arrogant) that provoked an angry outburst from Professor Zeisel, who had gotten out several years later. "Bruno, are you suggesting that you are a superior person because you had the good fortune of leaving Germany before I and others did? That is outrageous." Bettelheim in effect said yes, and the exchange that followed became a shouting match. The "discussion" never recovered from the acrimony. One of them, I don't recall whether it was Bettelheim or Zeisel, threatened a suit for slander. In either case, it would have been a mismatch, the psychologist going against the lawyer.

But then someone from the audience stood up. He was a short, round, and somewhat misshapen man. I recognized him as a member of the psychology department (not a colleague of Bettelheim's) who had written an interesting and well-received book on suffering. Bespectacled like virtually everyone else at the meeting, his face was soft and fleshy; his eyes had a kindly, humorous look that corresponded to the slow, almost ingratiating manner in which he spoke. He was the opposite in appearance and manner to Bettelheim and Zeisel, whose faces had strong, stark features and who spoke in a harsh German accent. The American-born David Bakan's appearance and manner were *echt* Ashkenazi. What he said was devastating. It cut through the absurdity of the quarrel between Bettelheim and Zeisel. Bakan directed his remarks at the self-congratulating universal Jew who had survived because he had understood the enemy and had known how to arrange an escape from his clutches. "I would like to remind Dr. Bettelheim," Bakan said in a deliberate manner that concealed its edge, "there was a group of Jews that knew the enemy long before anyone else. They knew the enemy, not because they were authorities on Nazism, but because they remembered: Haman, the Assyrian Greeks, the Romans. For them the Nazis belonged to an old life-menacing tradition in Jewish life. Who were these Jews? They were the Hasidim. Not the assimilated German Jews, who were incredulous when the Gestapo or the SS came to collect them. 'But I am a German citizen, my father served in Kaiser Wilhelm's army.' " The internecine conflict between *Yeckes* (German Jews) turned into one between *Yeckes* and Ashkenazi (East European Jews). I don't recall Bettelheim's response or much of anything after Bakan spoke. I remember thinking the occasion altogether extraordinary.

What did not immediately register on me was the oddity of my relation to it–or that of my younger colleagues with similar backgrounds. Where was I in all this? I certainly was not a *Yecke* and must confess that I always regarded the German Jew with ambivalence: I envied his cultural superiority but was repelled by his arrogance. He sounded too much like his Nazi countrymen. I was an Ashkenazi, but a far cry from the Hasidim who are its most vivid embodiment. Yiddish was our common bond, but it had become attenuated, if not abandoned, as I became educated and even a professor in a university whose spirit was much closer to the cultural ideals of the German Jews than of the Hasidim. It was not simply that I did not know what Bakan had told us about the Hasidim. I did not know because I shared Bettelheim's pride in his universalism. I believe I still do. But I now have a sense of deprivation and of isolation that in some obscure way I connect with the attenuation of Yiddish in me. One feels both the attenuation and the sense of deprivation in American Jewish writing. The Yiddishisms that sprout from time to time in the prose are like futile gestures to an irretrievable vanishing past.

My time at the University of Chicago ended when I received a fellowship to spend a year in Paris and an offer from Mount Holyoke, one of the Seven Sister women's colleges that include Wellesley and Smith College. I had asked my department at the University of Chicago for tenure on the basis of a published book on D. H. Lawrence as well as articles and reviews that I had written as the price for not going to Mount Holyoke. Apparently prematurely: the chairman wrote to say how much I was valued by the department, but I was told that I had to wait my turn. A senior colleague told me that there was astonishment in the department that I would leave the prestige of the university for a provincial college, and a women's college to boot. It was a foolish move, which would harm my career. I was as ambitious as any of my colleagues for academic success, but I was not happy at the university or in Chicago. An easterner and without a powerful incentive to remain, I saw no reason not to accept the offer from Mount Holyoke. So my wife, my two-year-old son, and I went directly from Paris to South Hadley, Massachusetts, where we stayed for only a year, dissatisfied—as I had been warned I would be—with the provinciality of the place. Mount Holyoke was the oldest women's college, it still had the atmosphere of the suffragette movement of the early part of the century: its feminism ardent, but prim and old-fashioned. I liked the students: they were bright, appealing, and industrious, but I couldn't bear my spinster colleagues who occupied themselves with their personal lives. So after a year at Mount Holyoke I accepted an offer from MIT, where I spent seven hectic years during the tumultuous sixties and early seventies.

I would be ungrateful, however, not to mention my friendship with Ben Reid, a multitalented colleague who was in fact responsible for my coming to Mount Holyoke. Although he was much older than I, he had been a classmate during my year in graduate school at the University of Virginia. He was pursuing his doctorate while teaching at Sweet Briar. I had evidently made an impression on him and years later, as a member of the Mount Holyoke faculty, he recommended my appointment to the faculty of the college. He was a gifted critic and scholar with an extraordinary command of the English language, a prose stylist, a poet reticent about his work, and a master biographer. His life of John Quinn, the New York financier, who supported the work of the great modern writers Eliot, Pound, Yeats, and Joyce, won him the Pulitzer Prize. He told me that he had discovered Quinn through photographs in which he appeared with the great writers. Who was this unknown among the great ones? He looked into the matter and discovered a man like himself, not in wealth, but in artistic desire. Quinn was an artist manqué, who lived through the accomplishments of the great modern artists. Reid was also a craftsman and carpenter. There was nothing, it seemed, that he could not do. But he was a deeply unhappy man, whose unhappiness, temperamentally ingrained, was deepened by his son's psychosis and suicide. I think of him in his alternations between sardonic comment and silence as a sort of goyish Shlomo Katz. A southerner from Louisiana, Reid loved to hear about my Brooklyn Jewish radical past and urged me to write about it before I was ready to do so. He is dead, and it is only fitting now that I am writing about that past that I remember him with affection.

My arrival at MIT coincided with the insurgence of radical sentiment on the campuses of America. The year of my arrival, 1967, was the calm before the storm of Vietnam. Most major universities were breeding grounds for the insurgent radicalism. But MIT was a special case. It was a strange place for the humanities. The sciences and engineering ruled the Institute; disciplines like political science, linguistics, and even music tended to be governed by the scientific spirit and so achieved an acceptance denied to the humanities. The soft disciplines like literature and history were marginal in the Institute. Most students did not take them seriously; courses in the humanities were like a drink at the bar after a hard day's work in the laboratory. Although the official policy of the Institute was to encourage the humanities (the engineering students could use some civilizing), its ethos was hostile to it. A mood of resentment pervaded the humanities faculty. So it was inevitable that when the war in Vietnam began to preoccupy the nation, the association of scientific technology with the war machine would become an occasion for humanists to strike out against the Institute. (To be fair, scientists, against the war also struck out.)

The year was 1968. Student rebellion against university authority would become a global phenomenon. The confrontation between the students and the police had just occurred at Columbia. On the days that I taught, I would have lunch with my colleagues in the school cafeteria. One day, one of them produced a petition protesting the behavior of the Columbia University administration in calling in the police. We were all asked to sign the petition. It was passed around the table and we all signed it. I returned to my office for my office hour with students. Not one student appeared, and I began to brood about the petition. Why had I signed it? What did I know about the events at Columbia? I was a Columbia alumnus, my sense of national patriotism weak, my institutional loyalty not much stronger, but why should I automatically join a protest without really knowing what I was protesting against? I was ashamed to admit to myself that I had signed the petition because everyone else at the table had signed it. If I had refused, I would have shown myself on the side of the unjust, of the oppressor. No one at the table had raised a question about the petition. The prevailing assumption was that if one had to choose between the students on the one side and the administration and the police on the other, the choice would be automatically for the students. Perhaps it was the right choice, but no one asked a question, no one hesitated.

Was I alone in the discomfort I was feeling? I tried to dismiss the feeling, it was done, over with. And what difference would it make? But the feeling refused to go away, in fact, became unbearable. I picked up the phone and called the colleague who had distributed the petition and told him that I wanted my name removed from the petition, explaining that I didn't want to sign on to anything about which I was ignorant. The voice on the other end was terse; he promised to do what I asked and hung up. I felt enormously relieved, even vindicated, though I can't say what I was vindicated for. Later I discovered to my dismay and anger that my name had not been removed. Rather, a line had been drawn through it for everyone to see what I had done. Or so I interpreted it. Only much later did I take some pleasure from the event—for in its ambiguity it was a true representation of what I had done and what I felt. It was a pleasure that said, "This is what I am, this is who I am. I will not ingratiate, I won't depend upon the approval of others." Most of our lives are lived in the possession of others. How often do we have the chance—no, take the chance—to assert our independence? How often do we say *noli me tangere,* don't mess with me? How often? Not very often. These are tests of character, times or moments of crisis, when you must choose between being yourself and being what others want you to be.

The radicalism of the sixties caught me, like everyone else, by surprise. The politics of my adolescence entered the university in a somewhat different form. The New Left declared its independence from the Old Left. It had no allegiance to the Soviet Union. On the contrary, it regarded the Soviet Union as an oppressive society, and at least in its rhetoric Stalinism was anathema to it. The fact is, however, that it supported movements in the third world that were Stalinist in their inspiration. The countercultural side of the New Left was more anarchic and erotic than the disciplined and puritanical Old Left would tolerate. Sexual liberation was a theme not to be found in the middle-class culture in which I grew up. I had endured the frustrations of middle-class puritanism as an adolescent, and my later interest in Lawrence was not entirely academic. Lawrentian sexuality was an odd, mystical affair, but I was attracted to the passion of his language, which for me translated into sex. Herbert Marcuse's *Eros and Civilization* and Norman O. Brown's *Life Against Death,* abstract and discursive, communicated some of the same excitement. But my "bourgeois" formation was too strong for me, and my sensibility too sensible, or maybe cowardly, to risk living at the "extreme tip of life" (Lawrence's phrase). I was not happily married, but polygamy and drugs were not for me. Sexual liberation was exciting stuff for the students—as was the politically sanctioned hostility to all authority. The politics of the counterculture was, in the narrow sense of the word *politics,* apolitical except in its militant wing, the Students for a Democratic Society (the SDS), which was decidedly political. Though the ideologies of the sixties were decidedly un-Stalinist, even anti-Stalinist, I kept recognizing the Stalinist type in the arrogance of the new ideologues: its intolerance of disagreement, its scorn for moderation. The party line changes, but not the impulse to enforce the party line. No one spoke of political correctness at the time, but it had already entered academic culture in the sixties. Among the ideologues were colleagues in my own department who had participated with the students in sit-ins in the administration offices, their rhetoric the rhetoric of condemnation. Jerry

Wiesner, president of MIT, a self-described liberal opposed to the war, appeared one day at a meeting of the SDS and tried to explain Institute policy only to be interrupted by the head of the organization, who told "the pig" that he was not welcome.

I wrote an article about the rhetoric of violence that was overtaking campuses and indeed civil life in America for the left-liberal *Nation,* a magazine with Old Left predilections. I sent the article to Trilling, who wrote back to express surprise that *The Nation,* given its history, would publish it. Given its history, the publication of my article should have been no surprise. The street language of the New Left, vulgar and terrorist, offended the sensibilities of the old "responsible" left. The opening paragraph of the article recalls the verbal atmosphere of the time.

The operative words are "pig," "bullshit," "motherfucker." It is the language of left militant students who find themselves "up against the wall." "The alma-mater fuckers" (Lionel Trilling's elegant phrase) thrust the new militant rhetoric into prominence first in 1965 at Berkeley, then in 1967 at Columbia. The Columbia episode made the new rhetoric a permanent feature of the political landscape. Perhaps the most memorable moment was Mark Rudd's denunciation of a faculty meeting with the cry "bullshit." The years 1965–67 are about the time when black militants expelled white radicals from the fight against racism. The machismo and ghetto energy of their language suggest that these white radicals are expiating for their expulsion—trying to prove to their mistrustful black brothers that they too can think black. . . . When criticizing the new militant rhetoric one runs the risks of falling into a humorless solemnity. The trick perfected by the Yippies is a quick capacity for modulating from impassioned denunciation to an extravagantly farcical jeering. By hoking it up to make the whole idea of institutional authority seem absurd, the language or gesture of militancy effectively disarms its adversaries. So what if a student smokes the president's cigars or scrawls graffiti on the wall? A censorious or disapproving response only reveals the critic to be uptight, the insinuation being that American puritanism, with its repressiveness and hypocrisy, is somehow implicated in the self-righteousness of American foreign policy.

I sympathized with the student criticism of the university's role in the war: "The classic definition that the campus is a place devoted exclusively to the disinterested pursuit of thought has been effectively discredited by the presence there of technological study and of Political Science departments that serve the interests of the Establishment." And in a liberal spirit, I said that if the university was to be an instrumental institution it should concern itself with

> the elimination of poverty, rather than . . . military hardware and the development of counterinsurgency programs. On the other hand, the view that the university must become a completely *instrumental* institution is indiscriminate and poisonous. Philosophical speculation, mathematical study, literary criticism: they constitute part of the intellectual pleasure, happiness and discipline of a humane society. Not only do they not require validation but one might suspect the health and value of a society or a political viewpoint that requires that they be validated as instruments of social change.

My rhetoric had some of the the the disabilities of the moment and the stridency of an immature polemicist. Although its animus was directed against verbal violence, it showed a genuinely felt sympathy for the militant response against the war; it had the virtue or vice of equivocal statement. I had been taught to respect complexity and ambiguity. So I spoke of "on the one hand" and "on the other," a formula sure to blunt the edge of my argument. Stridency was anathema to me, though I did not entirely avoid it.

If I hoped to propitiate and persuade the militants and ideologues, I was not only disappointed, but astonished by their reaction—nothing but scorn for what I had written. I was temporizing with the enemy. A colleague of mine photocopied the article, deleting one of the hands of my equivocal formulation, and had it anonymously distributed to my colleagues in the department. I was alleged to have sided with the enemy. It was now my turn to be enraged. Who was the enemy? You didn't have to be a Marxist to believe that the American presence in Vietnam was wrong—though the reasons for believing it varied. There were, of course, the pragmatists who supported it until they decided on its futility. There were those who opposed the war on the principle that we had no business intervening in the affairs of another country, especially in defense of a corrupt regime. And then there were those for whom Ho Chi Minh embodied the liberation of the Vietnamese masses. I had been down the Ho Chi Minh trail before, most recently at the time of the North Korean invasion, when I rebuked my father for suspecting that the South Koreans had not provoked the invasion. (My Stalinism had clung to me even as I was rejecting it.) When I marched in demonstrations against the war in Vietnam, I made sure to be as far as possible from the contingent that shouted the slogan "Ho ho ho, Ho Chi Minh, the NLF is gonna win." The shouts made me shudder, and I doubted whether I belonged in the march. To oppose the bloodiness of the war you didn't have to embrace the bloodiness of the Viet Cong. Wasn't it simply enough to get out of Vietnam?

Apparently not for the militants of the SDS and their sympathizers. What was needed, they felt, was a guerilla war against the university that stood as a proxy for institutional America and its war machine. However unjust it may have seemed then and seems in retrospect, the strategy was not irrational. The university (and I'm speaking generically now) presented itself as the most vulnerable of institutions, filled as it was with guilt-ridden liberals who heard in the raucus chants of the students the noises of their own consciences. Indignation against the war became an excuse for cruelty to those of weak and vacillating convictions and to those who continued to play by the rules of the institution. A distinguished elderly member of the faculty, who chaired the disciplinary committee of the Institute, became the subject of a photograph in the school newspaper in which his slightly porcine features were transformed in the face of a pig, the dominant metaphor for police brutality. At Boston University, a professor named Morton Berman was lampooned as "Martin Bormann," the name of Hitler's lieutenant.

Jerry Wiesner, the president of MIT, asked me to serve on the disciplinary committee concerned with the legal aspects of the political demonstrations and actions. I accepted the appointment; did I have a choice? Not to accept would be cowardly. Most of the actions consisted of obstructive sit-ins and sloganeering. Much of the anxiety in the panel discussions was provoked by reports of verbal, not physical, violence. There was considerable evidence of threatening and abusive language, but it was clear that little of the verbal violence spilled over into physical action. Nevertheless, the sense of outrage experienced by those who were the objects of abuse was so strong that for them verbal violence seemed the equivalent of physical violence. I shared the sense of outrage. In my *Nation* piece I quoted from an article by Jason Epstein in the *New York Review of Books* criticizing the squeamishness of Lionel Trilling's view that

> the moral ideas—or fantasies as he calls them—of political dissidents in our time have merged with a violent reality. It is as if he had come to take literally the violent political rhetoric of the moment and regarded it, as the authors of the anti-riot act, in a cruder way, had also done, as the moral equivalent of violent action, as if the moral rhetoric implicit in the occasional violent acts of political dissenters, and not the violence itself—their own and the official violence that stimulates it—were the true object of moral or judicial scrutiny.

I pointed out in response that the purpose of violent political rhetoric was

> to create the effect of violence in language. A man who is called a pig [that most unkosher of animals] is supposed to feel the cruelty of the insult in his gut. No one who has actually witnessed a confrontation could possibly take Epstein's line in the matter. Indeed, when the violence of the language ceases to be experienced as violence, the language loses its effectiveness. In order to maintain credibility the militants might logically have to throw bombs.

And yet despite these sentiments, I found myself in the role of protecting the trespassers and violators, many of whom I held in contempt, against those on the committee who wanted to punish them by expulsion and termination of employment. I did not need to urge against the turning over of the lawbreakers to police authority; even the most conservative members of the panel hesitated to cross that threshold. My views were shared by others and we mostly carried the day against draconian punishment. I knew that I would not receive the gratitude of those I had defended if they were to find out that I was their defender. I didn't want gratitude, for if I had received it, it would have diluted the pleasure I felt in the *principle* of resisting institutional retribution. In the decency of institutional response we would be making a sharp contrast with the behavior of the militants.

I stood for tradition in the eyes of the militants. Academic departments are divided between senior and junior members, those with tenure and those without. The juniors wanted to democratize the process: they too should have a vote on tenure. Hadn't I heard of 1789? We're no longer in the feudal ages, Goodheart. I might have replied, hadn't they heard of 1793, the year of the Terror? But such a reply would have been as fatuous as their challenge to me. They dismissed with contempt the reply that I made: that if they had their way they would be voting on their competitors for tenure, a conflict of interest. In their eyes I had an unworthy view of the unworthiness of people: I assumed that selfish motive ruled human action. "Participatory democracy" was the great battle cry of the militants. Everyone had a right to give voice to his belief and to act upon it. What it meant in practice became clear in large mass meetings in which consensus was sought on the resolutions of those who had strong voices. If five hundred people are present at meeting, you can rest assured that only those with force and confidence in their voices will be heard, and those who disagree or hesitate will do so in silence as the responding roar of enthusiastic assent approves every resolution. Participatory democracy becomes in practice the tyranny of the majority—a passive majority that follows strong leaders.

The cultural revolution was not all strident militancy. Against bourgeois puritanism, the revolutionaries showed their anarchic, comic side: drugs, sex, and sheer high-spirited foolishness. One of my colleagues assigned her students the task of roller-skating down the aisle of a subway train to hand out bonbons to bewildered passengers. Perhaps not so bewildered after all, because the craziness of the times was already familiar to most people. I taught D. H. Lawrence's *Women in Love* to a class absorbed by countercultural passions. There were students with strong political commitments against the war in Vietnam and for civil rights. There were students devoted to self-fulfillment or "doing your own thing." There were "touchy-feely" encounter groups, avatars of the New Age "lifestyles" that were coming into being. At one point in the discussion a male student, visibly disgusted with the discussion, lifted a pile of books and dropped them loudly on his desk. (Acting out was a fairly common phenomenon.) In the tolerant spirit of the time (the tolerance of teachers for the behavior of students, not the reverse), I asked the student in the mildest of tones, "What's the matter?" His answer: "Why all the cerebral talk about a book that's passionate and gets you in the gut?" I responded with all the professorial dignity at my command: "I know how to talk about the narrative form of the novel, its themes and language, but I'm not sure what one can say about the gut. What do you suggest?" A somewhat pompous reply. But the challenge to the student was fair game. Students were questioning and challenging authority. Why not give him a crack at taking charge? But he would have none of it. "Why ask me, you're the teacher?" So authority was still alive and well. But in engaging him I had clearly put myself at a disadvantage. I could tell from the expressions on the faces of the students, who were observing the contest with a certain fascination. A sudden inspiration. We had been talking about the wrestling scene between Rupert Birkin and Gerald Crich in which they strip themselves naked and achieve male bonding. "Ah, I know what you want," I said, "the rest of the class should leave, you and I strip naked and wrestle." "Yeah!" Laughter in the class. "Forget about it," I said, with a sense of satisfaction that I had finally risen to the occasion. The student was indifferent to the difficulty of the work. He did not want to have to struggle to understand what was complex and recalcitrant in it. He looked to reading for instance gratification, and if it was not forthcoming it had nothing to say to him—or the teacher who tried to express the difficulty had nothing to say to him. There was nothing eccentric about his response; it had become the going fashion in the academy.

The organizational discipline of the Old Jewish Left and its traditional bourgois values, perhaps more than my later acquired anti-Stalinism, enforced my suspicions of countercultural anarchism. The fellow-traveling Communist sympathizers of my parents' generation were bourgeois moralists in their private lives. God forbid (a locution available even to atheists in times of stress) that any of their children should not marry or come out of the closet. Professional success, responsibility, concern for others, in particular family, were driving values of our lives, values anathema to the counterculture of the New Left.

My rebellious student was the offspring of a movement of feeling that had started in the early sixties. I called its exponents "the new apocalyptists" in an article I wrote for the hundredth anniversary issue of *The Nation*. Herbert Marcuse, the author of *Eros and Civilization,* and Norman O. Brown, the author of *Life Against Death,* were its philosophers. Norman Mailer, Allen Ginsberg and the Beats were its artist practitioners:

> They advocate passion over the intellect, exalt the body over the mind, prefer the perverse to the normal, the spontaneous to the habitual, the risks of violence and disaster to the security of our ordinary modes of existence. They can best be described as apocalyptics, because they exist in a condition of expectation of some event of a demonic or catastrophic kind that will transform their lives. They are often politically radical, though the old conception of political struggle (its Marxian version, for instance) is superannuated. They might concede the importance of social reorganization, but the reorganization would presumably follow the revolution of the body and the consciousness of men.

The wedding of eros and politics produced a politics of impatience. Immediate instinct gratification was translated into a demand for immediate justice. Demands were nonnegotiable and had to be satisfied at all costs. Julien Beck of the Living Theater (no longer living) provided a striking example of the new revolutionary disposition:

> This society cannot offer peace, love, joy, honor, and fulfillment to its citizens, but in their stead, offers varieties of hatred, competition, greed, a life of senseless pain, trivia, and early death. A society that can attain affluence and still let people starve to death makes the brain go tilt; a society that can indulge in the Vietnamese war is insupportable to those who are trying to recuperate their holy feelings. A society that bases its affluence on useless toil in which millions of lives are sacrificed to the production of goods made not for use but for money, in which the mind must die in order to protect itself from thinking, because thinking is too painful if you have to live out your life in senseless drudgery—such a society must be transformed.
>
> Artaud's manifesto of feeling calls for assaults on the senses and the creation of cruel events in the theater, with the hope that such theatrical events will reach the spectator in the flesh, in the bowels, in the eyes, in the groin, there where he feels it. Then, once feeling something, other doors to the body of feeling will open, and, physically offended by the pain experienced in the theater, the physical spectator will no longer be able to tolerate pain around him in the world outside the theater, and the revolution will burst into action.
>
> The theater of Revolution must mean new forms of acting in which the space trip that the actor takes is worthy of the attention of the spectator. The actor must discover forms of behavior and experience that unite the physical body with the mind if he is to serve the needs of the public. The mental theater in which the body is only the stage must mutate into a theater in which all the senses operate, receive experience profoundly, answer experience profoundly, and resolve experience according to the truth of profound feeling.

Confrontation became the politics of choice. The voice of confrontation is that of exasperated indignation, a desire for immediate action, often without the benefit of reflection. Do anything, anything that will wake up our slumbering moral consciousness. Its tone of self-righteousness suggests that any question about the manner of formulating the issues is a kind of cop-out, an instance of bad faith. The peril of self-righteousness is injustice, where the interest is more in indulging one's indignation than in obtaining justice.

Black anti-Semitism was one manifestation of self-righteous injustice. The civil rights movement under Martin Luther King, which preceded the antiwar protests, came under attack from Malcolm X, Stokely Carmichael, the Black Panthers, and other militants. White liberals, many of them Jews, had been part of King's ecumenical movement. Now both liberals and Jews came under attack. The poet LeRoi Jones, who later changed his name to Amiri Baraka, let loose against the "joos"; black students at Brandeis University characterized its president Morris Abrams, a Southern-born Jew, as a Georgia cracker. Black militants resented what they felt to be the condescension of white liberals who controlled the agenda of the civil rights movement and wanted them "off their backs." But there was something deeper involved, a competition for the status of sufferer. James Baldwin, no anti-Semite, wrote: "One does not wish . . . to be told by an American Jew that his suffering is as great as the American Negro's suffering. . . . The Jewish travail occurred across the sea and America rescued him from the house of bondage. But America is the house of bondage for the Negro, and no country can rescue him."

There may be American Jews who absurdly compare their suffering to that of the blacks in America. But what should Jews say when blacks do not recognize Jewish suffering and resent Jews for having attained places of privilege in American society? During my time at the University of Chicago, I asked my neighbor, the editor of the African-American newspaper the *Chicago Defender,* why our black cleaning woman had not heard of the Holocaust. Not realizing that my wife was Jewish, she had complained to her about the Jews as privileged people who had never known suffering. Wasn't it the duty of the newspaper to inform its readers of what went on in the world? He told me that he sympathized with my view, but that he had been threatened with the loss of his adverisers' business if he repeated an editorial "best wishes" to his "Jewish brethren on the Passover holidays." Do we need to be reminded of the unfortunate role of the Jew as middleman, collector of rents, or as competitor in the market? Scapegoats too need scapegoats.

Black anti-Semitism predates the "apocalyptic" sixties, but in the sixties anti-Semitic sentiments became part of the rhetoric of militant black leaders. Racism and anti-Semitism release powerful memories and emotions, and one cannot apply different standards to the understanding of the two phenomena. If one tries to understand the emotional dimension of racism in the victims of racism, one must also sympathetically understand the emotional dimension of anti-Semitism in its victims. To say that the Jews have made it in American society and consequently the issue of anti-Semitism is fabricated, whereas blacks are suffering every minute of their lives, impressed and still impresses me as meretricious. A black militant like LeRoi Amiri Baraka Jones or an official of the Congress of Racial Equality (CORE) who says that Hitler failed to complete the job is not speaking out of the anguish of ghetto suffering. He too has made it, and he must bear responsibility for his utterances.

I was in a reactive mode, resisting what I believed to be the foolishness, excess, and even cruelty of the militant radicals, though not without sympathy for their cause, the ending of the war in Vietnam. I thought of myself as a liberal, but liberalism was viewed with contempt as moral weakness or, worse, as a bad-faith attempt to conceal one's complicity with the Establishment. In an article for *Dissent* on the susceptibility of *The New York Review of Books* to the politics of the New Left, I characterized the new militancy as an "assault on the complacency of the American liberal conscience." The New Left "was intimate with the failures of liberalism because in part at least it *represented the disaffection of liberalism from itself*." I resisted the disaffection as I would later resist the neoconservative assault on liberalism. But what did my liberalism amount to?

I was asked by *The Nation* to review a new book by Paul Goodman, *New Reformation: Notes of a Neolithic Conservative*. I wrote the review in 1970, at the time of the American bombing of Cambodia, when all hell broke loose on college and university campuses. Here was a sympathetic figure for the moment, an independent radical whose independence showed itself in his "perverse" self-advertisement as a conservative. His conservatism of course had nothing to do with any of the current American varieties. It was leagues apart from that of William Buckley. Goodman would turn to Coleridge and Arnold "when the vulgarity of liberalism gets me by the throat." When everyone in one's circle speaks the same political dialect, one has to find a language to express one's own individual ideas and perceptions. Goodman went against the grain to express his own positive ideas. Don't try to transform the world in one fell swoop. Learn to make changes in a piecemeal way, and change what needs to be changed. Don't call for change if you don't have a practical idea of how to change things: "To have no program rules out the politics of rational persuasion, for there is nothing to offer other citizens, who do not have one's gut complaints, to get them to come along. . . . Unlike other 'social critics,' I am rather scrupulous about not attacking unless I can think of an alternative or two, to avoid arousing metaphysical anxiety." Metaphysical anxiety was a speciality of the young militants, for whom Goodman had affection, but who needed his chastizing. So he made practical suggestions such as biennial checkups for everyone "to forestall chronic [health] conditions and their accumulating costs." He proposed "mini-schools" of about twenty children and four teachers, one licensed by the present system, another a graduating senior from one of the local colleges, perhaps embarking on graduate study, still another a literate housewife and mother, who can prepare lunch (pace Women's Lib) and finally a literate, willing and intelligent high school graduate or dropout. He made many other proposals, some eccentric, others eminently reasonable. I admired the spirit of pragmatic realism in Goodman, a salutary antidote to the apocalyptic spirit of the time.

The countercultural revolution of the sixties failed to transform American politics, which became increasingly conservative. During the decades that followed, *conservative* became a respectable word, while liberalism became disreputable. But the counterculture worked its way into society and culture. Sexual liberation, the woman's movement, and the celebration of ethnic identity are the legacy of the sixties. The "revolution" did transform the academy. It's a story that has been told in recent years again and again: the young radicals of the sixties who made the academy their professional home achieved tenure. If political and social institutions were resistant to radical change, literary and philosophical texts were vulnerable. Canonical works were deconstructed, ideologies demystified, "hegemonies" of nations and institutions unmasked. Activism turned into theory. Battle lines were drawn and one was expected to take sides. A new conservatism rose up, mostly outside the academy, to attack what it saw as a new barbarism. It had its own stridency to match the stridency of the ideologues of the left, and it shared with its adversary an intense dislike of liberalism. So I found myself in the middle, trying to steer a course between the ideological rocks on the left and on the right.

My days at MIT were numbered, and it was I who was doing the numbering. I was never pleased with the role of the humanities in the Institute. Humanists were second-class citizens. How seriously could we expect students devoted to the sciences and engineering to take what we had to offer? MIT students were very bright, and there were those who were serious about literature, history, and philosophy. A number of them dropped out of the sciences and had careers in the humanities and the creative and performing arts. (One of the impressive students in my course in Joyce was James Wood, who became the actor.) But it was hard for a teacher in the humanities not to feel that he had to legitimize his subject while teaching it. One time a physics major, just arrived from Japan, approached me after class in the beginning of the semester and asked me what were the most important pages in *The Odyssey,* the assignment for the week (he was terribly busy, he said, and had little time to read). I couldn't resist and recited some pages at random. As he began to take down the page numbers, I said I was only kidding. He looked at me, puzzled: "What's kidding?" Competence in English was not considered a requirement for admission to the Institute. Nor at the time were there courses in English as a second language. On another occasion, a precocious eighteen-year-old, already a presenter of papers at scientific conferences, came up to me after class to question something I had said in discussion. He told me how much he liked the class, and then with a look of embarassment asked in the most circumlocutory way how I had come to choose my profession. What I heard was "How could a grown man of intelligence devote the most serious part of his life to the teaching of literature?" We had been reading Othello and I recommended that he read the essays on the play by the great critic A. C. Bradley and then ask himself whether one could profitably devote his life to such work. In our next meeting, he told me yes, one could devote oneself to such work. I remember the episode with pleasure, but at the time felt no desire to have to continually justify my subject. Moreover, the well had been poisoned by politics. I was open to an offer from another institution, and it came in the form of the chairmanship of the department of English at Boston University.

John Silber had recently arrived from the University of Texas to become its president, full of determination to make it a leading university, the rival of Harvard, its nemesis across the Charles River. He was hiring new department heads from the outside to reshape and give dynamism to the university. He was convinced that it was second-rate or worse and that he was the man to take it to a new level. My task would be to energize the department. The interview with Silber lasted two hours, and it took place in the company of the college dean, who, it became clear during the course of the interview, performed the role of a kid-glove mediator. Silber is a small, compact man with fiery blue eyes and a lean, sharply angled face whose expression suggested that he was all purpose, no small talk. Silber was forceful, even abrasive. He was testing, not courting me, listening to what I said like a predator ready to pounce on my every utterance. I was expected to speak well and say the right things. When his thin lips widened in a smile, apparently with pleasure at what was being said, the smile was indistinguishable from a sneer. He wanted me to know his expectations, which seemed like veiled commands. Would I have the courage to take on the entrenched administration of the department and, in particular, the formidable poetry critic Helen Vendler, whom he delicately characterized as "Henry VIII with tits"? I said I wasn't sure what I would do until I became familiar with the department. Silber didn't seem satisfied with my caution and pressed me, only to be diverted by the dean, who, sensing trouble, changed the subject.

Silber reflected on his own career: how he had moved up the ladder from department chairman and dean of arts and sciences at the University of Texas to the presidency of a university and, implicit in his narrative, who knew what lay beyond. United States senator? Governor? President of the United States? In the interview he intended me to draw the conclusion that my ambition need not be satisfied with the chairmanship. Think of it, if I played my cards right I might become dean. And a parting shot: he believed in taking from Peter and giving to Paul. He wanted excellence above all. As I left the interview I did not ask myself who would decide what was excellent. I was so bent on leaving MIT that I simply thought of the interview as an obstacle to be surmounted on the way to an appointment. I would ultimately rue my failure to meditate on Peter and Paul.

As soon as I began my job, I detected a general apprehension among faculty and staff. The students lived in another space and their anxieties had different objects. The general apprehension I observed among the faculty and soon began to feel myself concerned President Silber. I had never taught at a college or university whose principal subject was the president himself. It became increasingly clear in a very short time that we inhabited a world (a small one, to be sure) shaped by a cult of personality. The personality in this case was more feared than adored, but perhaps that is true of all such cults as they are experienced. It may be that publicity transforms the fear into adoration in the eyes of an outside public that does not share the experience of living inside the cult. I'm not sure that it is quite right to speak of Silber's cult of personality: it was more a case of his ambition for it than an actuality. There was so much expressed discontent on the faculty, so much resentment at what was perceived as his high-handedness, that the faculty was in the process of organizing itself into a union just as I arrived. I was never a fan of faculty unions and of their leveling tendencies. We are not pieceworkers in a factory nor functions on an assembly line. We are individual scholars pursuing our disciplines at different levels of distinction. I had not lost my affection for the trade union movement, a legacy of the movement that had formed me, but I believed that the academy was an exceptional case; the collective mentality of unions did not apply to us. This view in theory was shared by most of the faculty, but their unhappiness was so palpable that they voted against the theory and for the union. I hadn't been in place long enough to experience the unhappiness, so I abstained. It did not take long for me to become a campus radical.

Silber bullied the faculty, and though my courage is not extraordinary, his manner always brought my blood to a boil. I had scarcely been on the job for a year and the union question was still being debated when I wrote him a letter complaining about the arbitrariness with which salary increases and various other perks had been distributed. All discriminations are in a sense arbitrary, and it is a hard thing for the just man who has the power and responsibility to make them. For the man who wants to be loved it is misery. I know because I think of myself as just and I want to be loved. It is always torture for me to distribute rewards to some and deny them to others. So what am I complaining about? Not the arbitrariness itself, but something else I felt in Silber: the pleasure in the display of power. If you want or love power for its own sake, you flaunt its arbitrariness.

This was not in my mind when I wrote the letter, but what I've just written drove me and drives me in general to complain. During the interview for my position, Silber had told me with a certain relish that he believed in taking from Peter to give to Paul. To reward merit, to be sure. As I got to know him better, I saw "the reward for merit" as an afterthought or a by-product and not as a reward for merit at all, but as a display of power. He was Yahweh redivivus, playing favorites with creatures who were not his creations. Before the vote on unionization, Silber asked to be invited to a department meeting in which he would try to talk my colleagues out of voting for the union, an unwise strategy it seemed to me. I had no choice but to accommodate him. At the meeting he spoke at length and then invited questions and comments. None was forthcoming, and I suspect he assumed that he had made his case successfully. On emerging from the meeting, he suddenly turned on me: "You had no business writing that letter," I said. "No business? I have a right to send a letter. If you don't like what I have written you can tell me in a letter." I had leveled the playing field, as they say, and Silber flew into a rage, which provoked my own, and we went verbally at each other in the street toe to toe like two adolescents. I was back in the streets of my childhood in Brooklyn. A crowd gathered, windows opened, and who knows when or how it would have ended if Silber's fountain pen hadn't burst in the pocket of his starched white shirt, perhaps from the sheer animation of his anger, forming a huge blue ink stain. I like to think that if *my* pen had burst the color would have been red.

I did not enjoy my little triumph, for I knew it would be short-lived. He had the power to mete out punishment and he was not one to refrain from using it. But I was also shaken by the surge of anger within me, over which I had no control. I had not decided to stand up to him, it simply happened. On reflection afterward, I realized that he too had exploded out of control, that despite his authority over me, he and I were reflections of each other. We were two peas . . . in fact, we had reversed roles. If indignation is the emotion of the powerless, it should have started with me. Since he had the power, he could have ignored my letter, his indifference only enhancing the impression of power. But he wanted to give more than the impression. He wanted to display it and to tell me that justice was on his side or that it was presumption to question his judgment, for it was like questioning justice itself. So his was the first explosion of indignation. He was stealing my thunder, forcing me to justify myself.

Silber's power showed itself not directly, but through the actions of his subordinates. Promises made to me before I was hired (new appointments, support for programs) were not kept. One appointment in particular was held hostage to the demand that we increase the workload of our faculty. The dean produced the demand after the offer had been virtually promised to a candidate, who accepted and took himself out of the job market. I told him that the young man, who had a wife and a child, was given every reason to believe that the position was his. The dean, an unconscionable instrument of the president, gazed stolidly and silently in response. I could not say to him as I once said to a customer-relations specialist who had sold me a defective product which I wished to return, "Put yourself in my (in this case the young man's) position." The pleasure of his being dean was that he was *not* in the young man's position. The young man was nothing more for him and his superiors than a means of humiliating me and the department. On another occasion, Silber denied tenure to a deserving assistant professor (a fine scholar and teacher) as a way of reminding me (or so I construed it) of the affront I and my department had delivered to his presidential vanity. She had the courage to sue the university and win her case in court. The university appealed the case all the way up to the Supreme Court and lost. Other acts of vindictiveness more trivial in the larger scheme of things had nevertheless a cumulative effect that was utterly demoralizing. President Silber was on a small stage, without a police force or an army. But one glimpsed in the trivial event and the sum of events an explosive desire to conquer and obliterate. He had unrealized dreams of action on a larger stage. Years later, he entered a larger stage, ran for governor of the state, and came dangerously close to winning.

We sometimes forget that people in power didn't always have it, and any affront to them must cast them back to the time before they possessed it, making them feel the precariousness of their situation and therefore their vulnerability. Anything you get you can lose. But this doesn't cover the matter. Silber is a powerfully built little man who suffers a physical disability. He has a congenitally short arm, and one might imagine that his life is marked by an inextinguishable memory of humiliation. Imagine growing up in Texas, the state of the two-handed quick draw, with a hand like that. It is a familiar story: the boy who is mocked by his schoolmates for his short height or his stutter becomes the ruler of a country, a corporation, an institution, but the ascent to power doesn't dissipate the memory—and indignation persists like an irremediable canker. Indignation cannot work against a despot, because its object has a heart of stone or is, like our president himself, the possessor of the emotion. When directed against him, indignation has an effect opposite to what it intends. It puts him in a rage. "Who are *you* to raise your voice to me?" The stress is on the first part of the question, not on the noise of the outburst. He cannot bear the independence implied by the indignation, which says: "I will not be ruled by others, however powerful. I will insist on my rights." If the indignant powerless man hears an echo of himself in the rage of the despot, it is because despotism is the form indignation takes when its possessor achieves power. The despot defends what he has, but that alone doesn't make him a despot. Like the powerless, he too is never satisfied, never appeased. What he wants is an illimitable satisfaction. I feel and know the emotion so deeply that I try constantly to give my genial and reasonable side every chance to assert itself. An apology will do, an extended hand, a realization that a mistake was made. Anything to avoid the disfigurements of indignation.

The faculty voted for a union. Among its leaders was my friend Fritz Ringer, a German-born intellectual historian, who brought to what would become an intense and difficult struggle the burden of his family's history in Nazi Germany. His father, who never joined the National Socialist Party, had been an engineer in a company that contributed to the German war machine. The Ringer family had come to America soon after the war. Fritz grew up in America with a powerful allergy to authoritarianism. In his struggles with Silber and his administration, he seemed to be fighting the battle that his father had not fought in Germany. Fritz has written an admirable memoir in which he describes the negotiations for a contract that took place between the union and the administration. He too understood the self-defeating dangers of indignation, and the memoir is filled with an acute self-awareness of the moments when he himself is swept by the passion. The negotiations failed, and the faculty went on strike for ten days, the first and only strike in which I have been an interested participant. No longer radical, I nevertheless experienced the pleasure and anxieties of comradeship on the picket line. The distinctions among full, associate, and assistant professor were leveled. Relationships among members of the faculty, always fraught with competitive anxiety, were never better. We were now a crowd of equals, thoughts about how each of us was *distinguished* from others in suspension. Unfortunately, the feeling disappeared after the strike was over. I sometimes feel a perverse gratitude to John Silber for giving me a chance to reexperience a sense of solidarity with others in behalf of a just cause.

My chairmanship turned out to be an exercise in frustration and powerlessness. From the beginning a number of colleagues mistrusted me, because I had been appointed by Silber. Surely I had been chosen to enact his program for the department. The fact is that he came to regard me with the resentment that he showed to everyone who refused to go along with him. My colleagues were suspicious to the point of paranoia, and though I could not be faulted for dishonorable behavior toward them, the poisonous atmosphere of the university affected these relationships. The fiery lieutenant in me did not always serve me or the department well. It may be that I was trying to prove my integrity to my colleagues by fighting every battle, regardless of the significance of the issue. If so, my angry reactions were not premeditated; the streets of Brooklyn had never been educated out of me. I had not learned early enough the importance of picking and choosing a battleground. I heard after leaving the university from a friend in the department that my "principled resistance" to what I and my colleagues regarded as despotism was not universally appreciated. They wanted me to fight their fight, but it was expected that I win. Losing meant even more trouble for the department. We eventually lost, and one is rarely forgiven for losing.

Be that as it may, I was chairman, and that meant that I had the power to decide matters that could seriously affect the lives of others—for instance, the hiring and firing of faculty members. Of course, departments are in a limited sense democracies, and senior colleagues share in the power of decision, but the chairman, if he wished, could decide certain matters without consultation. I don't—and did not—enjoy power. I took the chairmanship, I believe, because of a deluded notion about its prestige and because I thought I could accomplish something: make changes in the academic program and create a collegial department. A collegial department would have been no mean achievement. Academic departments are notorious for the unpleasantness of faculty relationships. Professors are aging adolescents, who have never left school, whose lives have been defined by the receiving and giving of grades. As students, they want to be recognized as the brightest, and as teachers and scholars they tend to regard their colleagues as competitors, envious of the rewards a colleague might receive (a salary increase, a promotion, a chair, a favorable book review, a fellowship). What I am describing may apply to other workplaces, but academic life exacerbates the egoism of the human condition.

Members of the department view the chairman nervously, for he is the source of recommendations to the dean about salaries, tenure, promotion, and leaves of absence. I was hardly on the job when at dinner in a restaurant following a poetry reading, the poet Anne Sexton, a member of our creative-writing program, her breath reeking of alcohol, asked me whether I meant to fire her. I had barely gotten to know her. Nothing that I had said, nothing in my behavior could possible have provoked her anxiety. It could only have been provoked by a combination of her insecurity and the impression of power in the title I had acquired. I assured her that I had no intention of firing her. The power that I was presumed to have unsettled me. I was in fact so unsettled and inexperienced in the ways of power that in this first event at which I had to sign the credit-card receipt for a large company of people in an expensive restaurant, I neglected to read the receipt in which the gratuity (a very large one) was included—and I wrote in another large tip. I realized this on my return home, called the restaurant the following morning, and had the extra tip withdrawn. Hardly a way to conduct the chairmanship.

A time came, however, when I had to exercise power. Another member of the creative-writing program (I will call him Ira) was completing a two-year contract and wanted it to be renewed. The position to which he had been appointed was a rotating one, an opportunity for accomplished writers to pass through the university and offer their wares to students. But the present incumbent ignored this understanding. He had been a college classmate of mine and appealed to our school tie to save his job. I knew that I had no choice but not to renew his contract. I tried to explain the reasons, reasons that he had been given when he first took the job, but he would have none of it. He was furious at what he saw as my betrayal of him.

Several years later I received a copy of a novel he had published in the mail. The inscription read "with affection." I began to read it only to discover that the story started with me. Surprise, shock, excitement: these are the emotions of reading about oneself in someone else's words. It was not the first time I had been put in a novel. My wise-cracking friend Leslie Epstein, the readiest wit in the East, tells me that it's a case of my SM: sheer magnetism. In *All the Little Live Things,* Wallace Stegner, probably never having read a single word I had written, threw my name into a rucksack of books of a sixties hippie student in California named Caliban alongside the likes of Søren Kierkegaard, Norman O. Brown, and Paul Goodman. He must have assumed from the title that an article I had written critical of the counterculture was a celebration of it. I was flattered and appalled. So much for truth. Later an academic colleague (not Ira) had made me into the moral hero of a mediocre drama of academic hiring and firing. He had caught some of my idiosyncrasies (the extravagant hand gestures when I speak, an unkempt appearance, my shirt hanging out over my belt). He added psoriasis, his own affliction, and when I expressed annoyance at his physical portrait of me, he denied I was the model for the character: "It's a composite portrait." Some composite—mostly the events of my life, my physical appearance, plus his psoriasis. I appeared again in a revenge novel by my ex-wife, who should have dedicated it to me, since our divorce unblocked her imagination and allowed her to vent her spleen. The lawyer will not betray the confidence of his client, the priest of the confessor, the psychoanalyst of the patient. But the spouse, who joins herself to another in the deepest of intimacies for better or worse, may broadcast their life together when the marriage ends and even before. To speak or to write the angers and resentments in marriage may be the way to recovery. Where the truth lies, who is at fault, is almost beside the point. My ex-wife's novel lost its sting for me. I knew where it came from.

Ira's novel was something else. The other novels irritated, but the irritation passed. This one, for reasons that were not immediately

clear, went deep and continued to trouble me. It tells the story of how
as chairman of a department of English, I (or the character that stood
for me) did not recommend the protagonist's reappointment to a position in creative writing and how my failure to do so triggered a bout of
alcoholism that nearly destroyed him. The novel mocks my scholarship. The protagonist (the author in disguise) expected better of me,
because we had been classmates in college over thirty years before,
though "he had never loved me." It does not tell the story of how out
of the blue, after years of not having seen and never having loved me
(knowing that I had the power of employing him), he called to ask me
to be the godfather of his son. I read his novel, appalled and yet
moved by his ordeal and rehabilitation. It was a "by your own boot-
straps" book.

The novel brought back college memories of the novelist. Embittered and sardonic, he possessed a large talent for language for the
evocation of scenes and atmospheres of Brooklyn in the late forties
and early fifties. He wrote stories about boys' clubs, cellar parties, male
camaraderie, gang bangs in an orchestral baroque prose that brought
Faulkner to mind. His teachers thought he might be the genius of his
generation. But whatever success he had did not diminish his bitterness. He published a book of stories to some acclaim and then, while
the world waited, he disappeared. Occasionally, there were rumors of
a novel about to happen. When one did appear, it failed to live up to
expectations. It took another fifteen years for him to write this novel. I
wrote back, "I was moved by your story, but less enchanted by the
portrait of the chairman and puzzled by the affection with which you
sent me the copy of the novel." And he replied with a patronizing
reminder of what all readers of literature should know: "Fiction is fiction, life is life, don't confuse the author with this jaundiced character."

Was he obtuse or did he believe that I was stupid? In the novel, he
presents a character who replaced him, a woman writer of some distinction whom I had agreed to appoint. The protagonist heaps scorn
upon her. Another character tells her what Ira has said, for he finds
himself in her next novel in the most unflattering light. His resentment
knows no bounds. Page after page, the protagonist rages against her.

Ira had written what would have been my own reply into the novel. Did he expect me to believe that the character in the novel who looked and spoke like me was not me? Did he think that the emotion of rage directed against the chairman could be in my eyes simply an aesthetic emotion?

I remembered the episode, vividly recalled in the novel, in which I broke the news that his contract would not be renewed. Our conversation took place over a meal in a Greek restaurant in which I told jokes in order to lighten the atmosphere. I felt immediately that I had stupidly miscalculated (Ira's narrative, lodged entirely in his own head, has no inkling of my own realization), for I sensed that he saw through my attempt to anticipate and propitiate his anger at the news. The episode is all about how he sees through me. I thought I was softening the blow in telling him that he had not been fired, since there had never been the intention of renewing his contract when he was hired. I was right in guessing that he heard this as a piece of legalism indifferent to the awful consequences of having a family and being jobless. The episode is charged with his own grief and anxiety and contempt for me. It brought to mind another episode, not depicted in the novel, in which he confronted me in a parking lot several days later and accused me of destroying his life and that of his family. I have always dreaded the possibility of professionally causing the suffering of others. I put my hand on his shoulder. He cast it off (*noli me tangere*), turned away, and walked off. The episode, as I say, is not in the novel, but the scene in the restaurant is charged with it.

Why had he sent me the novel with a note of affection? If he recognized the jaundice in his "protagonist," shouldn't there have been some effort in the novel to exculpate me, to understand my point of view? There I am, a target of his resentment, as if time were canceled and we were back in the past where it all took place. In having me read his novel, he was compelling me to reenact the scenes in a reversal of roles with me as the victim. He was paying me back. *I want you to feel as I felt.* The passage of time had not redeemed me.

The shock of finding myself in the novel, all but named, prevented me from going on. It was as if without warning an officer of the court had thrust a document of indictment into my hands. I closed the book and put it into a corner of the desk. Each time I returned to the desk, however, it was there as a temptation. A few days later I found myself absorbed by the story, my interest nourished as much by resentment as by curiosity. In reading and rereading the scenes in which I appear, I imagined my entering them to rewrite my part of the dialogue, telling him what I had not told him at the time: that he had tried to exploit a friendship that did not exist in order to hold on to a job to which he was not entitled, that for all his talent he had not written anything substantial and decent for years, and that according to student evaluations his teaching was only so-so. He had anticipated my response, for after the first two chapters I virtually disappear from the novel and the story bears me out. He had exposed himself more ruthlessly than I could possibly expose him. During his alcoholic binges he had shown himself to be a miserable son, an abusive husband, an irresponsible father, an unreliable friend, a bad colleague. Strange as it may seem, my resentment increased as I read on, for I could hear him saying: "I have shown less mercy to myself than I have shown you, and isn't my capacity for self-exposure a mark of my authority over you?" Self-revelation was entitlement, a familiar move in the antinomian game of justifying oneself in the very act of confessing one's sins.

I was struck by the irony of his self-justification to me. I was not simply a person whom he knew, whom he had cannibalized for fiction, but a critic, the mortal enemy of artists. The novelist resents critics when they invade his private life and speculate about his motives. He believes that the private life is off limits and irrelevant to the productions of the imagination. But the novelist has no compunctions about appropriating those in the circle of his acquaintance. The law of trespass, it would seem, does not apply to him. All he has to do is to assert the fictional status of his enterprise, and friends and family become the fair game of his imagination, prey to the malice of his language. The living person who offers up a protest that he has been betrayed and violated is made to seem pathetic and ludicrous. But why should privileges accrue to fiction? What is sauce for the goose . . . If words of fiction bite and scar, why shouldn't the person bitten and scarred be allowed to bite back without risking ridicule? And if the person is a critic, he may be able to speak some home truths about what being a writer signifies.

And yet the critic in me had to acknowledge his right as an abuser of persons. A writer breaks decorum and transgresses the norms. The imagination is uncivil. So I had been telling myself, my students, and the readers of the critical articles I published, and now the very proof of my views stuck in the craw. But even worse, the aggressiveness of Ira's "fiction" only underlined my *civil* incapacities. *My* imagination was cautious and timid. I feared offending family and friends. I did not have the courage or malice of my convictions. To be a writer one had to be able to write down one's most terrible thoughts. Whatever I wrote softened into fairness and judiciousness. My mind swung between the poles of "on the one hand" and "on the other." Judiciousness was my virtue, the virtue of judges and critics, and my judiciousness was of the benign sort, not the kind that sends people to prison. Fairness, the concern for others, is the bane of all creative action. The truly imaginative act requires an indifference to one's effect on others. The imagination is one-eyed, a heaver of stones, boulders that threaten to kill. The imagination is unloved even when admired, though it may excite affection posthumously, long after it has done its immediate work.

Ira, my critic's conscience told me, had done nothing more or less than what every genuine writer does in pushing against the limits of propriety, in resisting loyalty to anything but his "vision," his sense of what things are, always different from the received sense of things. The writer is a high-stakes gambler, risking friends, family, position for the possibility of producing something wonderful and famous. Whatever he had done to me, whatever he had intended to get out of me, I, the critic, the man of judgment, had to concede not only his right to what he had written, but its power as well. Moreover, my moderation and evenhandedness were not what they appeared or what I wanted them to be. If I had taken Ira's path, what would I have discovered: the envious, vengeful spirit perhaps in which I write these lines, while pretending to generosity in my praise of him? I apparently want it both ways, to receive credit for my fair-mindedness while getting in my licks at him.

A curious thing happened. In the course of reading the book, the impulse to avenge myself disappeared. I envied Ira the choice he had made long ago to follow the path of his bitterness, to make a subject of it, to express it without shame, and to let it lead him to the most self-revealing, the most embarrassing places. In order to write I needed the protection of someone else's text. I needed to hide behind the words and feelings of others. In Ira the distinction between fiction and reality was nothing but a fig leaf that allowed his inner reality to express itself. Disingenuous as he was in separating art from reality, he was the soul of truth in his fidelity to his miserable condition.

Months after our exchange of letters, I caught sight of Ira as I entered and he emerged from a movie theater, but I pretended not to have seen him. Did he pretend not to see me? I have since heard that he has gone west to teach in a small college, where doubtless the appointments committee took pleasure in his novel but drew no lessons from it. Unlike other potentially harmful commodities, books carry no warning labels. There is no FDA of literature, no contraceptives or prophylactics available to the unwary reader. If consulted by the appointments committee, I would not have provided the warning label. My critic's conscience would have forbidden it. What I have written here, believe it or not, is a letter of recommendation.

As a chairman or a dean or a president, your power derives from the institution you inhabit. But the power of a writer is his or hers alone, constrained only by the limits of imagination and inhibition. I have always harbored an admiration for the unaffiliated writer and intellectual whose only allegiance is to the transgressive powers of his imagination and intelligence. I have contempt for the empty academic suit whose identity is entirely institutional. I once thought of writing an essay on academic life with the title "On Being Institutionalized." The academic suit has never fit me perfectly.

I have taught at Bard College, the University of Chicago, Mount Holyoke, MIT, Boston University, and finally Brandeis University. I have been a visitor at Wellesley College, Wesleyan University, and

Columbia University. So I have traveled the spectrum of higher education in America as a kind of displaced person (a wandering Jew?) moving from one institution to another. At MIT I found myself at the uncomfortable center of the tumultuous politics of the moment. At Boston University I joined the rebellion against a petty but oppressive despotism. Earlier, at the University of Chicago, I rebelled against the coerciveness of the neo-Aristotelians. And before that, I mistrusted the herdlike hippie "freedom" of Bard student life. A sense of dissatisfaction with each institution made me move, harboring the vain illusion that I would find academic Eden somewhere. Is it fortuitous that I have wound up at Brandeis, the only secular Jewish institution of higher learning in America? An older colleague of mine once told me that Brandeis is where I belong, meaning that my work and temperament have an affinity with the New York Jewish intellectuals Irving Howe and Philip Rahv, who had taught there and have indelibly marked the institution.

Before joining the Brandeis faculty, I had in fact become a friend of Rahv during the last years of his life. He had severed his connection with *Partisan Review* and had launched the abortive *Modern Occasions*. Always in a rage against what he viewed as spuriousness, fecklessness, and stupidity, he viewed Jean Genet as a moral idiot, Norman Mailer a pornographer, the New Left a collection of political ignoramuses. His editorial character was sometimes overwhelming. *Trendiness* was his favorite word of disparagement of what proposed itself as the avant-garde, and he sought writers who would perform like troops in a battle in which he was the master strategist and tactician. He recruited me to to write an article attacking Norman Mailer as the exemplar of pornography. When I wondered why Mailer and not Philip Roth as well, he reprimanded me for my naïveté. Roth was a friend, an ally on other matters. Editorial character and strength do not always depend on fairness. I never wrote the article. Rahv was a bull in the china shop of the academy, a bluff-talking intellectual and literary critic, whose speech was a blur of indistinct words in which the attentive listener could discern a literary sensibility nourished on the reading of Henry James and Dostoyevsky. I have no idea what he was like in the classroom, but one of his students who became a fine critic, Stephen Donadio, has caught his presence and effect in the surprise Rahv presented as a man of exquisite sensibility under "the guise of a bearish not particularly cultivated fellow." In appearance he was the opposite of the elegant Lionel Trilling, but in sensibility a kindred spirit. Trilling's high style, filled with practiced hesitations, was in sharp contrast to Rahv's pugnacious polemical style, though Rahv admired Trilling's prose.

Ideology was a powerful negative in Rahv's vocabulary, usually an expression of the Stalinist mentality that *Partisan Review* combated from its inception in the thirties, when he and William Phillips rescued the journal from the John Reed Club and established its independent life. In a curious way, however, he retained his Marxism after he had criticized every perversion, or should I say version, of it. The Stalinists had betrayed Marxism, liberal fellow travelers were suckers for Stalinism, and the sixties radicals lacked the true revolutionist's understanding of history, strategy, and tactics. What was left was the negativism of the critic, who remained intransigently opposed to bourgeois society, but without any genuine positive alternative. Of course, this intransigence did not keep him from enjoying bourgeois pleasures. He knew the pleasures of the table. Rahv married well, if not happily. (He did not believe in happiness. " 'oose 'appy'?" he used to say in his Russian accent.) He was a genuine individualist who set his own agenda. There was nothing of the institution in Rahv's deportment, and Brandeis was the institution for him. I now occupy Rahv's office.

Though I have never felt at home in any institution, Brandeis has come closest to making me feel comfortable. I have come to enjoy the informality and intellectual seriousness of the institution, its *heimish*ness. And yet committee meetings have always made me uncomfortable. I find the endless discussion of inconsequential detail, the tone of discussion intolerable. I sometimes envy those who find comfort in their institutional identity. At meetings I have learned not to show how much I fidget inwardly—as if I were a person displaced in my own skin.

Five: On the One Hand

IN THE JEWISH schools I attended we were taught militancy on behalf of Jews and oppressed people everywhere in the only country devoted to the idea, if not always the practice, of liberating oppressed people. It did not stop us from siding with the Soviet Union against capitalist America. We were all expected to think in the same direction about our Jewishness and the important problems in the world. We were children: we didn't choose our politics, they were chosen for us. As you grow up, temperament sorts things out. It's not simply a matter of disillusionment. Yes, the revolution was a tyrant, the promised land a prison, so there was good reason to repudiate the movment. But let's assume the revolution was not tyrannical and the promised land not a prison. I still don't believe I would have been a comfortable presence on the left. I might have continued to make contributions to the cause, I might have delivered my vote, but always with reservations. I don't have the temperament for passionate commitment to a cause, nor do I have the passion of revulsion from it. Left, right, even center are all places that make me uneasy. You can't always refuse to occupy a place on the spectrum of politics or culture, but why does it always have to be the same place? I find myself listening to and resisting all attempts to confine me to a certain point of view. Politics has been an inescapable part of me. It was put there in my childhood, but it is in a sense an alien presence. The fact is that I have been critical of the left, but I have always taken it seriously. I wouldn't want a society that didn't have a place for it.

Let me begin again. I grew up on the left and in a sense have never outgrown it. My adversaries on the left will be surprised to hear this. I can't bear much of the talk I hear about oppression, exploitation, and victimization, especially the self-righteous tone of the talk. I know of course that there are victims (and who in history has been more victimized than my people?), that everything should be done to alleviate suffering and to remove the circumstances that make for suffering. But much of the talk leads nowhere or it may have a creative element, inventing victims where there are none. And yet I can't completely dissociate myself from the talk. I vote against the oppressors, and act on the parochial battlefields where I live and work. I give to charity, though I don't do it. (Giving to charity was frowned upon in the movement as a diversion from the necessary task of changing the system. Charity rests on the conviction that the poor will always be with us. Even if this is not the case, what would the anticharity ideologues propose as an alternative while the poor are with us?) I don't help out in soup kitchens or minister to those suffering from AIDS in hospices. I used to, but no longer demonstrate for justice. Moral laziness perhaps. But there is something else. Yeats said, "The best lack all conviction, the worst are full of passionate intensity." I don't mean to congratulate myself by claiming to be among the best. Yeats, after all, was being ironic.

I hear people on the left speak their indignation against a system they enjoy. Talk is cheap. If the system were transformed, they might be among the first to regret it, for their comforts would be disturbed. There are, of course, extraordinary persons who match their convictions with actions and for whom conviction has consequences. I don't particularly like the sour face and talk of Ralph Nader, but he is a man of conviction and consequence. He exists to make us all uncomfortable. It is odd that his cause is the consumer, for consumption gives pleasure and comfort. The sourness is the taste of self-righteousness. Is there a necessary connection between self-righteousness and conviction? There are times when I prefer the lack of conviction to conviction, an antidote to self-righteousness. We don't need to have an opinion about everything, a friend reminds me.

"The best lack all conviction": What would Yeats have made of our postmodern radical skeptics? They are in fact know-it-alls with the dogmatic conviction that we can never know anything with certainty. I was invited to deliver a lecture on the French critic Roland Barthes at Yale University. The department that invited me was filled with well-known exponents of postmodernist and poststructuralist theories. I was warned, "You are bringing coals to Newcastle." But I had something to say about Barthes that had not been said by others and took the risk. I spoke with force and eloquence; my mouth did not go dry as it often did on other lecturing occasions. The glass of water remained on the table untouched until the lecture was completed. (Pausing to drink only increases my nervousness. I fear that the pause diminishes the effect of a lecture.) The questions that followed the lecture were polite and were preceded by compliments. I sensed, however, that the comments were noncommital, reflecting some reservation about the lecture.

I soon learned what the reservation was about. No one in the audience was prepared to commit himself or herself until the master had spoken. The department (faculty and students) was in thrall to a gaunt, angular scholar from Belgium, Paul de Man, who spoke with an intimidatingly rapid-fire confidence. He had not yet spoken in the question period after my lecture, and everyone in the audience apparently was waiting for his lead. At the urging of the moderator, this most distinguished member of the faculty stood up and, affecting a certain reluctance, delivered a counterlecture, not really a lecture, but a series of evaluations of my claims: "You are right about A, wrong about B, wrong about C, wrong about D, etc., etc." I did not keep count, but my failures significantly outnumbered my successes. No reasons, no arguments, but papal bulls in effect excommunicating me from the subject.

What could I say in response? I did say, "You have given me grades without showing where I have gone wrong. You've asked no questions, so I have no answers." (Of course, he had all the answers.) I seethed for weeks afterwards, even more than when I had been challenged by the scholar at the Gauss lecture. I did have the consolation of learning much later, as did the rest of the world, that this famous scholar, who had tried to demolish my arguments about Roland Barthes, had been in his youth a journalist for a Nazi collaborationist newspaper. It gave a bizarre confirmation to what had been told to me about his presence at the university: that it was a form of intellectual despotism. The skeptic should be modest, because he claims to know the limits of his knowledge or may even be uncertain where those limits are, but the radical skeptic (de Man is an example) has the *absolute* conviction that knowledge is an impossibility, and he arrogantly dismisses all comers who claim to know something he doesn't know.

I am moved by a credible report of injustice, but resist deductions of injustice from ideology. The person who calls him- or herself a victim may or may not be one. An individual black person or an individual woman or an individual Jew is not entitled to the claim of being a victim as a deduction from the proposition that blacks have been enslaved and persecuted or that women have been treated as inferior or that Jews have been persecuted. We should want to know the actual experiences of individuals. The sense of victimization can lead to injustice. The victim strikes out against the victimizer, and the victimizer becomes the victim. Terror and counterterror. Does counterterror accomplish anything except contribute to the cycle of violence? A hard question. If not, what to do? Well, one can address the root causes that produce the violence. "Address the root causes" is a phrase to comfort the liberal conscience. What if an empirical study yields evidence of tangled causes of character and circumstance for which there is no obvious solution? I dislike the phrase as an automatic reflex in parlor discussion. It is riskless, a sop to conscience. Be careful, I tell myself, not to let your revulsion from victimization talk prevent you from recognizing when an injustice occurs and to care about it. There is injustice aplenty in the world without having to invent it.

The poet William Blake said, "I must create a system or be enslaved by another man's." Was Blake in control of his syntax? For it implies the possibility of becoming the slave of one's own system. Better mine than his, but do we need a system in which to live? Should we, can we resist any and all systems? Turgenev in a letter to Tolstoy: "Would to God your horizon may broaden every day! The people who bind themselves to systems are those who are unable to encompass the whole truth and try to catch it by the tail; a system is like the tail of truth, but truth is like a lizard; it leaves its tail in your fingers and runs away, knowing full well that it will grow a new one in a twinkling." Tolstoy's "system" may have compromised his art, but he possessed a moral passion to do good in the world. With his position in society, his genius, and his courage he made an enormous difference. He educated the peasants, spoke out against the pogroms, helped distribute food in a time of famine. Turgenev stood back from life to cultivate his art. Tolstoy was the greater man and the greater artist. There are also times when the worst lack all conviction and the best are full of passionate intensity.

And what of the conservatives? They offer a temptation, for they often make real sense about the world. Why have I resisted the temptation? The conservatives I know for the most part wear suits and starched shirts, and prefer bow ties on informal as well as formal occasions. No, they all don't dress that way, but those who do seem to be making a political statement in their dress. They speak well, their emotions are under control, and a sardonic note often enters their voices when they refer to a view or action on the opposing side. Contempt, disdain—as if the opposing view is unworthy of attention. The argument hasn't even achieved the dignity of deserving refutation. On the left, the dress is more casual, the note struck usually indignation or outrage. The adversary is evil, in bad faith, arrogant, reactionary. I am made uneasy in the company of either side when the conversation becomes political. I want to look beyond the periphery of an argument to assumptions I can't comfortably share with either side, and so I quarrel with both sides.

Neoconservatives are a special case. They are ex-radicals and ex-liberals who emerged as an immediate reaction to the illusions of the sixties, but they represent a deeper tendency that began with disillusionment with Marxism and went underground in the sixties. As a conservatism without roots, it has a curious resemblance to the object of its revulsion. Neoconservatives have the stridency of the radicalism they have abandoned. Why do they display such contempt for liberals? They think of them as Stalinists in disguise or as soft-headed fools. Leslie Fiedler once defined a liberal as a man with a *yiddishe hartz un a goyishe kop* (a Jewish heart and a gentile head). You have to listen or read for voice as well as sense. I hear in the accents of neoconservatism the old ideological patterns of the past. While traditional conservatives have the equanimity of those who have nothing to exorcise, neoconservatives, or at least those who are embittered ex-leftists, recoil from their past with particular intensity. I find them stridently confident, predictable, and even fanatical in their opposition to every liberal or radical tendency (homosexual advocacy, feminism) in their habit of dividing the world too neatly between good and evil. They tend to be intolerant of softness, hesitation, equivocation, the contemptible faults of liberals. I recall the same scornful guilt-inducing dismissal of liberals by Stalinists and sixties radicals. I think it a mark of strength in the liberal to scorn the scorners. In sketching a portrait of the neoconservative type I risk falling into the trap of ideological reduction. As with people on the left, I know admirable people of conservative persuasion who do not fit the type. The first humanizing wisdom about ideology is that type and reality do not coincide. It is a wisdom that makes possible friendship across ideological lines, though the friendships are difficult to sustain in proportion to the intensity of ideological conflict.

Two kinds of conservatives disagree. One says the American people are experiencing moral decline, the other says no, you can't condemn the people without being elitist. Conservatives used to cherish elitism, now elitism is a word they assign to contemptible liberals. And who are the people? Whether on the left or on the right, *the people* is a convenient abstraction to be bandied about for ideological purposes. I learned long ago to mistrust anyone's invoking of the people—as if they were a homogeneity, as if the invokers really knew the people.

Let's imagine for a moment that the person on the left was granted his wish, the person on the right hers (there! a solution to the problem of gendering pronouns), what would each wish? If their rhetoric is to be taken seriously, are we to believe that each side would wish the disappearance of the other? I suspect that the rhetoric corresponds to sentiment. The left dreams of a world without conservative callousness, what the conservatives call realism; the right dreams of one without leftist stupidity, what radicals call utopian hope. Each side acts as if it wants to rid the playground of seesaws, a totalitarian fantasy. It's not enough to grant the other the right to speak. Turning away from the other with contempt violates the spirit of the right—and, for the matter, the left. Intolerance is an instinct of the political life. We say everyone has a right to "their" opinion, but we often wish the adversarial opinion didn't exist.

Those who have remained on the left may have struggled with the painful reality of Soviet tyranny, but they have not always dealt openly with their disillusionment. They have never allowed the fact of the Soviet Union to put in doubt their convictions—as if the Soviet Union was merely corrigible error within their system of thought, the correction of which would never alter that system. In contrast, the leftist turned neoconservative made the Soviet Union the decisive mind-altering fact of their lives. Every item of left-liberal politics is brought into the experience of disillusionment. In both cases, there is a suspension of critical intelligence, a moral blindness. The neoconservative views the liberal as hopelessly contaminated by sympathies with a totalitarian regime, every program and policy for the general welfare on a slippery slope toward such a regime, but is untroubled by the history of conservative association with authoritarianism, racism, and anti-Semitism. Left and right are sensitive to each other's dark side, but pooh-pooh the dark side of their own convictions, the consequence of systematic thinking.

A wise friend of conservative bent, the biographer of Dostoyevsky Joseph Frank, says, "I try to keep the lines of communication open." He has friends on the left and friends on the right. So do I. My wife and I plan a dinner party. Should we invite the S's (on the left) and the

J's (on the right)? If we do, we risk disaster. Disliking a person's politics spills over into disliking the person. Who needs it? The coward in me would rather not reveal to the S's that I am friendly with the J's or to the J's that I am friends with the S's. I have been confronted with surprise that I am a friend of so and so by a friend who finds so and so beyond the pale. The most unpleasant part of it is my embarrassed response. Of course, a dinner of the like-minded might pass boringly without event. My wife's solution: don't have dinner parties.

I am not a joiner. I am reluctant to sign up as a member of any organization, because I generally can't find myself or my ideas in it. I try with only partial success to follow the example of the Cuban poet Herberto Padilla: "The only petition I sign is the one I write myself." I resist the passion for and the passion against, sometimes regretting it, for what I call my lack of conviction makes me lonely. It is not so much lack of conviction that defines me as a strong allergic reaction to fanaticism.

I have a theory. It arose in a conversation with a friend, a man of the notional left whose life comforts are disturbed mostly by personal demons and to a lesser degree when he looks at the troubles of the world beyond him: wars, oppression, exploitation. I told him of my surprise at the deductions of my salary check, a very large tax bite, and he said, "You sound like a Republican." And I said that we all have Republican instincts, meaning that we are all defensive of our interests, our money, our property, our children, our families. Generosity and self-sacrifice are occasional episodes in the system of our lives. I vote Democratic. I might vote socialist if the realization of the idea was the idea intended and not the tyranny it has become. But my instincts are Republican, and not only my instincts, but almost everyone's. Republicanism is the political id. Fortunately, we are also ego and superego.

What to do about the homeless? A liberal turned conservative, friend turned acquaintance, once asked me how I voted in a presidential election: "No wait, don't tell me. You voted for Dukakis, And I know the reason: it's the homeless, isn't it?" His voice was tinged with contempt. Didn't I know that the homeless will always be with us, no matter who is elected? He was probably right that it didn't matter who was elected. But I couldn't abide his disdain. And what if the election made a difference, he would still have voted for Bush. The homeless were beyond the horizon of his interest. The ordinary person on the left shares a revulsion toward the homeless, which he doesn't admit to himself. He walks past them, trying not to catch their supplicating glances. He may console himself with the thought that charity solves nothing; the system needs to be transformed, though he has no idea how the system should be changed. The person on the right is disposed to blame the homeless for making a mess of their lives, so he feels complacent in his unwillingness to provide government support, perhaps even to give a handout. It would only contribute to dependency or delinquency. The difference between liberal and conservative is a debating point. Both walk past the supplicating gestures without looking. The gestures threaten the comfort zone of our ordinary lives. The person on the right may have an easier time walking by the homeless. His convictions match his inaction. There is an older Tory right whose compassion for the unfortunate is the guiding principle, but they are not to be confused with the selfish right. The selfishness is less disturbing than the bad faith that haunts the right in their talk about freedom and virtue. The virtues incorporate too easily the gospel of capital accumulation.

Most conservatives, I suspect, dislike the state, because it is an obstacle to their greed. They want an unimpeded path to capital accumulation. They are right to see the state as often inefficient and unproductive and as the site of corruption. Private industry may also be inefficient and corrupt, but it lacks the enforcing power of the police or the military. So the liberal, taking all this to heart, must engage in a balancing act between a defense of the private and an affirmation of the countervailing role of the state in regulating private greed.

Dig deep into the assumptions of left and right and you arrive at conundrums. Conservatives affirm freedom and self-responsibility, liberals and radicals say we are the victims of circumstance and powers over which we have no control. Conservatives are realists who believe we need to accept the world as it is; radicals believe we can transform the world. We need to ask conservatives: if reality resists the will to change, what does our freedom amount to? The question for radicals: how do we change the world if power is elsewhere? Conservatives wisely caution us about the unintended consequences of any action we might undertake, but they seem unconcerned about the consequences of taking no action. Follow either position and you wind up confused. If forces determine our choices, do we choose? What about an intermediate position? We choose within constraints. But does that solve the problem? What determines the choice? Is there some psychological necessity that precedes and dictates choice? But maybe necessity leads to a fork, and necessity doesn't decide where it will flow. What is the it? I choose to stay with the questions, mistrusting as I do confident answers.

It doesn't matter whether it starts from the right or from the left, the rise to power always tends to corrupt. Yet power is necessary, for it holds things together. Out of power, there is the corruption of resentment. All hopes for universal justice, peace, and harmony are utopian—"nowhere," in Thomas More's sense. There is only more or less justice, more or less corruption. I mean this without cynicism.

I envy the poise of Tocqueville, John Stuart Mill, and Isaiah Berlin and their respect for the resistances in reality. Too many liberals care about the world but don't seem to know it. There is much to admire in the philosophical conservative mind, but conservative practice is something else, displaying as it does a hardness and scorn for anyone who doesn't respect the realities of power. The instincts of possession and self-interest are turned into absolute principles that can never be trumped by other concerns. The market is reality, a conservative acqaintance tells me. Opposing and criticizing it is like complaining about a river's current. My liberal conscience speaks up: the market takes different forms in different countries. Nothing prevents us from modifying the market to take care of its casualties. A radical friend is all indignation against the predations of the market and I say: the market is reality. There's a name for me in the stock market. I'm a contrarian. Is this perversity? I don't think so. I look for balance. If politics were a playground, I would choose a seesaw, sometimes one end and sometimes the other, and at other times I would stand aside to appreciate its movements.

I write from the point of view of aging. What should one say to the idealism of youth, its compassion for the poor, its activism to change the status quo, its principled outrage when power acts against weakness? How to respond to the indignations of youth, to my daughter Jessica's, for instance? She studies the plight of low-paid workers and welfare recipients and acts in behalf of what she sees as the failures of compassion in the system. She is reenacting, not imitating, the passions of my youth. Presuming the wisdom of age doesn't work, since age has perpetrated its own atrocities and follies. The young suspect that complacency, tiredness, a wish to have comforts undisturbed have been turned into a principle. Assume that to be the case, it doesn't make the intransigent youthful voice of principle less self-righteous. I heat up when I'm not allowed my uncertainty, when my refusal to go along, my hesitation about signing a petition puts me beyond the pale. I need to check my own proclivity for perverseness. The Padilla syndrome: sign nothing except what you yourself have written. The more I hear all the sides, the more I retreat from opinion. The older I get the harder it is for me to discern the consequences of a view I hold, or is it that in the past I cared less for consequences? The eye on consequences can paralyze the will. No political actor could safely follow a politics of uncertainty. Fortunately, I am not a politician or a journalist, who needs to have an opinion about everything. I am not giving advice about practice, only proposing an attitude, not for everyone and not for anyone all the time. When ignorant armies clash night and day, it helps to be able to go off somewhere in a quiet place and simply sit. Wisdom? Fecklessness? A sign of age? I grow old, I grow old.

Nothing irritates me as much as perverse arguers, those who never agree with anything you say. They say no to everything you say, or "Yes, but matters are more complicated." A discussion takes place between two people, the rhythm of the argument may be a continuous ebb and flow, and then a third person suddenly enters with deliberate gravity to slow the exchange in order to take the argument to a "deeper level." The deeper level precludes agreement about anything, since all is complication and uncertainty. What is my share in the perversity? The geography of the truth is not entirely on one side of the globe, and not always on the same side. At times we need to decide and act. I like T. S. Eliot's statement: "Scepticism is a highly civilized trait, though when it declines into pyrrhonism, it is one of which civilization can die. Where scepticism is strength, pyrrhonism is weakness: for we need not only the strength to defer a decision, but the strength to make one."

I am perfectly willing to settle into a conviction so long as I feel free to change my mind when the facts warrant it. Conviction can lead to fanaticism. But what about the perils of no conviction? You become a passive observer of events and are unable to commit yourself to anything. This is not what I have in mind. My life is so sedentary, so unadventurous in the physical sense that I want the intellectual risks of confusion and uncertainty. I want thinking that is like an unplanned trip, the destination unknown until I arrive. I am willing to wind up as a conservative or liberal or radical, but not to start out as one. Every trip shouldn't have to wind up in the same place, not because there is no truth, but because its location is not confined to a single place. And certain trips are to be avoided. I remember arguing with a follower of the political theorist Leo Strauss. He invited me into his assumptions and then began to construct his argument like a finely wrought chain, each link secured to the next. My mind slid effortlessly along the chain and suddenly found itself where it didn't want to be. But I couldn't find my way back; no link gave way under the pressure. I lost the argument, but continued to resist. The logic of the Straussian came up against my sense of life.

In the early seventies I saw *The Battle for Algiers.* Despite its obvious sympathy for the revolution, the film was remarkably evenhanded in presenting the horrific effects of violence on both sides. We were shown scenes of police repression and revolutionary terrorism. Two scenes in particular stick in the mind. In one scene a child is sitting on the terrace of a café on a bright day, eating ice cream. In the following scene a bomb explodes, destroying the café and everyone in it, including of course the child. The large student audience at Boston University, already filled with its own revolutionary passion, cheered loudly. I want no part of such revolutionary justice. Recently, my wife took me to see a film about the Zapatistas in Mexico, *A Place Called Chiapas,* sympathetic to the Zapatistas. Like *The Battle for Algiers,* the film was scrupulous in presenting all sides: the rebels, the government, the paramilitary, though there was no doubt as to where its sympathies lay. The persecution and suffering of the Mayans were unmistakable. The Zapatista leader, the masked Marcos, an educated white man from the city, came across as humane and appealing, though that is hardly evidence for his humanity. The film aroused in me the sympathies learned and fostered in my adolescence. I can imagine the cool, distant reaction of a conservative spectator, revising the story into a cautionary tale about the risks of revolutionary terror. If I recoil from revolutionary terror, I don't want to freeze my capacity for sympathy for the victims of established authority. A conservative friend of mine once said, "The measure of a society is the way it treats its disadvantaged."

Recently, I took a long walk on Madison Avenue with Bert Silverman, a childhood friend from my fellow-traveling past. We were reminiscing about old times. I suddenly asked him, "How do we differ from former sympathizers with the Nazis? Think what they have to do to deserve forgiveness, to forgive themselves. The Soviets were responsible for the deaths of millions, but all we have to do is condemn the system and say we were duped." We may experience a certain nostalgia for the time we believed in the cause without feeling guilty. There is even a residue of guilt for having turned against the movement. The past in memory has the glow of youthful idealism in spite of what we know about it. And the "renegade" who turns with vehemence against his past acts as if he has to prove himself against the claim of his early idealism. So what is the difference between the ex-Nazi and ex-Communist or fellow traveler? (As I write this sentence I feel a twinge of guilt, as if I have committed a sacrilege in comparing Communists and Nazis.) Whatever the practice, the ideals of Marxism were humane, the ideals of Nazi killers were not. We all know decent Communist sympathizers; a decent Nazi is an oxymoron.

I retain an affection for the ethos of comradeship in my early Marxist formation. No self-justification intended, nor exculpation of the cause. I think it bad faith or the absence of intellectual and moral rigor simply to say that the ideals were magnificent and betrayed in practice. The ideals themselves contained the seeds of betrayal. Stalinism was a monstrosity that had partial roots in Marxism (partial, because the authoritarian tradition of Russia has its share of responsibility). My son Eric's doctoral dissertation on the French Revolution reminds me that the Reign of Terror preceded Marx. Liberalism in its soft-mindedness doesn't have a clean record in relation to revolutionary terror, and it needs to resist any temptation to move again in that direction. But I can't share in the revulsion of the ex-Marxist for whom his past is nothing but blight. The ex-Marxist who devotes himself to revulsion from the left loses the sympathies that first led him into the movement. A sense of betrayal never leaves him and a resentful hardness takes over. He becomes immunized against susceptibility to any and all appeals for social compassion, and he does not lose the vehemence of the commitment which he is denouncing. If you reject the fanaticism of a cause, you must reject its tone as well, for the tone will give you away. I once said this in a letter to an ex-radical acquaintance, burnt by the sun, who had turned into a vehement neoconservative. I have never received a reply.

Like me, he had marched in May Day parades. He recalls them with a revulsion I cannot share. He remembers Irish hecklers standing alongside the marching route, proudly affirming their Irish roots. He wonders why he failed to experience a similar pride in his Jewishness. That is not the lesson I drew from my experience. The faces of the hecklers, Irish, Italians, Polish, maybe even Jewish, I don't exactly recall their ethnicities, were disfigured by hatred. After one parade, a number of them surrounded a friend of mine and broke his arm. However wrong we were about the Soviet Union, the hecklers get no credit from me. Their Irish pride and American patriotism on May Day were filled with hatred. Our marching and sloganeering was blind self-righteousness, our enemies abstractions of capitalism and imperialism. We had no desire to break arms.

The twin tenets of my Jewish education were pride in our Jewish identity and solidarity with the working class. None of our teachers suggested that they might be in conflict with each other. For us there was no conflict, because we were at home in the diaspora. Capitalism was the greater enemy than anti-Semitism. Marx knew that nationalism was the enemy of *international* working-class solidarity. Nationalism made you believe that your bond was with your countryman, whatever his class. Moreover, for the de-Judaized Marx (his father had converted to Christianity), the Jew not only represented an adversary faith, he had become part of the oppressor class. What Marx and his descendants did not realize was that national identity was deeper than class solidarity, that you have to work to achieve class consciousness. Most people are born into their national or ethnic identity. In the Freudian scheme, ethnicity is the id: look at the Balkans and countries of Asia and Africa. And yet, look at us Jews in the American diaspora: how easily our tribal identity has submerged itself into the mainstream. I have in mind my intermarrying children and their children. The ethnic id is not a universal.

Stalinism is worse than Nazism: I have heard this from neoconservatives. Not that they would discount the monstrous evil of the Holocaust, but somehow the horrors of the Gulag interest them more. I'm struck by how little the anti-Stalinist intellectuals of the forties and fifties devoted themselves to the study of Nazism, the main killer of Jews, Hannah Arendt being the most notable exception. Was it their involvement in radical causes that made Stalinism a main concern for them? Stalinism needed to be understood, whereas Nazism was simply evil. Why do we need to make comparisons of this sort? And if we make comparisons, does it simply become a matter of body counting? Millions more in the Soviet Union died than under Nazism, because the Soviet Union lasted longer, but for sheer numbers per year the Nazis take the prize. Body counting is a dismal science. Consider this: if the Soviets were worse than the Nazis, why didn't we join Hitler in the war against Stalin? Itzhik Feffer was killed by Stalin, but he had his moment in the sun when he could write "I am a Jew" with pride. Inconceivable this could happen in Nazi Germany. Imagine what the world would look like if the Nazis had won instead. We know what the world looks like after the victory of the Soviet Union and its allies: nothing to cheer about, but could we have conceivably made another choice?

I listened to a program on the radio devoted to the life of Paul Robeson and to my surprise was overcome by emotion. He was a man of extraordinary charisma in his physical presence and voice. An irresistible performer every time he sang or spoke, he would overcome whatever reservations you might have about his politics. In my adolescence, Robeson was "America to me." He sang in Yiddish, in Russian, in German, and in other languages as if he were a native speaker of each. He was the voice of the peat-bog soldiers in concentration camps, of the heroes of the Warsaw Ghetto ("Zog Nit Keinmal Az Du Geist Dem Letzn Vegg"), of the loyalist defenders of the Spanish Republic against the Falangist columns of Franco, and of course of the oppressed Negro people. Hearing him on the radio overcame the distance of four decades. His intransigence about racism in America and his unreconstructed loyalty to the Soviet Union destroyed his career. I had thought that Robeson had been a dupe of the Soviet Union, that he had somewhat blinded himself to the horrors of the regime, that if he had known what we know now, he would have withdrawn his sympathy from the regime. His sense of justice and injustice was simply too keen and universal to allow him to support injustice anywhere.

The narrator of the program, in the same tone of reverence and sympathy with which she told the rest of the story of Robeson's life, described a visit that he had made to the Soviet Union in which he had learned of the death of a friend, the great Yiddish actor Shimon Mikhoels, at the hands of the authorities and the imprisonment of another friend, the poet Itzhik Feffer. At Robeson's request, Feffer was allowed to leave his cell and meet with him in his hotel room, where Feffer signaled to him to be careful about what he said, indicating through gestures that the room was bugged. They carried on two conversations simultaneously: an innocuous spoken and a revealing silent one. With a movement of his finger across his neck, Feffer told of his imminent execution. Robeson, terribly moved, embraced Feffer. Without a change of tone in her voice, the narrator explained Robeson's subsequent silence about the episode and his continuing loyalty to the Soviet Union as reflecting a fear that if he told the story it would damage his credibility with his admirers and supporters. An odd explanation, for what would have been more credible than speaking out against injustice wherever it occurred? The narrator showed no awareness that in telling this story she had cast a shadow on Robeson's credibility. Why did Robeson persist in his devotion to Stalinism despite his knowledge of its horrors? Why do Christians maintain their faith despite what has been done in the name of Christianity? (I have since heard another explanation: the Soviet Union supported liberation movements in Africa and elsewhere and Robeson did not wish to do anything to jeopardize that support—a case of realpolitik.) Nothing in the voice of the narrative represented the dissonance of the episode in the story being told.

I can imagine a review of this program in the conservative magazines *Commentary* and *The New Criterion* in which all of Robeson's life would be transformed into a lie by this one episode. It is an event that reflects badly on him and more immediately on the creator of the program and the unmodulated reverence of the narrative voice. But I am unwilling to damn Robeson for it. Those who would condemn Robeson's life and career say nothing about those who shouted racist and anti-Semitic obscenities at him and his supporters on the road out of Peekskill after his concert. I don't know what was in his mind as he returned home. He was descended from a slave and spoke out against racial injustice in America when it was unfashionable to do so. He identified racial injustice with injustice against all human beings. And yet he failed to acknowledge it in this particular instance and perhaps in other instances as well. I suspect that he did not see the deaths of his friends as a reflection of the enormity and monstrosity of the Stalin regime. Scholars were already documenting the massive killing in the Soviet Union, but the documentation was part of a political struggle. It was not believed by the other side. Perhaps Robeson could not, would not, extrapolate the monstrosity from the fate of his two friends. His failure is unforgivable. And yet I cannot damn him. I resist the swing of the pendulum, the need to demonize every aspect of the world in which I grew up. Indeed, my refusal to demonize the past is part of my repudiation of Stalinism, which thrived on demonizing its enemies. In their wholesale revulsion from the past, the neoconservative converts from Marxism write and speak in the demonizing tones of the past. The Manichean construction of the world persists, only now they have changed sides. Now we have to choose between Pinochet and Allende, between authoritarian government and totalitarianism–as if there were no other choices to be made.

In my critical writing, I have found myself resisting the twists and turns in the evolution of the radical spirit in the academy–with concessions to its achievements. The war in Vietnam ended, the civil rights movement had its successes, but the dominant mood in the larger society took a conservative turn in the eighties and the nineties. The radical students who made careers in the academy sublimated their radicalism in the various disciplines they occupied, particularly in the humanities. Radicalism became theories of interpretation, its targets literary and philosophical texts and social and political institutions. Having failed to transform society, it also became disillusioned, and already, beginning in the seventies, the most radically skeptical of theories, deconstructionism, became the rage. Its aim was to unsettle our convictions about the possibility of objective truth, spiritual transcendence, authoritative discourse. It asserted a doctrine of uncertainty in the most certain of tones. Is it fortuitous that its originator is a French Jew, Jacques Derrida? D. H. Lawrence once remarked that the Jews, Marx, Einstein, and Freud have unsettled our universe: "We are all very pleased with Mr. Einstein for knocking that eternal axis out of the universe." Lawrence didn't really know what he was talking about in the case of Einstein, whose passion was to discover the divine order of the universe. God doesn't throw dice, he said. But Jewishness and a subversive radicalism (whether it takes a skeptical or an apocalyptic turn) have a long history of association. So do Jewishness and moderation. You should want to upset the applecart only if the apples are rotten. Derrida's deconstruction seems simply to take pleasure in upsetting the applecart. Apparently apolitical, deconstruction prepared the ground for the ideologues of race, gender, and class to stake their claims in the academy. The great books that we read in college and that I have taught for many years are now objects of suspicion, repositories of "false consciousness." Those who confidently find false consciousness in others believe that they possess true consciousness. And what entitles them to that belief? Radical skepticism and ideological dogmatism, it turns out, converge on the ground of intellectual and moral arrogance.

A reviewer of one of my books referred to me as an old-fashioned humanist. I prefer *unfashionable* to the pejorative *old-fashioned*. But I am not embarrassed by "humanism." It is a reflection of our modernist ethos that *old-fashioned* is an automatic epithet to be applied to humanism just as *wine-dark* is automatically applied to the sea in Homer's epic. Humanism is an intellectual vaccine against dogmatisms of all kinds. I think of it as a critical appreciation of the works of art and intellect past and present—*without piety*. If you're a critic, you can't afford to be pious. I like what the English critic, I. A. Richards, says about the artist: "[He] is concerned with the record and perpetuation of the experiences which seem to him most worth having . . . he is also the man who is most likely to have experiences of value to record. He is the point at which the growth of the mind shows itself." "Experiences worth having" and "the growth of the mind" are not the exclusive possessions of the artist. Readers, critics and "ordinary" people are capable in varying degrees of such experience and growth. If this were not the case, the artist's growth would be like a tree falling in the forest with nobody present to hear it. Part of one's growth is developing the capacity to discriminate and make judgments, to accept and reject with an uncomfortable mind, independent and without vanity. I love Matthew Arnold's sentences: "When one side of a question has long had your earnest support, when all your feelings are engaged, when you hear around you no language but one, when your party talks this language like a steam-engine and can imagine no other—still to be able to think, still to be irresistibly carried, if so it be, by the current of thought to the opposite side of the question, and, like Balaam, to be unable to speak anything *but what the Lord has put in your mouth.* I know nothing more striking, and I must add that I know nothing more un-English." I like to think of myself as "irresistibly carried . . . by the current of thought." I find myself a contrarian, not from perversity, but from a desire to resist any party whose language is like a steam-engine. Not wanting to be confined to an ideology or ethnicity or anything that would define me, I have the feeling of being an outsider, not a bad feeling when it is experienced as autonomy. It is the sentiment of the critic.

Fine for a seminar, what what about real life, what about our terrible century? Saul Bellow puts down the challenge: "You religious and enlightened people, you Christians, Jews, and Humanists, you believers in freedom, dignity, and enlightenment—you think you know what a human being is. We will show you what he is, and what you are. Look at our camps and crematoria, and see if you can bring your hearts to care about these millions." Primo Levi, the great writer and survivor of the camps, tells us with the authority of experience that "culture could be useful even if only in some marginal cases, and for brief periods; it could enhance an hour, establish a fleeting bond with a companion, keep the mind healthy. It definitely was not useful in orienting oneself and understanding." And his fellow survivor Jean Améry exposed the utter defenselessness of the agnostic intellectual in the camps. "In the camp he became an unskilled laborer, who had to do his job in the open—which meant in most cases that the sentence was already passed on him. . . . Camp life demanded above all bodily agility and physical courage that bordered on brutality," and the intellectual generally proved to be inadequate to the demand. But the internal situation is even worse. The intellectual found himself betrayed by the very qualities that were virtues outside of the camp: rationality, the questioning and self-questioning spirit. "Absolute intellectual tolerance and the methodological doubting of the intellectual become factors in his auto-destruction," Améry wrote. Rational questioning turns upon itself, and the man of reason loses confidence in his reason: "The intellectual . . . who after the collapse of initial inner resistance had recognized that what may not be, very well could be, who experienced the logic of the SS as a reality that proved itself by the hour, now took a few fateful steps further in his thinking. Were not those who were preparing to destroy him in the right, owing to the undeniable fact that they were the stronger ones?"

And yet Améry, an agnostic intellectual, a secular humanist, never took the fateful steps in his own thinking or behavior. He describes an episode in which he traded blows with a torturer with the full knowledge that he would only suffer more blows, because it was the only way that he could preserve his own dignity.

In Auschwitz he once hit me in the face because of a trifle; that is how he was used to dealing with all the Jews under his command. At this moment—I felt it with piercing clarity—it was up to me to go a step further in my prolonged appeals case against society. In open revolt I struck Juszek in the face in turn. My human dignity lay in this punch to the jaw—and that it was in the end I, the physically much weaker man, who succumbed and was woefully thrashed, meant nothing to me. Painfully beaten, I was satisfied with myself. But not, as one might think, for reasons of courage and honor, but only because I grasped well that there are situations in life in which our body is our entire self and our entire fate. I was my body and nothing else: in hunger, in the blow that I suffered, in the blow that I dealt. My body, debilitated and crusted with filth, was my calamity. My body, when it tensed to strike, was my physical and metaphysical dignity.

Knowing the temptations of nihilism, Améry persisted in his loyalty to the humanism of the Enlightenment: "I profess loyalty to the enlightenment, specifically to the *classical* enlightenment—as a *philosophia perennis* that contains all of its own corrections. . . . I stand up for analytical reason and its language, which is logic. In spite of all that we had to

experience, I believe that even today, as in the days of the Encyclope-
dists, knowledge leads to recognition and recognition to morality."
What makes this statement persuasive is not its logic, but the courage
with which Améry enacted it.

Levi too remained to the end a loyalist to a rational humanism. In
Survival at Auschwitz, he recalls a time when a particular passage from
the "Canto of Ulysses" in Dante's *Inferno* suddenly and inexplicably
came to mind.

> Then of that age-old fire loftier born
> Began to mutter and move, as a wavering flame
> Wrestles against the wind and is over-born;
> And, like a speaking tongue vibrant to flame
> Language, the tip of it flickering to and fro
> Threw out a voice and answered: "When I came . . ."

Puzzled about how or why it came into his mind, he nevertheless
finds that keeping the passage in mind enables him to defy the circumstances of his existence and to sustain him. One does not have to
know how the passage came to Levi's mind to be struck by how apt
the memory of the *Inferno* is in the circumstances. A modern reader of
the poem could hardly avoid thoughts of the Holocaust in the images
of horror and degradation in Dante's poem, beings frozen in ice,
buried in excrement, suffering the most excruciating pain without
promise of an end. The *Inferno* could be the poem of the Holocaust
were it not for the fact that even in hell the image of the human is preserved. It was Erich Auerbach, a refugee from Nazism, who empha-
sized the extraordinary humanity of the condemned figures in hell.
Severe as divine punishment may be, they retain their human capacity. Dante's characters are given the "freedom" to relive their earthly
pasts in imagination, a hell-defying imagination. When the pilgrim
Dante encounters them, their pasts, filled with suffering of a kind different from what they experience in hell, provoke his sympathy and
we remember them as they lived in the world. The *Inferno* in its inten-

sity helps us see the even more radical extremity of the Holocaust. Dante's hell is, after all, the work of an imagination, that of Dante's God, which also conceived purgatory and paradise. Purgatory and paradise are inconceivable in the mind that produced the Holocaust. Levi in effect becomes a character in a hell worse than Dante's and, unlike Dante's characters, undeserving of a place in it. Like Dante's characters, Levi "proves" in his very being the inextinguishability of the human face.

In stripping their victims of their humanity by turning them into garbage (killing them was not enough), the Nazis showed their contempt for humanity itself. Serial killers, they tried systematically to destroy all the "inferior" peoples of the earth, leaving only the Aryan, who is "more" than human. To be neither a human being nor a beast is to be not a superman, as the Aryan saw himself, but a monster. Levi acknowledges the partial success the Nazis had in depriving human beings of their humanity. He tells stories of victims who collaborated with the enemy in order to save themselves, but he does not acknowledge defeat. He is careful to note instances of people who managed to preserve their integrity and decency, no matter how extreme conditions were:

> I believe that it was really due to Lorenzo that I am alive today; and not so much for his material aid as for his having constantly reminded me by his presence, by his natural and plain manner of being good, that there still existed a just world outside our own, something and someone still pure and whole, not corrupt, not savage, extraneous to hatred and terror, something difficult to define, a remote possibility of good, but for which it was worth surviving.

Levi did not have the advantage of a faith and a sense of solidarity with those who share the faith. A confirmed Communist, like his barber, "never despaired," because "Stalin was his fortress, the Rock sung in the psalms." Moral reason and the cultural tradition (what Levi and Améry possessed) do not provide the sense of solidarity one finds in religious and political belief. They may be too weak as resources in extreme situations. But the examples of Levi and Améry should discourage us from dismissing their power. For them as for us they are the only alternative to the intolerable demystification of our humanity by the Holocaust.

Six: Heavy Breathing

THERE IS NO more powerful rebuke to our demand for justice than the vicissitudes of our life in the body: this is the great theme of the Book of Job. Illness reminds us that our happiness is never secure. We may dream of a return to paradise, but all such dreams are illusions. We may cry out against injustice, but we will never receive satisfaction from life. The dream of the transformation of self and world needs to answer to illness and the prospect of mortality.

We hear much talk these days about the body: relieving pain, curing disease, prolonging life. Some scientists even explore the possibility of immortality. A scientist friend of mine tells me that cells are not intrinsically mortal; their mortality is an accident theoretically preventible. The goddess of the dawn, Aurora, gave her lover immortal life, but neglected to give him immortal youth. She forgot to consider her lover's quality of life. Tennyson wrote a beautiful poem, "Tithonus," in which Aurora's lover, eternally aging longs for a death that will never come. While the scientists make discoveries, we become sick, grow old, and die. Illness, aging, and dying are our deepest experiences.

I don't make obscene phone calls, but people sometimes hesitate before they respond, because I'm a heavy breather. I have what is called late-onset asthma, the kind that suddenly appears in middle age after a crisis like divorce. Children may outgrow their asthma, but its late-onset version is a rest-of-the-life sentence. In theory asthma can disappear as suddenly as it appears. But I don't know of a single case of late-onset asthma disappearing. Does asthma distinguish between the innocence of children and the guilt of adults? Of course not, but that is a thought in the mind of an adult asthmatic. Unlike emphysema, which destroys the elasticity of the lungs and is fatal, asthma seems like, but is not, a psychological disease because it doesn't leave a mark on the body. The only traces it leaves are indirect ones, scars from pneumonia, to which asthmatics are particularly vulnerable. A manual my doctor gave me says that asthma is not an emotional or psychological disease, though emotional stress can exacerbate symptoms. I once consulted a psychoanalyst who told me there was no psychological cure, but he could help me cope with the anxieties of having the disease. I am a reverse skeptic. There may be no evidence of psychological origins, but that doesn't rule out the possibility.

It began when I was visiting friends in the Berkshires for a weekend of what I hoped would be a lull in the anguish of recriminations between me and my ex-wife, anxiety about my children, and resentments toward lawyers and the legal system in general. A number of childhood friends had converged on the summer home of the warmest, the most generous of friends, and it felt like a return to a childhood Eden, a childhood of course I had never really known. After lunch we took a long walk to settle the meal. The host proposed that we play touch football. We were scrimmaging for no more than five minutes when I caught a pass and suddenly had to struggle for breath. In terror I began to inhale and exhale rapidly. (Later I learned this was the worst possible thing I could do. When the attack comes, one must avoid panic and breathe as deeply and as slowly as possible.) I bent over instinctively, panting strenuously for what seemed an age. The terror increased as nothing seemed to change and the breathing became more and more difficult. I could see the anxious, helpless looks of my friends, and hear voices discussing what to do. I thought I was going to die. I felt desperate, but I also felt an emotion of–I'm not sure what to call it, guilt? I imagined the grief-stricken expressions of my parents, the desolation of my children. Why guilt, why not just plain terror and fear for myself? And then the attack subsided. It would be the first of many.

It had come without warning, although there were anticipations in a chronic cough that I had acquired in the preceding months. As a child, I suffered from hay fever, so my susceptibility to asthma should not have been a complete surprise. But the first attack was so sudden and overwhelming that I experienced it as a bolt from the blue, a visitation from an alien force that had nothing to do with me. In the days that followed, the attacks varied in severity; the shock of a sudden attack wore off, but it was replaced by alternating moods of fear, despair, and denial. The feeling of being unable to catch my breath is one of utter helplessness. There seemed to be no prospect of relief. But I didn't succumb, because of an instinct that compels me to take breaths, no matter how difficult it is to breathe. I can imagine someone who has the prospect of frequent severe attacks contemplating suicide. But during an attack suicide would be an impossibility, because the compulsion to breathe is irresistible.

Asthma is not all attack. It is a chronic condition, depending on its severity, of wheezing, the production of clotted sputum, tightness in the chest, postnasal drip, skin rashes; it is life-threatening; it can lead to suffocation if not treated. In some sufferers attacks are infrequent and the chronic condition is in abeyance, so for most of their lives they are asymptomatic. In others (and I am one of them), even if you learn through the use of medication to stave off an attack, there is always a wheeze or a tightness in the chest or a dull sense of diminished breathing.

I began a search for a cure, going from one doctor to another, never satisfied with the treatment, which as it turned out was always the same. The difference was in the attitudes of the doctors. Asthma doctors for the most part are an irritable or indifferent lot, because they deal with patients who are neither curable nor terminal. The patients just keep coming back, and though they fill their coffers, the doctors must feel that their work is something of a scam. They are like the railings of a highway overlooking a ravine. They are there to make sure that you don't career off the highway into oblivion. You live in constant fear that you may at any time lose control of the wheel.

There was the Boston Brahmin, Dr. Thomas Elliot, courteous, correct, candid about the limited knowledge about asthma despite countless books on the subject. He died on me. Robert Markoff was cut from completely different cloth. Coarse, aggressive, impatient, he reminded me in his behavior of the army doctors who examine you for draft classification. I was on a line of patients, to be given a series of tests without explanation, indeed without a word. When asked a question, Dr. Markoff would bristle in response. After a year I decided I had had enough. My next doctor, Bromberg (I remember only his last name), was young, eager, friendly, but confused. Hours seemed to pass between the various phases of examination as he ran from one patient to the next. When he returned to you, he had to remind himself who you were. On the recommendation of a friend I quickly changed to a charmer, a middle-aged immigrant from South Africa. Dr. Saul Fogelman *was* charming and seemed knowledgeable, but his casual and sometimes distracted manner distressed me. Phone calls constantly interrupted the examination. I had the distinct feeling that my visit was unnecessary, that both he and I knew what was the matter and what had to be done without the visit. He told stories about how people managed before the invention of the new drugs. One story in particular moved me. During the steamy summers, a father in western Massachusetts would wrap his asthmatic son in blankets and, in the dark early-morning hours before the sun had risen, climb a nearby mountain to the top, where the air was thinner and clearer; there he would cradle him in his arms and wait hours, if necessary, for the boy to breathe normally again. Something in the telling suggested a certain disdain for our present dependence on drugs. It seemed to suggest a weakness of character. Dr. Fogelman admired the heroic past. He shared my interest in literature and asked to see what I had written. I began to suspect him when I met a fellow sufferer at an academic conference. She had recently been afflicted with a particularly severe form of the disease. She wore a mask that covered her nose and mouth while walking in the street. She asked me what my peak flow reading was, and I astonished her by not knowing what she was talking about. The peak flow meter is a device for monitoring one's breathing capacity; a diminishing capacity is a warning sign of a possible attack. When I asked Dr. Fogelman why he hadn't provided me with one, he said he didn't believe in it, as if it were a matter of faith. After a serious attack during which I called desperately for help, but could not reach him and wound up in the emergency room, I decided to change doctors. But not before I was hospitalized.

Away from the doctors, my life is uneventful. Three A.M. is the dark morning of the soul (in the circadian rhythm of the day, this is the worst time), a tickle or constriction in my chest ominously signaling the filling of the lungs, several coughs, one or two of them yielding phlegm, then a shortness of breath. In a prone position, the asthmatic is always at risk that his lungs will fill with fluid. I sleep with several pillows in a propped position. Not good enough. A sense of isolation grips you, even if your soul mate has been sleeping close to you. This has been a frequent, if not daily, event for umpteen years. It has become part of who I am. A chronic disease, unlike a passing one, becomes part of one's character, one's self-definition. One wakens to it as to a familiar that one may perhaps resent. In time, however, it becomes impossible to imagine oneself without it. Asthma has been my routine almost as long as any routine in my life: going to school, teaching school, marriage, parenting. It has made my identity, and like any routine, it tests my will and stamina. I wonder what would happen, how I would feel, if my asthma disappeared. Would it be a loss, a sense of something deeply part of me gone? Would I feel liberated or deprived? A grotesque question.

During an attack I try to divert myself with listening to the radio or watching television. Music is less satisfactory than the speaking voice, because a speaking voice suggests a human presence that can help me and take me out of myself. Sometimes I struggle against the waste of time of an attack by trying to read or write, as I am doing now. Early-morning TV is my distraction. I have seen Ronald Reagan in *Shanghai* and *Bedtime for Bonzo* several times, but the main fare is the endless recycling of news and commercials, especially the commercials promising salvation: relief from pain, removal of skin blemishes, restoration of hair, the delights of junk food, escape from daily labor and tedium to sunny, watery climes. One commercial seems specially addressed to me: a woman in distress inserts an inhaler in her mouth and has immediate relief from wheezing. I know all about inhalers, and they are useless in the middle of an attack.

I turn off the TV and face the reality of the dark. Alone, I fantasize my death and count the number of people who will attend my funeral. Maybe, as with Ford Madox Ford's funeral, only three people will be in attendance—my wife and children. The size of your funeral is your final grade, it says how important you were in the world, how much you meant to people. My uncle Sam had thirty, mostly family members. Two hundred thousand people followed Sartre's coffin to Père-Lachaise. I don't even have a cemetery plot. Nor have I decided how to dispose of my body. Back in bed I try to fall asleep. At the break of dawn, I open one eye, squint at the clock on the night table, and see a blurry hour hand at the 5 position and the minute hand at the 10. The first glimmering of sun lightens my thoughts, my breathing becomes easier, and the usual anxieties about the prospects of the day return. I continue to lie in bed late into the morning, among used Kleenex, clutching a tissue in one hand and an inhaler in the other as a provision against an asthma attack. When I do get out of bed, I move directly to my study, spending hours among books and papers. On the days that I am not at the university teaching, I phone to break the monotony, still in my pajamas into the afternoon like Oblomov, the valetudinarian in my genes. The papers strewn about my study come to resemble Kleenex. Faded yellow lined pages of notes that come to no conclusions, fragments of ideas, the debris of thoughts without consequence to be discarded along with the used tissues.

There are a few things to do around the house, such as connecting the garden hose and sweeping the front porch. Time to write, the time that never seems to free up. On most days, I have reasons or give myself excuses for a slow start: bills that need attention, phone calls to be returned, a visit from a repairman, a visit to a bank. But even when

I am bereft of excuses, the fatigue from the night's struggles leaves me inert. While eating breakfast, consuming pills, making my ablutions, and dressing, I turn on the radio and listen to the news chatter. I am a slow dresser, partly from distraction, partly from fatigue. Dressed and ready, I look at the clock and am no longer astonished to find that it reads ten o'clock. I know I should avoid the newpaper, but find it irresistible. The *New York Times* is a quagmire, I should be reading the *Boston Globe* to save time. I start with the sports pages, then the editorial pages, and finally the news. It is now eleven o'clock.

I go to the back deck of the house, sink into the butterfly chair, pad and pencil in hand, ready to write, and often find that I have nothing to say. No memory drifts up from the past, no anger or resentments are flaring inside me. Yet I have a need to write. I look up at the trees and hedges of our lush garden, watch the squirrels chasing each other, and listen to the birds I can't identify, except for the intolerable grackles that make a racket rivaling the worst of city traffic. A black cat appears on the deck. Has he come to jinx my day? The deck is open and only partly shrouded by trees. The summer sky (on this particular day) is beautiful and cloudless, but I am unprotected from the sun. Precociously sensitive as I have become to all threats to my health, I seek a place shadowed by a tree, knowing that I will have to move again as the sun seeks me out. In addition to being dangerous to the skin, the sun is an immense distraction. So why not go back inside? I enter the house and sit down at the kitchen table, but to no avail. I have been in a suburban stupor for days. The semester has ended, the grades are all in, but I find I can't relax. As my energy returns, my mind is gripped by an uninspired busyness.

Often I awake from a night of troubled dreams, glad to escape. But writing means looking for trouble, and now that I'm awake I can't find it. Maybe a phone call or a letter will disturb the day, but it is already late morning and the summer air has begun to hang heavy, like a metaphor for my mood. I remember a scene from the film *Bye Bye Braverman* (based on Wallace Markfield's *To an Early Grave*), in which a blocked writer sits at his desk, neatening piles of paper, sharpening pencils, getting up, walking about the room, peering out through the window, sitting down and typing furiously for a minute, gazing at the paper in the typewriter, pulling out the paper, crunching and tossing it into the wastebasket in disgust. Give it up, I tell myself. Why not go out for a walk, maybe the juices will stir? Or call a friend and suggest a game of tennis? The phone rings. I stand up, move quickly to the phone to anticipate the voice machine that kicks in after three rings, only to be greeted by blankness when I lift the receiver. Probably a computer message that misfired–another metaphor for my present state.

At a loss, I go to the television room, plunk myself down on the BarcaLounger, pick up the remote command, and turn on the television set. Television at eleven-thirty in the morning! Quiz shows, commercials, talk shows, commercials, soap operas, commercials: I cruise back and forth between channels, irritated as much with myself as with what I see. Is this a foreshadowing of my retirement? Television in the morning as a compensation for lack of inspiration. Here's a theory of work: a mechanism of activity to fill time in the absence of inspiration.

Some writers when they have nothing to say summon up their powers of observation and description. They can describe a natural scene at length, name all the flowers and trees. Description becomes a place marker for the imagination while it fills up and finds the path of action and event. I don't have the requisite powers of observation and description. Wordworth counseled a wise passiveness, allowing the winds of inspiration to blow in your direction. I am passive, but don't know how wise. Half awake in the wee hours one morning, I was visited by something that induced a rapid heartbeat, which lasted several hours. My wife lying close to me could hear it. I tried to take my pulse but failed to find it. I felt the beat in my neck, and started to count against the clock: 125 beats per minute. I called the doctor, and he told me to come to his office immediately. His count was 150 beats, twice the rate of my normal heartbeat. He sent me to the hospital emergency room, where they inserted a calcium beta block, applied pressure to the carotid artery, and had me bearing down as if I were moving my bowels. After about an hour the rate of heartbeat fell to seventy-five. The inspiration may have been medication that I take for asthma. Not exactly what I am waiting for.

A perfectly good subject, illness may even be a source of inspiration. There is illness and illness. In a preface to Dostoyevsky's short novels, Thomas Mann notes that they "do not constitute one-tenth of his actual published writings," and he goes on to say "that of all the novels Fyodor Mikhailovich carried with him in finished form, so to speak, and which he narrated enthusiastically and in detail, not one-tenth was ever put on paper. [His friends] say that he required practically no time at all for the elaboration of these countless outlines. And then we are expected to believe that disease represents an impoverishment of life!" Disease as inspiration. It can enter the mind as a productive activity. My illness is a challenge to my equanimity, a limited inspiration. I may envy the teeming brain of a Dostoyevsky, but I would resist the Faustian bargain and choose to stay put in an arid place, grateful for any rain that might come my way.

I decide to go for a walk around the track in the town's sports field. Maybe physical movement will stir the mind. On the track, I look about at men, women, boys, and girls of all shapes and sizes, some with earphones, others in conversation, still others giving their full concentration to the movement of their bodies. There is a slender, muscular lady with a haggard, determined expression on her face who seems to be a permanent fixture on the track. She walks quickly, her arms swinging in a wide rhythmic manner (almost as if she were race-walking). She looks neither to the left nor to the right. I call her the robot lady. My younger retired cousins have devoted their lives to walking. Every morning six months of the year they set out for a walk for days and days in foreign places, one time from one end of Britain to the other, twelve hundred miles from Land's End to John o' Groats, the length of the country. They have climbed Kilimanjaro, walked the Dolomites, reenacted Darwin's journey to the Galapagos, submerged themselves in the scuba zones of the sea. They are fit physical specimens in late middle age, bright, energetic, and outward looking. Their thoughts are objective and cheerful, never gloomy or introspective. Or so it seems when I talk to them. They are all activity, outward to the world. They walk to discover the world. I make circles (the geometry of inwardness) when I walk.

I have been asked about my plans for retirement now that I am in my late sixties. The expected answer is Italy, England, some exotic place in the Far East. It is assumed that work has been prison and retirement will be release. For me travel is a break from routine, not liberation. The great temptation is inwardness; the risk is that I will have nothing to say. I often find visual novelty a distraction. I am on the track to introspect and find something to say. What an odd need, what a strange compulsion. Is it a compulsion or a defense against the exhaustion of physical effort, a reinforcement of my sedentariness? My circular walks are minimal concessions to my need (everyone's need) to alter one's position from time to time, like turning in bed at night. I want the stillness of focus, the undisturbed freedom of random thought. So what do I think about as I walk? The petty humiliations of everyday life: an awkward turn of phrase where grace is expected, greeting someone as you walk past and receiving no greeting in return, being angered by a receptionist in a doctor's office only to find the anger misdirected, then having to cope with her sullen scowl as you walk by her desk every time you visit your doctor. An authority in my profession, I am a suppliant in the doctor's office. And what about my authority? I look into the passive-aggressive faces of certain students, become distracted, and falter.

I think of my friendships, most of them pleasantly in place. But a perverse sentiment doesn't want to leave well enough alone. Increasingly, I have the odd sensation of isolation from other people, even from close friends of long standing. A. talks too slowly and at great length about himself. But through all the "communication" I feel that he is wrapped in his self-regard—not from vanity, but from insecurity. B. talks rapidly, too rapidly: there is rarely a pause for our minds, our souls to truly meet. His eyes are turned inward toward his subject. Then there is C., who speaks sparingly, as if he is often at a loss for subjects, and I am expected to fill the vacuum. At times I have the vain thought that I alone have the capacity for genuine spontaneous communication, for the back-and-forth flow of energy and feeling, but

I know that I too am on the list of inadequacy. I sometimes hear myself forcing conversation, ingratiating myself, self-dramatizing, and I can sense that I have produced awkwardness in others. At other times, I relax into myself and cease to care about my effect on others.

Scarcely a day passes in my life when I don't regret an action or speech. I wait in line at the bank, two tellers are free, a white woman whom I know and a black woman whom I have never seen before. I approach the counter of the white woman, because I know her, though the easier path was to the black woman, and I sense at once a wistful resentment in the black woman's face. I almost anticipated it. Am I guilty of racism? I leave the bank knowing that she couldn't possibly know my real motive, and that I couldn't make things right. Could I say to her, I didn't go to you because . . . not because you are black? I have been looking for trouble and now I am finding it. It can come from the outside: a dunning letter from the IRS, a quarrelsome colleague, an unhappy son or daughter. I don't speak of real tragedies. The mind can stir up trouble with no prodding from the outside.

During my walk around the track, a constriction in my chest slows me up and then brings me to a stop. It must be my asthma acting up. I move slowly to the spectator benches on the sideline of the field and sit down, head resting on my hands. Swept by fatigue and the weakness of hunger, I wonder whether I will be able to make it back to my house. I had miscalculated the time for the walk. Four o'clock in the afternoon is my time for a "fix," my most mindless pleasure, a small coffee and apple square in a pastry shop in the center of the town where I live. This day I have missed my fix. I sit for a while, hoping that the fatigue will pass, but it doesn't pass. There is no accessible phone to call my wife, and she may not be at home. It would be humiliating to ask a stranger to take me home. Is this my adventure for the day?

What is the worst that can happen? I will ask a stranger, and with this thought my fatigue disappears. I get up and make my way back to an empty house. The butterfly chair on the back porch seems to beckon and I sink in as the fatigue—or is it lethargy—returns. I pick up the pad of yellow legal paper and force out a sentence, but nothing follows, and I experience self-disgust about the waste of time. Time, the puritan's nemesis. The puritan conscience is satisfied by the completion of particular tasks, by an amount of time set aside to work, for instance, nine to five. Conscience is enforced by the presence of others engaged in similar or complementary tasks. But the writer alone with or without a thing to say has the gnawing sense of work undone. The urge to write, strong or weak, is ever present. The writer may have to force himself to clear his mind of this gnawing sense in order to write. Can he? When I retire from teaching, will the gnawing sense intensify?

If I can't write, I should read or do *something*, but I know that if I do something, I will not be able to concentrate. I will have given in, and guilt will distract me. Maybe I should put my papers in order. I reenter the house and go to my study, open a drawer of my desk (the miscellaneous drawer in which I put things indiscriminately), and look through the mess of papers, opened envelopes (frayed envelopes depress me), postcards. I begin to toss things into the wastebasket, carelessly and confidently at first, then hesitate. Should I toss or keep? I can't decide, so I toss, then worry that I might live to regret what I have tossed. I examine the contents of the wastebasket and return items to the drawer. I lack the courage to rid myself of debris. How hard it is to discard pages of what I have written or even to delete sentences. There is magpie in me, a fear of giving up anything that might at some time be of use. The magpie is of course a threat to accomplishment. While looking through discarded notes that have been saved just in case, my mind is in a mechanical or distracted state. I look for something that might bring me back to my subject and get me going, but instead find myself going down another path. I come across a postcard, which reminds me of that wonderful meal we had in Bars, in the Dordogne—only fifteen francs for a five course meal. It was in 1975. My wife-to-be and I were renting the farmhouse of a poet friend, who would die of cancer in his late forties. My children were with me and getting better acquainted with their soon-to-be stepmother. It was not an easy summer. In a rush of self-revulsion, I fantasize throwing everything out and clearing the decks. And then the fantasy turns into reality. In a sudden access of courage, or is it the guilty reflex of my cowardice, I empty the drawer again and toss and toss.

I am a misplacer of things. My personal library is an accumulation rather than a collection, which means that I never quite know where a book I need is. I begin looking for a book I had misplaced, but to no avail. Another book catches my eye. The author is a friend who sent it to me with his compliments. I pick it up and peruse it–a solid achievement, and I experience a twinge of envy. I turn to an old stack of letters and begin to read. Letters of recommendation galore: "LM is one of the best students I have had in thirty years of teaching." "RM is very intelligent and articulate." "MP writes with remarkable insight and lucidity"–all have my enthusiastic support. Here is writing about nothing. (I recall a letter my department at Bard College once received about a candidate for a job from a distinguished professor of Spanish origins: the candidate was a "*haciendado* of the imagination, roaming plantations of thought." I never managed to achieve a striking metaphor in one of my letters.) A colleague of mine says that he could publish his letters of recommendation under the title *Collective Fictions*. A writer's subject is trouble and that is why he is always looking for it. There can be no stories about happy marriages, as Tolstoy tells us in *Anna Karenina:* perfect friendships leave us with little to say, success stops the imagination in its tracks. Happiness, as every writer instinctively knows, is an ending. So writing depends upon risking the comforts of the self, maybe even its very existence. My asthma is trouble enough.

We are given speech to communicate and writing to remember. When I read what I have written in the past (an essay or a journal entry), I am surprised at what I have forgotten, and regret not consistently keeping a journal. The unrecorded days are like days not lived, or like ephemeral body functions: eating, eliminating, and all the bodily processes of which are unaware. But writing is not only the recording of event, it is also the creating of it. Sometimes I think that writing is an obstacle to experience, an ulterior motive that gets in the way of it. The fear of forgetting makes you turn away from what you are doing and go for your notebook, or if your notebook is not available, your mind retreats from the experience in order to fix the event. It is not hard to see why Flaubert and Kafka saw writing as an unnatural act, an exchange for living. Kafka also thought of it as an ax that breaks the frozen sea within. Joyce's Stephen Dedalus views it as stasis, an arrest of the flow of experience. For D. H. Lawrence, writing is the expression of vitality: it is life itself. So many different, even contradictory views of writing. I used to prefer Lawrence's view, but now think that Flaubert and Kafka are closer to my experience. I am mistrustful of Stephen's aestheticizing of stasis and of James's aestheticizing of emptiness, but something in me inclines in that direction. I experience an illicit pleasure in the elusiveness of the subject—like a detective looking for a culprit.

The need to write is not a universal. I don't mean of course the need to write a letter of application for a job or to one's parents or children or friends in distant places. I mean writing for its own sake. *Need* is a weak word for those who write for its own sake. *Compulsion* may be more like it. The desire to communicate doesn't explain it, for we give what we write to friends with whom we could speak. (There is no communication like speech.) What explains it? Is it that we want approval for having conceived and formulated an incisive thought, an interesting story, a beautiful conceit? When we converse, we rarely stop to consider what we have said, the way we have said it. Our pleasure is in the rush and energy of exchange, like the embrace of bodies. Writing fixes what is said for contemplation. When I write, I often close my eyes and try to imagine the next phrase, the shape of the sentence. I am not compelled or distracted by someone else's face or speech, as I am when I speak. I prefer writing to teaching, because writing is the condition of autonomy. When I write I need please only myself; pleasing others is after the fact. To live is to be responsive to the distractions that life offers, to write is to be able to incorporate without being distracted. A voice of skepticism: "You're romanticizing and mystifying writing. You write to please, to gain approval and rewards." Well, yes and no. If the answer were only yes, it would be hard to understand why we who continue to write in the knowledge that recognition and approval will not come our way continue to write. Maybe there is the lingering hope against all odds that recognition will come. But what if we were told by a voice that had complete knowledge of the future that recognition would never come and still we continued to write. Not that writing always gives pleasure, it is often tedious and frustrating. I ask a friend who is often in a dark mood how his writing is going. "Half the time," he says, "no, most of the time I think that what I am doing is crap." I don't have to ask him why he continues to write. It is his anxiety and his relief from anxiety. If he went cold turkey and suddenly stopped, he would experience withdrawal symptoms, the dark mood would become utterly black. Here's a guess: the irresistible subject of writing without a subject is the self, whether it be its making or unmaking.

I return to the porch and my butterfly chair. A siren sounds in the distance. I write, "A siren sounds in the distance." A door closes. I write, "A door closes." A neighbor in a corner house beyond the hedges that surround my house calls out for her cat in a sing-songy voice that drives me up the wall: "Chlo-o-oey, Chlo-o-ey!" I have never seen the neighbor, so she has become for me the name of her cat. A radio blares out rap music from a car. Neighbors' voices rise and fall. I try to make out what they are saying, but hear only an occasional phrase. So I listen for intonation, for the emotion. How do I sound to others? I've heard my voice on the telephone voice machine, surprised how gravelly it has become, a smoker's voice, though I don't smoke. These are all place markers for the imagination, and I am still at the same place. I wonder whether the butterfly chair is the ideal seat for writing. So I get up, reenter the house, and move to the kitchen table with a forced determination, still having nothing to say. Give it up, my body tells me, but I persist as I would not if I were exercising or playing a game. Like sinners, writers keep the faith even when grace doesn't descend. We wait and wait for something to happen, fearful that if we turn away, we may miss the moment.

On a visit to Lake Como in Italy, I met the father of a friend of my wife's, who as it turned out suffered from severe asthma. He had been forced to retire from his business in order to devote himself to his illness. When we met him, he was living in a villa on a mountain overlooking the lake. He was a burly man, inflated by the heavy dosage of prednisone he was required to take (prednisone makes the body retain water). When my wife and I arrived at the villa, we found him in his swimming pool. We immediately fell to talking (fell is the right word) about asthma. He was surprised I was so thin: "You must be immune to prednisone." His case was much worse than mine. Incapacitated for years, confined to house and bed, he had almost given up hope. He was saved however by someone who had told him of a sanitorium in Davos, Switzerland, the site of Mann's *Magic Mountain*. His wealth enabled him to spend several months there, and if Davos did not magically transform his life, it saved it. He urged me to go to Davos. It was a stunning idea, an opportunity to experience what Mann's characters had experienced. It would turn the humdrum of heavy breathing into a kind of glamour. I played with the idea, but remained stuck in the humdrum and never went. The figure of the Italian has stayed in my mind as a figure of possibility.

Recently, I reread Mann's novel and came across a passage in which an asthmatic resident of the sanitorium at Davos (a hunchbacked Mexican) suffers an attack: "He suddenly could not get his breath and would then grab his neighbor, a man or woman, in the iron grip of one of his long hands, hold on tight as a vise, and drag his struggling, panicky victim, now shouting for help, down into the pool of dread with him." The passage made me realize that the novel was a comedy of illness and dying. Anatole Broyard, intoxicated by his own illness and dying of cancer, called the novel "the great definitive romance of illness, a portrait that, I would say, speaking as a connoisseur now, will never be equaled. [Mann's] description of life itself showed how precarious it was: 'a form preserving instability, a fever of matter . . . the existence of the impossible-to-exist, of a half-sweet, half-painful balancing, or scarcely balancing, in this restricted and feverish process of decay and renewal, upon the point of existence.' " Broyard is infected (good word) by the suggestion in Mann of a symbiosis between creativity and illness.

The novel gives us more than one view of illness. For the Jesuit Naphta, "illness is what makes [man] human. . . . The dignity and nobility of man was based in the spirit, in illness." For Settembrini, the man of the Enlightenment, illness is reactionary, a form of irrationality that can be cured and ultimately banished from the world: "It is outdated and ugly. It comes from an era of superstitious contrition, when harmony and health were considered suspicious and devilish, whereas infirmity in those days was as good as a passport to heaven. Reason and enlightenment, however, have banished those shadows, which once lay encamped in the human soul." What foolishness in both of these views, the one fetishizing illness as a sign of spiritual distinction, the other imagining a world completely transformed by reason. Naphta justifies the suffering of the body with the promise of heaven, Settembrini imagines the transformation of the body into a condition of perpetual health. Would that that were the case.

It was at Lake Como where I met a distinguished American respiratory specialist, who was participating in an international conference, to whom I told my story. And his response was: "Unacceptable." He wrote out the name of a Boston doctor whom I have been seeing ever since. Dr. Frank Mason (all the names of doctors I have given are pseudonymns) is a virtuoso medication prescriber: sixty milligrams of prednisone tapered down to five during a period of a week, six puffs three times a day of flovent, two puffs twice a day of serevent, uniphyl once a day. Dr. Mason has taught me the discipline of the asthmatic: how to anticipate symptoms through medication and not expose myself excessively to the elements: severe cold, stifling heat.

Asthma attacks are triggered by allergies to dust, to plants, to foods; by changes in weather, by stress–the possibilities are endless. The allergist tests for them by pricking the skin of one's back and arms a hundred times for reactions. The asthma sufferer is lucky if he can find the villain or villains. All he has to do then is refrain from eating chocolates or nuts or . . . But in my case the villain has not been found. Little red blotches of allergic reaction appear on my skin, but none of them is significant enough to be the allergen that provokes the attack. My asthma is anallergic.

Imagine the following scenario: a paranoid state with a highly equipped army at the border, always anticipating enemy incursions that do not occur. Instead, illegal aliens slip through from time to time or a change in the weather produces an ominous cloud formation that suggests enemy troops on the horizon. The nervous commander, always ready to react, orders the troops to fire; occasionally in the confusion a soldier is hit with friendly fire. This is the condition of the asthmatic body, its glands prematurely firing or misfiring defensive secretions to annihilate nonexistent enemies, causing inflammation of the airways and constriction in breathing. Asthma is the war of the body against itself. Why, the doctors don't yet know. At a holistic center where for a brief period I sought help, the therapist asked me to close my eyes and imagine an invading army of bacteria, which I would surround and defeat. It struck me later that if my body was paranoid, why should I be encouraged to imagine an invasion? I also thought it odd that a holistic center should have on its staff an asthma specialist.

So the disease becomes an existential condition. I am allergic to life itself, as far as I can tell. The cure would be to seal me in a large vacuum chamber. On the other hand, I can turn my "condition" into sensitivity, which causes me to see and feel things differently from other people. I understand how Proust may have regarded his asthma as a blessing, but you need the gift as well.

You need to be a scholar to remember how and when to take the medicine. Dr. Mason reminds me that I *am* a scholar, but this is hardly my favorite subject. Dr. Mason is an impressive figure of a man: tall, handsome, a major doctor in the profession with a no-nonsense attitude. In the beginning he cautioned me about making the change from Dr. Fogelman: "Don't transfer your records yet, you may not like me." Odd for a doctor to say. But I soon discovered what he meant. He has a passion for doctoring. In his office at six in the morning, he takes calls from his patients from six to seven. He insists that you call him, so that he can monitor your progress. He questions you closely about whether you had taken the medicine as prescribed, and if you have forgotten he scolds, the way a father scolds a child. I am a year younger than he, and sometimes he intimidates me as my father used to intimidate me when I was a kid. So I prevaricate and alter the truth if I have forgotten to take a pill or haven't tapered the medication as prescribed. And then pay for it in my dreams. Dr. Mason has become the most significant authority figure in my life. He is driven and drives others. The nurses roll their eyes at the pace of his activity, his constant demand for quick action. He is obsessed with accomplishment, with making a difference. He is like a poet or painter of genius whose art is his life. Asthma is his canvas, a detached object. To think of it as having a soul or a spirit would mystify it, and prove an obstacle to its treatment, so he has little patience for the affect of suffering, except as a route to understanding the illness. He is not atypical in this respect. The suffering of a patient may be as professionally irrelevant as the color of an organism to a molecular biologist. But color is important. A student of mine who had been a professional nurse noticed my fingernails turning blue at the beginning of a mild attack, a sign of oxygen deficiency.

When Goethe prophesied that the main institutions of modern civilization would be the theater and the hospital, he foresaw my own existence: hours of difficult, heavy breathing in front of the television set where I seek the diversion that will relax my bronchial tubes and a calendar full of appointments to doctors: Dr. Mason, the internist to test my blood for diabetes, the endocrinologist to protect me against bone loss incurred by the taking of prednisone, the ophthalmologist to check against cataracts, all potential side effects of asthma therapy. (Osteoporosis is my particular affliction—a woman's disease, and I've got it: 70 percent of the normal bone density of men of my age and build. One in five people who have it is a male, and I'm that one. It has no symptoms in its dormant state, but like a pellet of explosive in the body, it can turn your bones into powder.) For efficiency's sake, the doctors should arrange themselves on an assembly line and examine me as I pass them by.

Dr. Mason has made a difference, but the price is high. Like a military man who wants a decisive victory and refuses to temporize with the enemy, he deploys all the force at his command. My medicine cabinet is an arsenal of prescribed drugs. An excessive use of the inhaler can produce palpitations of the heart. On one occasion they were so severe and continuous that I had to be rushed to the emergency room where the doctor applied a finger to my carotid artery and restored my normal heartbeat. He warned me of the danger of trying to perform the remedy myself. The wrong kind of pressure on the artery can kill you. I become apprehensive about the toxicity of medical cures. So I decide to seek an alternative, or rather a complementary therapy. Acupuncture, some say, cuts the phlegm. Do I dare to tell my doctor? I tell him while he is writing a prescription and he shakes his head dismissively. "There's no scientific evidence for it. If the patient feels better, it may be nothing more than the placebo effect." I reply feebly, "I'll settle for the placebo effect." Dr. Mason doesn't want to discuss the matter—as if it were beneath contempt. He picks up his dictaphone, summarizes the results of the examination, and then to my astonishment speaks of the *long* conversation we had about acupuncture. The long conversation had lasted no more than thirty seconds. But I have no complaints. Dr. Mason, unlike any doctor I have ever known, is always there for me.

The acupuncturist, unlike Dr. Mason, is a small, discreet man, economical in his gestures and speech. He could never explain the method, only describe it. The body has meridians that the needles activate. He told me there were different styles of acupuncture, and his preferred style is to prod the skin with a moxa, an herbal powder which he ignites and applies with a needle until the skin warms to the point of becoming uncomfortably hot. After every application, he would take my pulse to determine whether it had an effect. His taking of the pulse was a subtle affair, gently feeling it repeatedly from different angles. He couldn't explain what he learned, though a symptom that things were not what they should be (that the energy level is not quite right) is that the pulse is slippery, or as the Chinese would say, "a pearl on a disk." "The Chinese see the world in metaphors," said the acupuncturist. I had six sessions, the minimum number required to judge whether the treatment was working. I couldn't say it was, and the treatment ended. Since there were no promises, I didn't feel cheated. But the experience inexplicably made asthma more of a mystery. My wife thought it made my hair look different, curlier, richer in texture. So maybe it made a difference.

I have given up the search for a cure. Call it a cop-out. Aren't there enough clues in my story about the cause or causes? A divorce, a paradise I never experienced, a father who intimidated me. Actually, I don't trust all these memories. My father also loved me deeply: oh, there's another possibility, perhaps too deeply. But where does all this lead? It doesn't change anything: the constrictions and secretions recur. So I've raised false expectations that this is a detective story, with clues scattered throughout and forming themselves into a solution. The truth is that this is a story about accommodation and about becoming philosophical; those interested in psychological thrillers can stop reading here.

I am fortunate to be an academic, as my work consists of teaching, reading, writing, and thinking. All other activities are diminished by asthma. Walking, especially up a hill, becomes a struggle. On a long walk around Walden Pond with a friend, I had to hold on to trees periodically. My friend teased me about my "hugging trees." Thoreau might have approved. I don't observe carefully when I walk or drive: the distraction of breathing turns me inward. Any household activity— sawing a piece of wood, lifting a garbage can, mowing the lawn— leaves me breathless. As does lovemaking, during which a little wheeze in my chest is my constant companion. My wife calls me Wheezer—which rhymes with geezer. Asthma is an old man's disease: it slows the walk, "You are old, Father William." So I sit at my desk or in an easy chair with papers and books on my lap, disgracefully irresponsible. It is my wife who has to put out the garbage on the cold days when the frost bites into the chest. It is she who must run up stairs to find my misplaced inhaler in anticipation of an attack. It is she who . . . A perverse thought: my asthma is a refuge—from the world, from the requirement to be active. It confirms me in my sedentariness. As my gregariousness dissipates with age, I want the excuse to be alone. Another thought strikes me about the resemblance between the scholar's activity and the effluvia of asthmatic breathing: they both seem unprovoked and gratuitous, the products of excess serving no function except their own production.

Asthma is the narrative of repetition, the workday extended into the weekend. The occasional crisis, a severe attack, produces variation, but even an attack is a repetition of a previous one. You are never free of it or struck down by it. The famous nineteenth-century doctor Sir William Osler said that asthmatics pant their way into old age. So does everyone else who lives into old age. Why then take notice? Dr. Mason says that Osler's remark was a disaster for asthma research. Why fund it if it's not a killer?

Unlike cancer, which seems to be striking all around me. I have friends with brain, prostate, stomach, pancreatic cancer. That is drama. My friend Bob Nozick has just undergone surgery. He's had his stomach and spleen removed. On awakening from anesthesia he told the doctors that he didn't have the stomach for another operation. He has been the golden boy of philosophy and experience: handsome, brilliant, the inventive maker of arguments and distinctions, a lover of women and loved by women. As a philosopher, he moved from analysis to wisdom, and now, struck down, he exemplifies the lessons of the examined life in his attitude toward the prospect of dying. He is all cheer and self-possession: "My only sadness is that I think of myself as a protector and I'll be leaving behind those I've loved and protected." Not a false note in this. I remind him, does he need to be reminded, that he began philosophy inspired by the example of Socrates' heroic defense of it in the *Apology*. I tell him that he reminds me of Socrates' farewell to his disciples in the *Phaedo*. He lacks the stereotypical Jewish complaining voice. "Oy" has an ironic place in his vocabulary, always accompanied by laughter. You would never hear it coming from the depths of his being. He jokingly paraphrases Henry VIII in T. S. Eliot's *Murder in the Cathedral:* "Who will rid me of this body?" Is it possible that I write this out of envy? How stupid! The sword has not delivered its final blow, so Bob must wake every morning to the thought.

I think of my friends and the effect of illness upon friendship. Friendship is the frank exchange of intimacies, so what happens if the space of intimacy is more and more occupied by illness? Who wants to hear of another person's illness unless it is a trade-off for hearing about your own, or the satisfaction that it is not you who is suffering—who wants the guilt of experiencing the satisfaction? Illness can corrode friendship if it becomes an endless obsession with one's body. We all know the experience of not wanting to listen to others when we are ill, because listening interferes with an indulgence in *our* pain, *our* needs. Dignity, however, requires that we listen. We cultivate reserve, we silence our needs and listen to others without pleasure. Unless we are Jews, who have the gift for suffering and communicating it—of turning suffering into the spontaneity of our relations with others. This is the birth of Jewish comedy: the awareness of the grotesquerie not of suffering, but of its indulgence.

What happens when two people compare illnesses (we might call the exchange comparative suffering)? One or both might want the satisfaction that his or her illness is the more serious, the more painful. You think you have it bad, listen to me . . . Or the motive may be the opposite: to seek consolation that someone else is in a worse condition. Samuel Beckett's Mercier suggests that we don't need others to achieve this consolation: "When you fear for your cyst think of your fistula. And when you tremble for your fistula consider your chancre." Does this make things better or worse?

I am drifting from my subject, asthma, which has a venerable history. It is a Greek word, adopted by the Roman Seneca, who wrote of his own asthma and gave it the nickname of the doctors, "rehearsing death," because the asthmatic feels as if he were breathing his "last gasp." But the attack turns out to be "a squall" of brief duration. "One could hardly, after all, expect anyone to keep on drawing his last breath for long, could one?" Seneca wrote. I did. One night I breathed as if it were my last for eight hours straight. Dr. Markoff once told me that with time asthmatics become aerobic athletes. While breathing hard and continuously, I must have asked myself Seneca's question. Of course, given the fact that it is Seneca, we should expect what we get: pithy reflections on life and death. For stoicism, I turn to the Romans, not to the Jews, who do not suffer with equanimity. Noted for his patience, Job is also remembered for indignation. For Jews (and Job is one, if only in this respect), there is a limit to patience, and when that limit is reached all hell breaks loose. Rehearsing death holds no terrors for Seneca. He reminds us that since we were not conscious of distress before we were born, we should not anticipate distress after we die, when we will be returned to our original prenatal state. A sophistic evasion, because the anticipation does not arise from the prospect of death, but from dying, the terrifying change or transition from one state of being to another.

Did Seneca write the extended passage while having an asthmatic attack? Who knows? His stoic reflections seem to be his way of talking himself out of an attack while experiencing it. His breathing, he tells us, becomes more regular, more tranquil. The rehearsal for death leads not to the real thing, but back to the distress of living.

Susan Sontag cautions us against turning illness into a metaphor: "A disease of the lungs is, metaphorically, a disease of the soul. Cancer, as a disease that can strike anywhere, is a disease of the body. Far from revealing anything spiritual, it reveals that the body is, all too woefully, just the body." But the body is not just the body. It may be the "place" where the mind takes its toll and reveals itself. And even when the mind does not make the body ill, it is tested by the body, which finds out whether you have the soul of a whiner or a stoic and measures the strength of your will. What Sontag perceives in the displacement of physical suffering to the spiritual and the symbolic is a disrespect for the pain of the sufferer, for it turns the victim into the guilty party. But metaphor also bestows meaning. In literature illness, catastrophes, accidents are always metaphors or occasions for significance, or else why have them make an appearance? An accident like Ivan Ilyich's fall from a chair while hanging a curtain is a judgment, a fall from grace. The illness that ensues and will kill him is not even given a name: it is an *it* that becomes more and more ominous as the tale unfolds. Tolstoy refers to a floating kidney, but that is not where the main interest lies. Sontag speaks of the naming of a disease as damning, but not naming it is more damning, because it makes it elusive, mysterious, and overwhelming.

Here are two contradictory views of asthma. I walk around the track on an athletic field and see an elderly man with a racking cough, breathing hard, spitting stuff, and glimpse what I might look like to others. The other view: in the splendid German film *Celeste,* which gives us the life of Proust from the point of view of his housekeeper, there is a memorable scene in which Proust suffers an attack and calls to her for help. She appears with a breathing apparatus for relieving symptoms. As Proust inhales the vapors, Celeste, close to him, breathes in sympathy. The camera pans away and from the distance, there is the appearance of a love scene, the romance of asthma.

What is illness, how do we decide if someone is ill? One has symptoms: pain, aches, rashes, unusual secretions, an awareness of bodily events (we are unaware of our bodies when healthy). Illness is relative, measured by our relations to others. If people were born with one arm, one-armed people would be the norm. "But illness may prove fatal": that is no argument. All of life is fatal. This is the consolation of the chronically ill. It takes time to settle into an illness, but if one does life becomes normal. One needs to banish thoughts of what might have been, one needs to stop making comparisons. All of the above are just words if the pain is unbearable, or if one can't breathe.

An illness may be a judgment of a wasted life. A chronic illness is a caution against all dreams of self-transformation, the cowardice of the body. It tells me what I cannot do, what I dare not do. But illness may also be an opportunity. Teddy Roosevelt overcame his asthma and became a Rough Rider. Jackie Joyner Kersee runs with fury, despite the fact that her racing victories end with asthmatic gasps. In my case, asthma is a form of imprisonment, a confinement to sedentariness, to a life of reading, spectatorship, and writing. Writing is the only action that doesn't make me short of breath. The most famous of asthmatics, Proust, wrote long sentences. He breathed in his sentences as he could not breathe when he walked. Chronic illness narrows our choices, even helps us find a calling, a vocation. It is the quintessential condition of self-discovery, the boundary of existence that tells us what we are and what we are not, who we can be and who we won't be. One adjusts to the boundary the way Gregor Samsa adjusts to his insect body in Kafka's *Metamorphosis*–though never completely. The spirit, weakly or strongly depending on its strength, rebels from time to time. It says, "I am my illness." It also says, "I am *not* my illness."

In times of physical despair, I think that I have traded body for mind. All our literature, Semitic and anti-Semitic, presents bookish Jews, sick in body and soul, feminized into passivity. For centuries, the Jew was kept from the land, segregated in ghettoes. He learned to compensate as a handler of the abstractions of money and ideas. He lived an inward life because he was denied the outer world. In America he could work the land if he wished, but he had lost the habit. The Yiddish writer I. Raboy, author of *Der Yiddisher Cowboy,* is an anomaly. The American-born Jew engages in sports. He plays tennis and golf. But Jewish heroes of sport are few: Hank Greenberg, Sandy Koufax, basketball players before the sport was dominated by blacks, and a few boxers from the era of Murder Incorporated. In the dispersion from Eretz Israel, the Jew left behind the heroism of Moses, the Maccabees, and Bar Kochba. Itzhik Feffer's poem is a rant of yearning for something lost in the diaspora. In the Zion of Israel we have a return to the physical body and to the health of the tough Jew. The Jew of diaspora may have lost his faith and even his language, but he can be recognized in the anxious activity of his mind.

Seven: Mother Right

IN WRITING ABOUT yourself, you write about other people. How can you avoid doing so unless you are a hermit? And even hermits have at one time in their lives lived among other people. Unless you are Romulus or Remus, you have been brought up by adults. So the question is how to write about other people: family members, friends, acquaintances, foes? My own experience of being a character in someone else's story (and more than once) has made me sensitive to the transgressiveness of writing about others. A critic of the current rage for writing memoirs accuses certain memoirists of a narcissistic exploitation of people supposedly nearest and dearest to them: wife, husband, father, brother-in-law. She quotes the prophet Micah in support. She is on to something, and I take what she has to say to heart. But unless memoir writing is turned into an exercise of continuous censorship or simply banished from the republic of letters, the risks of exploiting and appropriating the lives of others is always present. And the risks seem particularly daunting when the other is a parent. I am about to write about my mother.

I have scruples about how much I am prepared to reveal about myself. What and how much of the people closest to me am I prepared to reveal? There is a First Amendment assumption in writers of courage and imagination that anything goes. The writer has an absolute right to his experience. But isn't there an obligation to respect and protect intimacies between yourself and your family, between you and your friends? When someone has spoken to you about some deep and troubling matter in confidence, aren't you required to be discreet and keep the confidence? Wouldn't you be betraying a friend or relative if you revealed the confidence? The First Amendment protects your right to say anything, but it doesn't justify it.

And what is the justification? A reverence for the imagination, which now has become a god. Scripture enjoins us to abandon family when the choice is between family and God. It is now what the imagination enjoins. And even if one is without imagination, the very act of writing has acquired the aura of the sacred. I sense pretension in all this, an excuse for small or no talent to indulge itself. But I can't dismiss the impulse, which I find strong in myself—as strong as my need to check it. It was Augustine who understood better than anyone before or after him that to confess was both to learn and to realize oneself. In our social lives we arrange our faces to ingratiate, we speak to please, because we desire to be ingratiated and pleased and in the process we obscure, if do not lose, our souls. In St. Augustine's world, God was the other to whom ingratiation was intolerable; the space between self and God was reality. In our secular world, writing has become the potential space of the real. But at what price? Think of all the sacrifices of family and friends the writer is prepared to make to achieve his reality. The egomania of writers is notorious. God is a humbler, a source of love for one's neighbor. The writer, who substitutes himself for God, loves no one but himself, that is, his imagination. Nothing else can compete with the imagination. Cranly asks his friend Stephen Dedalus in *A Portrait of the Artist as a Young Man* whether he loves his mother and the man of imagination replies: "I don't know what your words mean." Could there be a greater alienation from common humanity not even to know what the words mean? Or is Stephen simply being difficult?

A friend who is writing a memoir (everyone seems to be writing a memoir these days) tells me of a writer he knows who uses his family (father, mother, spouse, brother, sister, son, daughter) without compunction to tell his stories. My friend says children are off limits. What's the principle? Affection? Well, don't we have affection for father and mother, sister and brother? We owe our children the freedom to make their lives. They are growing, forming, making choices, perhaps incapable of making choices. In writing about them we put them in our power, place them at risk, if we don't actually decide their fate. Auden said, "Poetry makes nothing happen," but writing can destroy. My friend said one's children are off limits. So are spouses. Write about a spouse, and he or she becomes an ex-spouse. The writer who exploits his family defends himself by saying that he is hardest on himself in what he writes. Perhaps, but suicide doesn't justify homicide.

I agree with my friend that children are off limits. But what of the rest of the family? I am not Stephen Dedalus when he says that he doesn't know what love means. I cannot muster the icy courage, the ruthless commitment to the truth of my experience to transgress every boundary and violate every taboo. My imagination is not so precious that I am required to follow all its imperatives. I am not even sure what its imperatives are. On the other hand, the committed family or tribal loyalist can only write sentimental propaganda. I am not justifying myself, but simply stating the facts as I see them. Loyalty plays in my writing, but it is only one side of the inner conflict I experience, for which there is no resolution. This is the part of my story that I have struggled most with. It is written out of respect and love. The struggle has been to be as truthful as I could be. If I have transgressed boundaries of privacy, I hope it is for the sake of understanding and not for the prurient pleasures of self-disclosure.

My father died in 1981 from heart failure. Mother accepted his death stoically, for she had already anticipated it a year before when he fell forward facedown in a subway car, unconscious, vomiting his guts out. My son Eric, their sixteen-year-old grandson, who was with him, begged in vain for help from the other passengers. They retreated from the scene in horror. Eric grabbed the train door at the next stop and held it while he shouted for help. Father was given little chance to survive. All the same he lasted for a year. When he died, eighty people appeared at the funeral services. At the gravesite, the rabbi guided me through the kaddish, the Jewish prayer for the dead. As my atheist parents had provided me with no religious training, my knowledge of Hebrew, the sacred language, was pretty much confined to the Hebrew element in Yiddish. But neither my parents' atheism nor mine was relevant to the burial of my father. A Jew dies, and the son says kaddish. Kaddish is remembrance; without it, one has only one's own words. I did not have the words following my father's death. *Apicoiris* that I am, I nevertheless felt deprived of the tradition that my family had rejected. My secular upbringing provided me with no ceremonies for the great events of life: birth, marriage, and death.

My mother was dry-eyed through the services. Her tear ducts had been irreparably damaged when a pressure cooker heating on the stove had exploded in her face. It had burned her face and injured her ducts so that she could never shed tears. The dry-eyed grief was terrible. A year later, before the memorial service, she spent sleepless nights worrying whether the stone she had ordered to be set upon the grave was too small and insignificant compared to the larger ones in place on either side of the grave. If it had already been set, she could still have it dug up and replaced. She thought of hiring a broker to arrange for a new stonecutter. Father deserved better. I appealed to her aesthetic sense, reminding her that distinction lies in smallness.

At the memorial service, I spoke of how my father, who was accompanying my mother, had died while giving directions to the cabdriver. Mother had held him dead in her arms while the driver had rushed out to find a cop. (In Paris at the time on sabbatical, I was awakened at two o'clock in the morning by a cousin with the news of my father's death and left with my wife for New York the following morning, to the chagrin of the landlady of the apartment we rented. She was worried, she told us, that our tragedy was a disaster for her: she would be losing the rent.) If my father's body wasted away during the last year of his life (he had been two hundred pounds in his prime, reduced now to 120), his mind remained bright and alert. To the end he knew what he was about and where he was going. In intensive care, his nose and mouth were filled with tubes; he couldn't speak, so he wrote on a piece of paper: "Don't worry I ain't goin' yet." He lingered for a year, frustrated that life had closed in on him. Housebound. How he hated being confined! I spoke of his interest in politics, in particular the politics of the state of Israel. He had long ago given up on the Soviet Union. Politics had been important to him because his life had been altered by politics in a profound way. As a young man, he had been uprooted by World War I and the Russian Revolution. In America he remembered the Russian Revolution as a great upheaval, but also as a liberating event that would create a just society for all Russians, gentile and Jew. When it became clear to him that the Russian Revolution was the opposite of a liberation, he was quick to condemn it. His politics, I said, was a politics of justice. He had a great sense of justice and injustice in every area of his life. He was always good for his word, always trustworthy and reliable. He had a temper which was quickly provoked when he thought that something wrong or bad had been done.

And then I spoke of his relationship to my mother. It is customary to say that the deceased was a devoted husband, but the bond between them was deeper than the bond of any other couple I have ever known. I was the only son, the only child, and, addressing the small gathering of family and friends, I told them what they already knew: the enormous investment of feeling he had made in me. A large part of him lived through me; whatever success I had he thoroughly enjoyed and when I suffered he suffered too. He was also one of my severest critics: he never praised me simply to make me feel good, and he knew how to joke at my expense—like the time he asked me to shave a gray beard I had grown because it made me look years old than I was. He would introduce me to acquaintances as his grandfather. I praised his intelligence, his moral gifts, which in the scale of eternity count for everything. There was so much of his temperament in me, his virtues (I would like to think) and his faults, that I knew he would be alive in me as long as I lived. These words were my kaddish.

The memorial service took place in the rain. I had written my eulogy in ink and the words ran with God's or nature's tears as I read them. But I myself, strangely, never summoned tears either at the funeral or memorial service. I meant what I said about my father, but I was not really mourning his death. I stood at the graveside of this admirable man dry-eyed like my mother, while the skies were weeping. I am reminded of the monologue by Sholem Aleichem that I used to recite in which the narrator, a teller of tall tales about America, describes three kinds of funerals: the rich man's (the day is bright, the sun is shining), the man of middling means (the day is overcast, the sun occasionally peeps through), and the pauper (the sky is dark with pouring rain). My father had a poor man's memorial service, which my words tried to redeem.

The death of my father cleared the path to mother. Father and I growled at each other. We fought over my appearance and my conduct. He had a strong sense of what I should be and do, and I fought back for my independence. But all the intimacy was between Father and me, Mother always a figure on the periphery, rarely speaking but anxiously concerned. I remember once sitting in a car with her and feeling how rare it was to be alone with her, and suddenly—or was there provocation? I can no longer recall—she spoke almost matter-of-factly of how from my early childhood there had always been a strong bond between me and my father, how all the talk and intimacy had excluded her. I have little memory of mother speaking much while father was alive. He was the talker, the person with ideas, the bon vivant with the boundless energy of sociability. There were family dinners, delicious meals prepared by Mother, but all the social pleasure was generated by my father. She spoke without resentment but with the conviction that I should know that she knew and that somehow she approved because of its importance for Father and me. I had a pang of guilt and wanted to assure her, but I couldn't; I could see that she didn't want assurance. Only the truth, only the truth. Maybe she was glad that my father fully occupied me, that she was off the hook. But now the path was cleared and we could no longer hide from each other. In the eighties of her life, I discovered a remarkable woman. She lived alone for fifteen years after my father's death, and now, for the past four years, in her late nineties, she has been living in a nursing home. This is the story of those years.

At the age of eighty-eight my mother began to read Wittgenstein— or read about him. On a visit I brought with me Ray Monk's superb biography of the philosopher to read, and put it down on mother's coffee table. She perused the book, was fascinated by the photographs of the family, read a passage or two: "This is a strange man. I would like to read it." She fixed her attention on Wittgenstein's tormented relationship with his father and with Jewishness, and though she claimed that the philosophy was above her head, she caught something of its charm. Wittgenstein compares a language game to two men playing catch. One of them catches the ball, puts it in his pocket and walks away. He doesn't know the game. She loved the simplicity and the rightness of the example. I told her about a novel that had been written about Wittgenstein, *The World As I Found It,* by Bruce Duffy. I obtained a copy and she devoured it, but made a discrimination: "This is not the biography. The biography is a masterpiece." My mother had always enjoyed reading, serious reading (she loved Jane Austen's novels), but this interest in Wittgenstein was extraordinary. When I told friends about it, they were astonished and amused. They asked me about the level of her education and were even more astonished when I told them that she had not completed high school. What drew her to Wittgenstein was her sense that his genius was connected with his suffering. My mother has her own share of suffering. For years she has suffered from arthritis, her back and legs a constant source of pain. Although she has the gift of entering into the suffering of others, she derives no consolation from it. She understood the wisdom of Wittgenstein's remark "Another person cannot have my pain."

In other parts of the world, death is a huge maw that consumes thousands, millions of all ages. She was saved from the ovens of Europe. She is among the lucky ones, living in the comparative safety of America. But she has never recovered from the tearing up of her roots. What haunts her and what she has unwittingly communicated to me is the disaster waiting around the corner. In some obscure way there is a connection between her physical suffering and her uprooting. And yet she has always nourished a weak hope that relief would come, perhaps even a cure. She equivocates between resignation, *"Dos i dus"* (that's the way it is), and "Maybe tomorrow will be different." There is a Jewish hope in all this. "Almost always," the great sociologist Max Weber writes, "the theodicy of suffering has originated in the hope of salvation." Notwithstanding her atheism! Despite her complaining, she has the stoicism of the long-lived. Her stoicism is a kind of vaccine to immunize herself against the fear of disaster. For her now there is aging, the unrelenting medically slowed deterioration of the body, the indefinite postponement of dying. Without diversions, she directs a steady gaze upon her body, monitoring every change like a doctor's machine. She searches for the cause of her pain with the weak conviction that the discovery of the cause will evaporate it, or that even if it will not alter the pain, at least she will know. With a scholar's passion, she pursues the implication of a doctor's remark, of an unexplained test result, but gets little satisfaction. The doctor only half remembers her condition. He disappoints her as a poor student disappoints a demanding teacher. Questions should have answers.

What has not aged is her mind. It was never young, because it had endured too much at an early age. But it is the sharp and fastidious mind of a perfectionist, rarely satisfied. The perfectionism reveals itself in her domesticity. When she shopped (before entering the nursing home) she would pick through items of food, clothes, shoes, endlessly, looking for flaws, unbelieving if she had not found them. Unbelieving too that prices have multiplied thirtyfold since she had last bought a dress. When she found it difficult to shop she would order food by phone, but always with the apprehension that a tomato would have a soft spot or a chicken would be spoiled by the time it arrived or that the bag would contain three rather than four zucchinis. If mother had ordered a bottle of wine in a restaurant, she would more often than not return it after sniffing it, not from any perversity, but because her sharp scent and demanding palate would have discovered something not right in the bouquet and in the taste. I am fantasizing about the wine, but she has returned items and whole packages of food. When I shopped for her I would go nervously from store to store, never certain that I had picked the right thing. The rare occasions when my wife and I succeeded in getting her out of the apartment and into a restaurant, she would express astonishment at the prices and the poor quality of the food. Once, after eating in a fine gourmet restaurant specializing in nouvelle cuisine, she needed to run to the bathroom to throw up. Her whole life has been devoted to disgorging the impurities of the world.

During the year I spent in France on a Fulbright scholarship, my parents came to visit. It was their first trip to Europe since their flight from Russia in the twenties. We traveled together to Normandy. What I remember even more vividly than the magnificent cliffs of Etretat is mother's indecisive shopping in the clothing stores of a nearby village. She went from store to store, but nothing looked or fit right. At one point my father left the store and exploded with rage at her inability to make up her mind. It was a comic reversal of the situation of the husband distraught over the profligate spending habits of the wife. Behind the indecisiveness, of course, was her perfectionism. She would not waste a penny on something that was not absolutely right.

Mother exists out of time, where there are no periods, no eras, no fashions. Fashion is provisional, the imperfect state. She can buy a dress or a suit only with the greatest difficulty and always, on the rare occasions when she does buy, with dissatisfaction. For fashion is the corruption of the moment, the distorted shadow of the real–that which passes because it cannot satisfy for long. Her apartment was filled with furniture and furnishings purchased over sixty years ago, when she was first married. Whatever she possessed was carefully preserved and inventoried in her mind, so that she could retrieve whatever item she might need or want at a moment's notice. She needed no lists to remind her where things were. She seemed to have been born with the instincts of an archivist, embodying the principle of continuity, a resistance to the disruptions, the obsolescences of modern life.

Her perfectionism showed itself–still shows itself–in her command of medication. Every morning she places her pillboxes before her, carefully opening each one of them, removing the requisite number of pills, closing each box, making sure again and again that they are tightly secured. One morning when I visited her, she had forgotten whether she had taken a particular pill and panicked, not because of the pill, but because she had "forgotten": "This has never happened before." Fear of Alzheimer's? When I tell her, "I always forget things," she replies, "*You're* not me." Her mind has always been a data bank of memories meticulously recalled. Family members would call to verify a recollection of an event that had occurred ten years, twenty years, thirty years, forty years earlier and her authority never failed. Once a quarrel arose over the birth year of her younger sister. She was convinced that she was a year younger than she was, but Mother, who had raised her after her own mother died, knew that this was only the vanity of her sister refusing to acknowledge the reality of old age. And she gave no quarter. The truth is the truth. As always she marshaled evidence; the birth certificate had vanished, but marriage dates of brothers, school-registration dates, dates engraved on tombstones, all the lines on the graph converged on her sister's real birth year and nothing could change it. The eightieth-birthday party given by my aunt's children nearly turned into a fiasco as my aunt announced to bewildered celebrants that she was not eighty. Mother was stone. My mother's memory, fortunately or unfortunately, is an astonishing power. Even in very old age she has forgotten nothing: the distant, middle, and immediate past. She remembers not only her own past but my own better than I do. But it is not simply a matter of recollection: the past is present to her. The desolation of her orphaned state has survived the seventy years of relative and increasing comfort in America. She is proof that memory is not an unequivocal virtue.

A perfectionist is a judge. People have always passed through her life to be scrutinized and judged. Whenever I introduced a girlfriend about whom I had serious feelings, my parents disapproved. In inspecting her appearance and behavior, Mother tried to be discreet, but she was obtrusive to me and to the object of inspection. She listened but rarely spoke, and her silences would make my girlfriend nervous and awkward. It was no better when I introduced my (first) wife-to-be. My father and mother both disapproved and prophesied that no good would come of the marriage. They were proved right, but there was something self-fulfilling in their prophesy. My first wife, who was impulsive and lacked tact, constantly stirred the pot. She served strange and spicy meals they could not eat, wore clothes they thought unseemly, put on airs of superiority. She ignored all my signals and plunged headlong into trouble. When we broke up, much of the blame was placed at the feet of my parents. I had taken their side. I resented my parents for the harshness of their judgments, but I understood their point of view. I was torn between wife and parents. Caught in a drama my parents had created without wanting to, I was enacting a fate they had foretold. The marriage came to a bitter end, but they did not gloat, they grieved–for me, for my suffering, for the innocent casualties, my two young children.

Anyone who has ever met my mother and is attentive to her presence has remarked on her alertness, her judging eye. She will not be condescended to because of her age. Two friends of mine met her at my daughter's wedding, one a novelist, the other a literary scholar. The novelist brought up her reading of Wittgenstein with the intention of paying her a compliment, but she would have none of it. She was not a child to be praised for displaying an unexpected achievement. "She saw right through me," my friend said. My other friend found himself sweating as he discerned that she was not an old lady to be trifled with: "There's an unshakable integrity about her." Charm in others produces flickers of pleasure, occasionally a sustained joy in things, an outburst of pure comic delight. But she sniffs disapproval, grudgingly concedes the rightness of something like a piece of pastry or the juiciness of a grapefruit: "It's Okay." Her palate has been a keen analytic instrument for analyzing the ingredients of food.

What has given her joy is the sense that she is in the presence of greatness: Fyodor Chaliapin's voice, Nureyev's leaps, Heifetz's tone, Horowitz's virtuosity. Scornful of religion, contemptuous of God-talk, she views the great singers, dancers, violinists, and pianists as gods. Without knowing anything of philosophy, she sensed in Wittgenstein another god of the spirit. The heroic figure in mother's family was her grandmother, a wise woman who lived to be more than one hundred. She was a sage to whom people came for advice. Mother loves to tell the story of a moment at the dinner table when her *bubbe* removed her teeth, put them in a cup, and proceeded to eat. The teeth were decorative, not made for chewing. My mother, a little child then, was so impressed by her grandmother's feat that at night in bed, she tried without success to remove her own teeth. It is a story that she has told me a number of times. Somehow it is linked in her mind to her *bubbe*'s distinction. It is an expression of power, like my mother's own, for her life has always been a stripping down, a reduction to what was essential. I imagine my mother triumphing over every disability, every failure to function, sustained by an indomitable will to survive. My mother, incidentally, has almost all her teeth.

For years mother had no guests in her apartment. Since my father's death, she had become a virtual hermit. Apart from visits from me or her grandchildren and the occasional surprise ring of the doorbell, mother lived in isolation–until her entry into a nursing home. But the voices of friends on the telephone connected her to the outside world. If a ring of the doorbell stirred anxiety ("Who could that be? I'm not expecting anybody"), the ring of the telephone, loud and sudden, was clearly welcome. She would drop anything she was doing or holding and go promptly to the phone. No one had to wait for more than two rings. She also kept a mental record of when someone called and how often. The frequency of the calls measured the character of the caller, character being consideration for others. She herself was meticulous in keeping in touch with friends and family by phone and returning calls promptly. Sometimes when I visited her I watched her speaking to her friends as she lay in bed on her back and complained in a quiet and relaxed voice. The only effort she was required to make was to speak. She did not have to move or to gesture. She could close her eyes, unobserved by the caller. The intimacy was not with an embodied person, but with a voice. The phone insulated the friendship and kept it safely at a distance.

Living away from her, I would worry about her isolation. "Shouldn't you have help?" The answer was predictable: "Where can you get good help these days?" Mother's standards would be very difficult to satisfy. She did, however, covet her neighbor's East Indian housekeeper, whom she would occasionally meet in the hallway and talk to. The housekeeper would from time to time do her a favor and shop for her. Her employer, a ninety-six-year-old man, lived in the apartment catercorner to my mother's and became aware of the meetings and the favors. Wizened, squint-eyed, usually distracted, he began to fix a sharp eye or rather cock an ear when my mother made conversation with the housekeeper. He kept his door slightly ajar, so that he could hear what was going on in the hallway. He must have had a hard time distinguishing what they were saying from the continuous sound of television coming from his apartment and from the open doors of other apartments. One day he confronted Mother, screaming and waving his cane at her: "Keep away! Keep away! She belongs to me." "The idiot!" she hissed to me afterward. "All I said to her was that if you can pick up a few vegetables for me on the way to work, I'd appreciate it. I have no intention of taking her from him. The idiot." And she didn't entirely back off. She had no intention of stealing the woman, but she refused to be forbidden to speak to her. One morning, she saw a suitcase in front of the old man's door; when she looked again in the afternoon the suitcase was still there. She started to go to his door, which was, uncharacteristically, closed, to knock, but thought better of it. What did it mean? In the evening, a neighbor told her that the old man had suddenly taken ill and was rushed to the hospital. His suitcase had been packed, taken out into the hallway and forgotten. A curious business. Where was the Indian woman?

Mother told me the story inconsequentially, bemused. I asked the obvious brutal question: "If something happens to the old man, then the Indian woman will be available. Are you going to ask her to work for you?" She had been complaining about a need for help and about the incompetence and dishonesty of the help. All suggestions from me, from other members of the family had been rejected. But this Indian woman with the lovely manner and the gentle voice had won her over. Ah, but she belonged to someone else. Now she might be free. "We'll see," Mother said. The prize was hers, but she wasn't sure she wanted it. Her independence was too precious a possession.

I accompanied my mother on one of her trips to an opthalmologist and on entering the waiting room noticed a familiar face. It was the face of a ninety-year-old woman, a friend of my mother's whom I had not seen since the funeral of my father many years before. This woman had managed to retain the features of younger days, and surprisingly to me, they had remained etched in my consciousness. My mother had been speaking to her by phone several times a week, but hadn't seen her for many years. I told my mother, who is hard of seeing, that her friend was in the room and she seemed to straighten with anxiety. I said, "Why don't you go up to her?" She hesitated, then approached her friend and spoke her name. But there was no sign of recognition. She repeated her name and still there was no response. She then retreated to the bench where I was sitting and observing, clearly in distress. "How I must have changed?" The first thought was for her own appearance. Vanity is the last emotion to disappear.

Both my mother and her friend had changed remarkably little during the past fifteen years, but this was the waiting room of the near blind. My mother wondered whether she should try again. Meanwhile, the doctor had called the friend in. Mother decided that she would wait for her to reappear, and when she did, she approached her and this time spoke her own name: recognition, delight, tears, animated discussion. From a distance I could hear the familiar sound of complaint, this time coming from the friend. My mother held her hand with a quiet dignity, uncomplaining about herself. I thought: complaints seemed to be reserved for intimacies with her son. I didn't think that Mother and this friend were particularly fond of each other when they were younger. But the wear and tear of aging seemed to have "purified" their relationship and they could now concentrate on essentials. The friend looked up and recognized me: "How well you look! How you have filled out!" She remembered me as a skinny kid of twelve. A month later, my mother called to tell me that her friend was "no more. She was tired and just gave out." And I heard her own mounting fatigue, as if the end of her friend were an omen of her own end. Friendship is the last link to life, stronger perhaps than her bond with her son, with whom there is the disaffinity of generations. The friend is that other voice not always in tune with yours, but striving for a life-sustaining connection.

The phone in my house rang in the middle of an August night. "Sorry to disturb you," said my mother, urgently but with a sense of consideration, "but I fell on my back in the bathroom. I thought it was all over, though somehow I managed to crawl back to my bed. I think I broke something. I need you." She was calling from the floor of her bedroom after having crawled to the telephone. She had also called the neighbor who had a duplicate of the key to the apartment. The neighbor gave the key to the superintendent, who let himself in. The ambulance was on its way. This was not the first time. I got up, packed my bag, and waited for the first shuttle flight to New York. I spent five grueling days with Mother, who insisted on her self-sufficiency, though in fact I became practical nurse, dishwasher, errand boy, crisis manager. But why not, wasn't she all these things and more when I was a child? She went on endlessly about her pain: "I've never experienced such pain, not even years ago when the pain in my back was so severe that every movement was agony." She said this with an uncharacteristic whine as she moved an improvised walker (a folding chair) and was about to collapse. I caught her. It was a terrible moment, for she felt like a bag of bones and I imagined at that moment life escaping her. But her hands gripped the chair frame like a vise. I was sure that she would bring the chair down upon herself. I told her to relax her grip, but the grip grew tighter, like the desperate act of a swimmer who is drowning. Only my shout made her relax her fingers and trust me to hold her. Her pain was palpable, without words. I thought she would die in my arms.

She recovered slowly. I could sense the mind beginning to work again, remembering the pills she must take, the checks she must write, the calls she must make. I imagined her body deteriorating, wasting, virtually evaporating, but the mind persevering, hardening in its determination to survive. If the will alone had the capacity to insure survival forever, that will would inhabit my mother. I am agnostic on the question of whether Mother will live forever. I made gestures to console, a brief caress of the forehead, a kiss on the cheek. She passively received affection with a look of grievance, as if to suggest that the affection was propitiation for the guilt of not having loved her as I had loved or she believed I had loved my father. Or so I read her look.

It was clear to me that my mother could no longer manage by herself. I called agencies, churches, synagogues for help. A series of women showed up for the job as helper. First a blowsy Jamaican arrived with a friend who suspiciously sniffed the atmosphere in the apartment. I tried to be genial, but I could see the cool stare of my mother. Later: "Can you imagine, she removed her shoes after she walked in. *Siz mir gevoren finster in die oign.* (My spirit sank.) Can you imagine going to my grave in the company of such a person? Out of the question." Next was a tall, broad-shouldered Irish woman in her fifties, impeccably dressed, all aglitter with painted nails and large earrings. Mother looked dazzled and frightened. She hardly spoke as the Irish woman told horror stories of elderly persons and the pride before the fall: literally, the falls that make for broken hips, severe contusions, strained ligaments. "It's the pride of independence, of not realizing how frail you are." (Spoken in an Irish cadence.) The lesson was clear. Old lady, you better put yourself in my hands. Mother listened, impressed and fearful. "Such a fancy lady. Is this someone to clean my house? She said light cleaning. I know what that means, a dab here and there, finished and then hours in front of the television. Who needs such an impressive woman?" My heart sank; I thought she would never agree to anyone and I would become mother's prisoner, her permanent practical nurse and errand boy.

And then, miracle of miracles, a Russian lady appeared, also impeccably dressed. "Beautiful," Mother said, but I could see no beauty. They spoke Russian and I sensed the warmth in the lushness of my mother's speech. Russian turned her from dry to wet. Russian had been the language my parents spoke when they wished to keep me in the dark. Russian contained secrets about other people, or, as I dimly suspected in my childhood, about myself. I had neither the curiosity nor the will to crack the code. I may have even found some comfort in the knowledge that they lived in a language I did not inhabit. It was the place where they left me alone. If I had entered that space, I would have been in their . . . no, they would have been in my life totally. And now the Russian lady and Mother were speaking the language I do not understand, but they were speaking without complicity, without the intimacy that had always excluded me. I could tell from my mother's expression that she was forming impressions and arranging them in a judgment about the kind of person who might become her companion, and I could tell that it would be a mixed judgment with enough that was favorable in the judgment for us to hire her. (Several weeks later, she told me that the Russian lady was okay, but full of pretenses about what she knew: medicine, politics, literature. "She even confused Pushkin with Lermontov. I set her straight." I was oddly grateful that I did not know Russian. It was as if I could entrust Mother to the Russian lady because they shared a world I did not possess and into which I did not have to enter.) It was a match and I closed the deal.

The Russian lady, dressed to the nines, arrived at eight-thirty in the morning, all cheer and energy with only a slight trace of the melancholy for which the Russians are famous. She served Mother breakfast and then sat herself next to her. Soon she was telling her about her life, how her family was rich before the revolution, how they hid tangible wealth like jewelry in false closets, how when they came to America they put diamonds in baby shoes. Customs would never inspect babies. She was a grandmother, but the details about a husband were unclear. "There's a man who wants to be with me," she said. "Sick wife. What should I do?" Mother, for years confined to her apartment, gave advice. She had learned from television and from telephone conversations that people now lived together without being married. They learned about each other before getting married. Sometimes they didn't marry. "We're now hanging on the question of what she should do," her voice quickening with new energy. Without realizing it (for she was still full of complaint), she had been rejuvenated by the Russian lady.

The honeymoon was short-lived. Mother phoned to tell me a story. From her sickbed, she had called a locksmith to have the locks replaced, because the doors had become difficult to open. The locksmith had arrived, replaced the locks, and given her an extra set of keys, which she had carefully placed in a tray on a chest of drawers. But the keys had disappeared; or had she, uncharacteristically, forgotten where she had placed them? With her walker she moved about in every room, opening drawers, inspecting surfaces, searching in pockets, but she found nothing. "I didn't want to tell you this, to upset you after everything that had happened, but you have to know." And then the denouement: two days later, the Russian lady opened the drawer of a chest next to Mother's bed and, lo and behold, she dug in and between papers found the keys. The Russian lady did not know that Mother had already inspected the drawer, indeed had removed every item, laid it all on her bed, and carefully looked at the contents, doing all this while knowing that she could never have put these keys in the drawer. It had flashed immediately through her mind that the Russian lady had had the keys copied, and that at some propitious moment when she was away the apartment would be robbed. What made it more sinister was the affection the Russian lady lavished on her, the soft words, the kiss on the forehead when she left. And worse, the insult to her intelligence: "She thinks because I'm old and physically weak that my mind is feeble. But I didn't let on that I suspected her. I'm not afraid. I know she won't do anything to me now. She has a good job. The plan is for later. We have to fire her and replace the locks. She has done a terrible thing to me." Indignant, hurt, Mother, with the cool, calculating part of her brain, would play the game, wait out the week, before I came down like an avenger to dispatch the Russian lady.

We could not fire her immediately because there was no one to replace her. She *was* solicitous of Mother's every whim, praised her as a wise woman from whom she had much to learn, spoke of her as her *"mamitchka."* "She wants to be on my good side, so that she can settle in for good," Mother said. I sensed trouble. She would be very hard to get rid of. "She asks me whether you and I are in touch, and I tell her of course, that you call me every night." I suspected that she wanted to take my place. Mother also had her suspicions. "Why shouldn't she be happy in her job? She has a picnic here. Very little to do. She brought me roses for Mother's Day." *I* had not sent her roses. But I didn't hear a reproach in her voice so much as a warning about a wily competitor. "I didn't want her roses, but I didn't want to insult her either."

Meanwhile, she called her friends and broadcast her discovery. One friend, a particularly close one, was disbelieving: "Maybe you forgot where you put the keys." "I never put them where she found them. But anyway I was so frantic that when I searched for them, I looked in that drawer, took out all the contents, the keys were not there. So *she* put them there, I'm sure." But the friend remained disbelieving and Mother, always most perceptive when insulted, knew that her friend thought she was fantasizing, maybe that she was paranoid, that her mind was *averbutl* (going senile). "Can you imagine? I never thought she was so stupid. She doesn't believe me." I heard the anguish of deepening isolation, another turn of the screw; it was not enough that she was in pain, now she was not believed. With her mastery of the arithmetic of life she may have put two and two together and suspected that her pain was not believed.

And yet the new cheer and energy in her persisted, though Mother would never have acknowledged it. Simply having to figure out how to get from place to place, how to make sure that things got done, keeping her eye on the Russian lady to make sure that she didn't pull a fast one, like asking for more money than she paid out when she shopped, had given her energy. "She says she respects me, respects my intelligence, and that she has already learned a great deal from me. She uses too much oil when she cooks. I made her understand that I don't like it. She's beginning to see how I like to do things." I was certain that Mother would not fire the Russian lady. The anxiety about the keys would become the suspense of her life, something that would even sustain her and keep her from despair. "I'm not afraid," she said. She was declaring not only her courage but her intelligence as well. "She has no reason to steal from me now. Why should she, she has *some* job. I'm not senile, I'm clean, the apartment is clean, she doesn't have to bathe me, she has very little to do. She reads, watches television, her taste is terrible. Anyway, we'll leave things as they are."

Mother fell again and fractured hip and shoulder. The family, or what is left of it, descended on the hospital to support me and to reveal itself: the alarmist, the brooder, the cheerful advisor. I was given all sorts of advice and warning. "This is an enormous burden"; "You have to plan ahead"; "Ah, you didn't withdraw her money, it will all be used up"; "Watch out, don't be consumed by this, you have your own life to live"; "Look at the positive side, she came through the operation, what a fighter." Aunt, uncle, cousins walked into the recovery room after the operation: Mother was no more than a wraith; all the color had been bleached out of her so she had become virtually indistinguishable from the sheets that covered her. Distress was written over her sister's face. I had to steel myself against all the pity and concern that seemed to emanate from the family. It was as if I was about to perform an extraordinarily difficult athletic feat and was not expected to succeed. They were there to keep me company and I wanted solitude to indulge my anxiety.

I escaped from the hospital and took a cab back to Mother's apartment, where I was sought out by the telephone. A call came from another cousin. I heard in the voice his own grief about his failed career and burdensome mother: "It's tough, first the rehab, then the new living arrangement. My mother went through it all—went back to her apartment. She had house care twenty-four hours around the clock. She wasn't satisfied with the care, so we had to call the agency to ask for a replacement—and then another replacement and another. It was a nightmare, drove me and K. [his wife] crazy, and then some of the help asked for money on the line. One time we didn't have the money and the expression of the woman's face made me feel that she would take my mother hostage, that when we left she wouldn't take her to the bathroom, that she would let her wallow in her piss. Such fucking bullshit. It's a jungle out there. No heart. Everyone wants their piece of the action. And then the kvetching and whining." My cousin had a powerful command of the tough-guy cliché; he was the complete sentimentalist who had only contempt for sentimentality.

Another call, this time from the Russian lady: "Where is your mother? I come to apartment and ring the bell. There was no answer." I told her what happened and heard real distress in her voice. And immediately I thought that this was her chance to use the keys. She didn't have them. What she did have was a genuine concern for my mother. I changed sides and now believed with her friend that she had forgotten where she had put the keys. I would tell Mother that she had a friend in Lisa.

Mother's pain subsided, but the recovery took a long time. She had to be bathed and fed and have her excretory functions managed by nurses, female and male. "It is so humiliating," she said. When I visited her, she looked away and up to the ceiling: tears would have formed in her eyes if she were capable of them. "I've had little, but I had my independence, my own apartment, my friends." She had of course not seen her friends for years. The telephone had been her line to the world. Now she would have to move away to live in my city, and though the telephone would not disappear, the sense of distance would change everything. "But you can still call your friends," I said. "It will not be the same. I never wanted to be a burden to you." "You will be less of a burden if you stop saying you don't want to be one." She became pensive and with a gentle nervousness kneaded the sheets that covered her. I was seized by anxiety. Not only her life, but my life, our lives would change inalterably. She would become my daily concern, her worst fear. Would she heal and walk again? And even if she healed, she had lost her independence. Vulnerability was the deepest fact of her life. The doctor said she was strong, warning that in whatever condition she would go on a long time and perhaps with an undiminished lucidity, like Tithonus, who, as Tennyson said, helplessly observed "cruel immortality consume" him. Sitting next to her in the hospital, she suddenly broke the silence and put a surprisingly firm hand on mine. "I will try to accept this, what else can I do?" Tears blurted from my eyes. I said, "I love you, Mother." "I love you, too." We had spoken the words to each other spontaneously.

The staff was astonished by her age–ninety and she still had her teeth and the full command of her faculties. She shared a room with a woman twenty years her junior who was a talking machine: "She never stops. She talks. I fall asleep, I wake up. She's still talking. And she eats like a horse. Last night was terrible. She had to go to the bathroom twice, which means in the commode, and the nurses just let her stay on the pot, the stink was terrible." When Mother was in agony and the nurse did not respond to her ringing, the chatterbox hobbled down the corridor for help. "When she left the hospital she embraced me, hugging me and kissing me again and again. She said she would never forget me. I was moved."

When I told mother that she could not return to her apartment, her head tipped upward; her lips pursed in pain, as if they were fighting back tears. She didn't speak. "You will return and be alone. I'm in another city. Even if you have help, what if a problem arises, who will be there to help?" She gave no response; she was fortifying herself against the pressure I was applying. I felt a surge of anger, so I too remained silent for fear the anger would speak itself to her. Everybody I spoke to understood her point of view, her desire for independence. Anxiety woke me at four in the morning and I thought I would never be rid of it. I decided to withdraw the pressure: "What do you want? You decide." "You know what I want." "All right, if that's what you want." Tears, or rather the shadow of tears. A smile. She took my hand and kissed it. I felt or rather she made me feel like a judge who had released a prisoner in an act of mercy. This cautious woman, whose every thought anticipated trouble, was prepared to risk her life alone in the most intimidating city in the world because it was her home, where she had lived for more than seventy years. Though friends had moved away, disappeared, or died, it was her life: familiar, certain, even safe. "You are choosing your apartment over your family." "I know." She herself was bemused by the fact, but she felt no guilt or at least she made no excuses. She could not afford to deny the truth of her feelings.

She began to walk again–with a walker, then, tentatively, with a four-pronged cane. Amazing. In two weeks she would be released and

I would drive her home. When she reentered the apartment, she uttered a cry–like someone returning to a lover. There was no contest between family and apartment. In no time, she settled in, and before I left to return home I exploded unaccountably. We had packed her up in the belief that she would be moving to live near us and now we had had to unpack her. I was bristling with resentment. I wanted her to understand what we had been through. I must have shown my anger, because I could see it penetrating her expression: she seemed amazed by it. Back in her apartment with the winter days upon her, incapacitated, alone, she put on a cheerful voice whenever I would call, so that I would not be irritated by her complaining. The episode of the keys had been consigned to the past. The Russian lady was back for three days a week, but for the most part my mother was by herself. "Can you manage alone?" "Yes." Why hadn't I appreciated her bravery? She wanted the dignity of her independence.

Not long after my mother's return home, I received a phone call from my uncle, the former Trotskyite, with whom I had argued in my adolescence. He was now in his eighties and had long abandoned the politics of his younger days. Two muggings and a passion for the state of Israel had turned him into a conservative and a devoted member of a temple congregation. I understood from what he told me about his role in the temple that in discussion he would side with tradition against change. He was the pillar of conservatism, always checking the reformism of Reform Judaism. A craftsman, an organizer, a traveler, an eater of vast amounts of food, he was a man of cheerful disposition, opposite to my mother's–with vitality and a sense of adventure. From time to time, he would pass out after a meal and would have to be taken off to a hospital. He had cancer of the prostate, a triple bypass, but never a complaint. Nothing could dissuade him from changing his plans or breaking a habit that gave him pleasure, whatever the consequences. On a trip to Guatemala, he had insisted on traveling to the jungle, the neighborhood of guerrillas at war with the government. His wife (my mother's sister), sensible but no match for her husband's desires, put up resistance, but went along in a state of anxiety. He must have overeaten the evening before their arrival in the jungle, for he passed out, as he had done numerous times before. The guerrillas suddenly appeared as if on cue from behind the bushes into the open space in which he lay. My aunt's anxious account of what occurred never made clear how the government negotiated with the guerrillas for their return to Guatemala City. My uncle (American-born) lived life to the fullest.

I had not seen or spoken to him for a while, partly because we lived at a distance from each other (he in New Jersey, I in Massachusetts), but also because of an estrangement that had set in between my aunt and my mother, her sister, an estrangement that had involved me. He called to ask me for something, and I was glad to hear from him. He told me of a controversy in his temple over the question of whether to grant honorary Jewish status to non-Jewish spouses of members of the congregation. "Honorary Jew," he said, "what does that mean?" My uncle was firmly opposed. "Of course the spouses should be made to feel welcome, but being or becoming a Jew is no easy matter. You are born to it, or if you want to be converted you must earn it. Being married to a Jew is not enough. Being a Jew is a very serious thing." I listened amused and at a distance from my uncle's account. As he spoke, an old joke from my childhood came absurdly to mind. A kid walks into a luncheonette and says, "Make me a malted," and the man behind the counter extends his arm and points to the kid: "Poof, you're a malted."

The point of the call was the request that I send him a copy of "Ich Bin a Yid." He would have it translated and then use it in his defense against honorary Judaism in the temple. "I want the congregation to know something about what it really means to be a Jew, historically speaking, the suffering, the struggles, the devotion to the Book." I was surprised. "You've forgotten, Caesar," I said, using the nickname that commemorated his habit as a young man of reciting Mark Antony's famous speech over the body of Caesar, "that it's a Stalinist poem. Feffer speaks of drinking from Stalin's cup of happiness." "It doesn't matter. I'll cut out the Stalinist sections. I remember how wonderfully you recited the poem, how it used to move everyone." My ex-Trotskyite, now conservative uncle wanted a Stalinist poem to affirm Judaism to his fellow congregationists. How strange. I agreed to send him a copy, if I could find the poem.

Several days later I received a call from his daughter with the shocking news that her father, a man who everyone marveled at for his energy, his exuberance, his optimism, had suffered a massive stroke and was paralyzed on his left side. During the week that followed, I called several times, hoping for signs of recovery. Despite the paralysis and the fatigue and distraction that result from a stroke, my uncle's mental faculties were essentially unimpaired. His wife, my aunt Ruth, his daughter, Elisa, and his son, Jay, were with him constantly, speaking words of encouragement, expressing their love, asking questions. Jay said it was as if he had fallen into a deep well and they would have to find a way to reach and extricate him from it: "It's hard, it's frustrating. You know how positive and cheerful my father is, how cool. And now he cries when certain things are said to him." I mentioned my promise to send "Ich Bin a Yid." Maybe, I suggested, it could be read to him. But neither his wife nor his children read Yiddish. (My uncle, a latecoming passionate Jew, had not given his children the Jewish education I had received.) So I decided to record the poem on tape and send it. When I spoke next to my cousin, he told me how moved my uncle was when it was played to him. He cried and asked that it be played again and again. But I did not experience the impact until I visited him. My uncle asked that the tape be played, but it couldn't be found. It must have gotten lost when he had moved from the hospital to the rehabilitation center. But my cousin had the copy I had faxed. So I read the poem aloud as he lay on the bed, his eyes closed, his wife and children present.

> The forty years in ancient times
> I suffered in the desert sand
> Gave me strength
> I heard Bar Kochba's rebel cry
> At every turn through my ordeal

And more than gold did I possess
The stubborn pride of my grandfather
I am a Jew.

As I read, he wept, his wife and children wept. I too wept.

I called my uncle from time to time, and though his speech was slurred and my questions not always responded to; his mind, when focused, retained its sharpness. Before the stroke, he was a person who rarely displayed emotion other than cheerfulness. Now his moods swung between weepiness and hilarity. Jokes made him laugh uncontrollably. On Yom Kippur, I called and he said he would not ask God for forgiveness, God should ask him for forgiveness. My aunt told me that though he was without bitterness about what had befallen him, he had lost his faith—but not his sense of Jewish identity. It took him a year to die.

The effect on my mother was profound. The stroke she believed was a punishment for the the way he had lived, for his profligacy. She didn't mean it unkindly. If only he had taken care of himself. With his death, a new sadness seemed to eat away at her. Eleven years his senior, she regretted that she had not gone first. Shortly after his funeral, she began calling every day, reporting a new affliction: dizziness, growing blindness, a sprained foot that made it impossible to go to the bathroom, pain in her spine. And always there was a general misery. When I would suggest a course of action, for instance, moving to an assisted-living arrangement, she would respond, "I can't. I don't feel good. I'm deteriorating, getting worse every day." "But that is no answer. You have to be rational." "I know I'm irrational." Every day seemed to bring an increasing rigidity and indecisiveness in her about what had to be done. "Should I decide for you?" I could hear the tone of indecisiveness in my own voice. No answer. "I'll decide for you." No answer. One morning I called and said that I would put a deposit down on an assisted-living arrangement. Almost immediately after I had hung up, she called back to say "Don't do anything." She spoke of regretting her life. She had no one to blame but herself and was sorry for what she was doing to me. But no amount of awareness could change her. She was overwhelmed and wanted help, but at the same time refused it. I silently blamed myself for not having been more persuasive earlier, not having kidnapped her, as even her doctor had suggested. He had advised me to perform a deception, that is, to bring her up to Boston, my city, for a brief visit, place her in an an assisted-living arrangement, and make the visit permanent, whatever her wishes might be. How could I coerce another person to live where she did not want to? But I suspected that my lack of persuasiveness, my *laisser-aller* code, was fed by an anxiety that she would be too close and would consume my life.

My grandfather suffered a stroke in his late fifties and never fully recovered. He became mostly deaf and virtually lost his speech. He could speak some words, but the syntax of sentences had deserted him. We communicated through shouts or a primitive hearing aid that we used for more sustained exchanges. Zeide lived with us for most of my childhood, wrapped in silence. I was the apple of his eye: he called me *"bebbele,"* he taught me how to play dominoes, checkers, chess. Mother was the always the solicitous daughter, who knew his suffering and loneliness. Inconceivable that he would live anywhere but with her or her brother. Inconceivable that mother, now twenty years older than my grandfather when he died, would live with me. She knew, I knew that we could not live together. I believed, still believe that my mother will live beyond a hundred, into my old age. I had already in fact passed into the zone where she lived and felt my body reenact my mother's suffering and her anxiety about the world.

I told myself that I needed to break the hold she had on me—of always answering the call. I would force her to come to live near me by resisting her calls for help. But I doubted that I would succeed. I told her that I also had a life: "I can't fly down every time you need me anymore." "I know, I know," she said, but the knowledge caused no change. "I can't move. I can't dress myself. I can't . . ." "That is why you need to change your situation." "I can't change my situation." The complaints persisted: dizziness, excruciating pain in her back, but there was now a new and deeper note of despair, a weakness in the voice—and a long, drawn-out moan. "Oh, I've made such a mess, such a mess." "You can change things right now." "Oh-oh-oh, I'm so dizzy." Avoidance, resistance. "I can't come down on a moment's notice." "Don't you want to see me?" And the question so plaintively uttered entered me like a knife.

Was I being manipulated or was this an authentic cry of despair? Was something happening to her? Was this the beginning of the end? I decided to speak to my New York cousins who had promised to visit her. They would tell me what to do. The day passed slowly, agonizingly, as I waited for their call, but when it came it resolved nothing. "Your mother hasn't changed dramatically; she's paler, but what's different is her agitation. She was sitting there, kneading her legs, saying she was worried about becoming a burden to you. When I said something about her moving to Boston, she became silent. I think I understand why you must be at your wit's end." That night I awoke from sleep in the middle of the night with palpitations that lasted several minutes.

I had to satisfy myself, so in the morning I called Mother to say I would be down in two days–on Monday. At five o'clock in the morning of the day following my call I was awakened by a ring of the phone. "There is no linen, no sheets, no towels. You must bring linen and sheets." Bizarre. "Mother, do you know what time it is? You call me at five in the morning to tell me that you don't have sheets for me. That's crazy." "It's important that I called you." My mother's voice had her familiar gravity. I was enraged.

On Monday I flew down to see my mother as I had never seen her before. Her Russian companion, Lisa, was in tears as Mother sat at the kitchen table, distraught, moving her pills about like a shell game. She had a puzzled look on her face, a look I had never seen before. Her mastery was gone, she could not figure out her medication. Lisa looked at me with gratitude. "Oh, dear, she is terrible. She not eat. I thought . . . I'm so glad you come." My mother glanced up, saw me, said nothing, but began to eat with apparent appetite. "She eat," Lisa said, "because you here. You come like a god. Oh my, oh my."

I decided that she must be taken to the doctor. Simply getting her to the taxi and from the taxi to the doctor's turned out to be an ordeal.

The walk from the door of the apartment to the elevator, from the elevator down the stairway to the exit of the building to the cab, from the cab to the entrance to the doctor's office was interminable. In his office, she sat patiently; we spoke to each other, but she didn't always focus on what I said. After the examination, the doctor called me in and told me in her presence that my mother had changed: "She is confused, and will have to go into a nursing facility." Mother looked imploringly at me—as if she understood and didn't understand. Back in the apartment, my mother surprised me by eating half the lasagna I had bought. I thought maybe the doctor was mistaken. The time passed slowly and painfully until it was time for us to go to bed, she in the bedroom, I in the living room. I had grown up sleeping in the living room of our three-room apartment. I was returning to my childhood.

During the night, the hallucinations began. I heard a stirring in the bedroom and got up from the sofa to observe her entering the other bedroom, opening the ancient secretary that contained her papers to examine her checkbooks. "What are you doing?" "It doesn't add up." "What doesn't add up?" "It doesn't add up." "Stop it." She opened a side drawer and turned to me with the revelation that Lisa, her companion, had been stealing from her. "Where is the envelope of cash? Where?" "Maybe you put it elsewhere." "No, I put it here. I always put it here." I opened all the drawers and found the envelope. "Look, here it is." She looked at me with a smile of sorrow: "Ah, she tried to steal it, but couldn't find it, because I put it elsewhere. But . . ." I experienced a surge of anger, and led her silently to her bed. I returned to the sofa, only to hear her stirring again: this time she was standing before an open drawer of the chest, fingering her underwear. She noticed me and said with a look of despair: "I have no underwear." The chest of drawers was filled with clothes bought many years earlier, meticulously cared for, but in somewhat frayed condition. "What are you talking about, look at how much underwear you have." I pointed to neat piles of underpants and bras. "No you don't understand, you don't understand, I have nothing to wear." I insisted and argued—only to encounter her familiar stubbornness. She continued to finger her bras. I implored: "It's late, go to bed." But she remained standing near the chest, obsessing over the bras. I grabbed her firmly and spoke harshly: "Go to bed." And she raised her face, put a hand to her forehead and gazed at and beyond me with a look of terrible pain on her face. "Such pain," I murmured, as if I were ventriloquizing my mother's voice. "Such pain." She lay down and I returned to the living room.

An hour later, she appeared somnambulant in the dining room that adjoins the living room with a magnifying glass in hand, and I observed her peering through it in the dark at a piece of paper lying on the kitchen table. I got up and walked quietly behind her: "What are you doing, Mother, what are you doing?" "I'm looking for Joan's phone number." (My wife's number, which of course was also mine and which she knew by heart.) "I must call her." "Why?" "You're having trouble breathing." (She was imagining that I was having an asthma attack.) "But I'm fine. I'm perfectly all right." "No, this is important. I must call Joan." I led her gently back to the bedroom. How could I have been so dim-witted as not to see that she had undergone a transformation, that dementia had set in? Why hadn't I seen it–instead all the craziness of the last few days had seemed like an exacerbation of her familiar stubbornness. In several days, without anyone close to her (me, my wife, my cousins) realizing it, she had lost her reason–and devastated us with guilt for not having perceived it.

The following morning I arranged for an ambulance to take her to the hospital. Lisa, her companion, and I accompanied her in the ambulance: the mood was somber, as if it were a trip to the cemetery. In the emergency room, the doctors stood around her, discussing her case, while she had a scowl on her face–an expression of disgust with life? The doctors suspected that she was suffering from malnourishment and dehydration. She expressed concern to the doctors about what she was doing to me. Attendants wheeled her away, and I left to return home to Boston.

The next week or two were spent in an anxious search for a nursing facility. At a loss about what to do, I called friends who had been through similar crises. They suggested my calling other friends and professionals they know. Advice: make sure there is no smell of urine, that the staff is friendly and shows concern for the residents. I visited seven nursing facilities, a number of which were quite impressive: handsomely furnished and beautifully landscaped with trees, shrubs, flowers, terraces, and gazebos. Inside there was the appalling look of disintegrating and crippled bodies, twisted faces, injured eyes, and the sounds of dementia. I learned that it was important for the corridors to be wide enough to navigate through a field of wheelchairs and walkers. On one visit, walking through a narrow corridor, I was grabbed by a demented woman with long, bony fingers and sharp elongated nails, in a wheelchair, who pulled me toward her and kissed my hands. I managed to extricate myself, but on returning I forgot her presence and she grabbed me by the belt. It was as if she were holding on to a lifeline. Her grip was amazingly powerful, and nurses rushed to my aid to release her grip. I decided that the facility was not for my mother, nor, obviously, for me.

Meanwhile, my calls to the hospital yielded little information. The CAT scan showed nothing. She was dehydrated and undernourished, with a low sodium count. The worst of it was the responses of the medical staff. When I called the doctor to ask questions, he impatiently brushed me off by saying that he was in the midst of a consultation. He called back to say that since my mother was not eating, I had to make a decision about whether she was to have a feeding tube inserted in her stomach. She had told me in the past on several occasions that she did not want to be resuscitated if her mind or body had deteriorated to a point where life would be intolerable. The doctor had diagnosed her condition as chronic dementia. In an agony of indecision I said nothing for a minute or so and then hesitantly said, "No, my mother would not want the tube under the circumstances." I hung up and felt a wave of guilt sweep over me. I then called a social worker to find out whether my mother had received a psychiatric evaluation. She too displayed a similar impatience—New York style? She didn't know. No one seemed to know, but she did give me some valuable information. Did I know that no nursing facility would accept my mother if she did not have a feeding tube? I would have to take her home and watch her die. I immediately called the doctor to tell him I had changed my mind. My mother would have a feeding tube inserted in her stomach. On Friday I received a call from a social worker with whom I had never spoken, telling me that my mother would be released the following Monday. "You better have several facilities to which we can refer her," she told me. "I was never told that I needed several facilities." "Well, you better get on the stick." "On the stick?" And the fiery lieutenant in me exploded.

But I had no choice. Two appointments and two visits later produced the required facilities. I flew down on Sunday only to discover on Monday that Mother was not being released and that the doctor had given no instructions. I received no apology from the social worker. Several days after my empty-handed return from New York, I called the supervisor of social services to complain, and shortly afterward I received a craven call from the offending worker apologizing for everything. "We're shorthanded, the pressure, the . . ." I interrupted her with a cold "You're forgiven" and moved on to business.

I had chosen the facility with an available bed the day my mother would be released from the hospital. The choice of a nursing facility is like a relay race in which you have to perfectly time the passing of the baton. My mother's doctor called to say that she had made an amazing recovery, her wits had returned, but she remained very weak, eating very little, with a feeding tube still in her stomach. On the day of her release, I accompanied my mother in the ambulance (New York to Boston—a seventeen-hundred-dollar fare): the medical attendant was a twenty-six-year old veteran of the Gulf War, with an admirable passion for caring for the sick and communicating the medical knowledge acquired as a biology student in college and a medic in the Gulf War. During the course of the trip, he constantly consulted a pill book, containing information about medication and its intended and side effects—and he explained to me as no doctor has done what my mother was taking and why. He himself had gone through a period of depression after the war: "No eighteen-year-old should have to see what I saw—dead bodies to which you grow indifferent." As he told me of his experiences, my mother uttered an occasional moan, and the attendant turned to her with concern and adjusted the blanket that covered her.

The ambulance arrived at the nursing home, and my mother and I entered a new phase of our lives. In her mid-nineties, this most habit-ridden woman, who had lived a life of unchanging days for years and years, who dreaded every change as if it were catastrophe, would have her life changed in the most dramatic way. From independence to senile dependence. But she was not senile: she had her wits, her lucidity, her sardonic articulateness (it had all come back), though her mental powers could not command her body, which had weakened into chronic lethargy. The feeding tube had restored her mind; perhaps it was only a matter of time for her body to be restored. On visits, I found her lying down with an arm covering her eyes as if she wished to block out the space into which she had entered. I would prod her gently into wakefulness. "You should try to walk. It's no good to lie in bed all the time." She would look at me in the way that she had always looked at me when I have been foolish and obtuse in her eyes, as if to say, you don't understand, you don't know how I feel. Uncharacteristically, I avoided a quarrel, not wanting to upset her.

Now that she had recovered her wits, I asked her whether she remembered anything of her collapse. I had hoped that she would remember having admitted that she had made a mess of things, that for the first time in her life she would acknowledge that she had been in the wrong. But she had no recollection of having confessed to me that she had made a mess of things. I have in my possession a note she wrote and left on the coffee table in her apartment in which she addresses me as "my dearest son" and writes of my "noble advice" that she move to Boston to be near me. "I should have taken your advice. I deeply regret that I did not." I didn't show her the note. If I had, I am sure she would have been bewildered. With the restoration of her wits, a sense of righteousness had been restored to her. She was not responsible for her age or her infirmities, and it would be the height of meanness and unreasonableness to want to hold her responsible for her collapse.

In the nursing home, she resumed her complaining, mainly about the food. "No salads or fresh fruit and vegetables—everything comes from cans." We (the caregivers) are urged by the administrators of the facility to be forthcoming in complaints and advice to them. The home, we are told, is dedicated to the well-being of the residents. The genes of complaint and indignation have been passed on to me. "I would want *my* son to be such a strong advocate like you," a social worker once told me. I have lived up to the compliment and made my mother's views known to the nurses, therapists, and administrators. One evening for dinner, a plate with a banana and apple was put before her. "I bite into the apple. Let me tell you. In the old country, it would have been food for pigs. And the broccoli they served—it was like buckwheat kasha." She has taken to reminiscing about her childhood in the old country—not about the squalor that drove her to emigrate to America, but about the variety and abundance of available cherries: red, pink, white, purple. As she remembers, she seems to savor their taste.

My mother was a remarkable cook. She made wonderful pea soup, hot and cold borscht, a cold soup of greens, rice, scallions, dill and sour cream (*schav*) beet patties with chicken (*kafteln*), wonderful stews (*zharkoia*), knishes, and countless dishes that I took for granted without knowing their ingredients. It was always a great treat for my friends and relatives to eat at her table. No one's knishes could compare with hers: onion, potato, and kashe knishes enveloped in the most delicate flaky crust. She would spend hours stretching the dough to the breaking point. The knishes melted in your mouth. Cooking was a religion to my mother, and only the finest ingredients were admitted into the food. When she tasted food that she hadn't prepared, she could sort out the ingredients and pass definitive judgment on their quality. She did not keep a strictly kosher household, but she had a kosher bias and a reverence for good nutritious food (no fancy haute-cuisine notions). In the nursing home, compelled to eat nondescript institutional food (hamburgers, mashed potatoes with heavy gravy, excessively salted tuna fish or chicken salad, hot dogs and beans), she experienced a sense of outrage, as if something sacred had been profaned.

She started a revolution. I call it the cottage-cheese revolt. Every time she asked for cheese, the waiter presented her with American cheese. "Too salty," she would say, and push the plate aside. I asked the dining-room manager to offer her cottage cheese, and the next day the waiter produced cottage cheese. The effect was electric–her companions at the table now all wanted cottage cheese. I sensed in the administrators of the facility an unease about mother's presence. She was too alert for her own good. Unlike the wits of most of the residents, hers were intact, her sensory apparatus as keen as before her collapse. She could taste the difference between a canned pear and a fresh one–and her refusal to eat the canned fruit was felt to be a threat to the order of things. "The people at my table look enviously at the plate of cottage cheese they serve me," she said. "I feel very awkward. I don't understand why the others can't be served cottage cheese if they want it. What's the harm? Would you believe it, one of the staff members came up to me and asked me whether I would agree to sit at a separate table. They don't want me to put ideas about the food that's being served into other people's heads. Can you imagine–all this over cottage cheese?" The following day on a visit I walked past the bulletin board in front of the dining room and saw that cottage cheese was on the menu. The revolt had succeeded.

And then there was the complaint about mistreatment. Hostages to the nurse's aides, who do most of the menial and grim work of tending their basic needs (bathroom functions, showering, dressing, cleaning up), the residents depend upon their goodwill. Like children, they whine and cry out, "Nurse, nurse, nurse, come here right away, come here!" It is easy for the authorities to discount grievances, because many are *non compus mentis* and the complaints are the emissions of deterioration and extravagant neediness. Mother is different. She is fastidious, demanding, and truthful. Her stories can be trusted. But how could we expect the administrators to know this right away? Wonderful Jane, the Jamaican nurse's aide with the captivating smile, had suddenly turned on her. Mother: "She tells me to shut up, and while showering me turns on the cold water. It's Christmas, she expected and didn't get a gift." She is an interpreter of the old school.

There is one correct interpretation of Jane's behavior, and it is hers. Knowing she was telling me the truth of what occurred, I needed to contain my rage. Whatever I did or said, I had to keep in mind that mother was a hostage. If I complained and it had no effect, Jane could take revenge. The solution: a belated Christmas gift, and Jane is all smiles again.

I went to an administrator to discuss a matter having nothing to do with the food, but the subject came up. The administrator was at a loss about how to satisfy mother. She didn't say so, but her stiffly correct manner said to me: "Your mother is simply unreasonable. Nothing will satisfy her." I admitted that mother is fastidious in her tastes; a lifetime of sheltered eating (she had avoided restaurants and institutional eating all her life) made it difficult for her to eat the food of the facility. But she may nevertheless be right about the quality of the food. I was concerned that my remarks may have registered on the administration as a personal insult. I regretted that I had spoken, and knew that I would have to consider moving Mother. But where? This was one of the best homes, beautifully cared for, well run. For the most part the staff was competent and kind. I needed to tell myself not to despair–they can't boot her out until we're ready to go. But where could she go? How could we be sure that the next place would be an improvement? And what if she wanted to move again? What if . . . My mind became a site of alternative scenarios, each one with its share of problems. There was no one to tell me to act or not to act–and if there was someone, how would I know whether the advice was reliable? It was up to me; it should be up to mother, who has all her wits, but she was indecisive: "I'm in limbo."

The power of decision was taken from me. She was struck down by a severe flu (everyone on her floor was afflicted) and was completely helpless again. She had lost her appetite, she couldn't lift herself to go to the bathroom. Would she recover from this new blow? The possibility of a quasi-independent situation for her–assisted living, as it is called–evaporated. It would be unwise to move her even should she recover. And recover she did.

Mother's first roommate was catatonic. On the floor below, there were livelier residents, more mobile and expressive. The director of social services suggested that she move downstairs, but no, she was not ready. She took a peek at the room that she had been offered, but didn't like the view–a car lot. "But, Mother," I said, "think of your view inside the room, your roommate lies there all the time, asleep or half awake, and says nothing, absolutely nothing, how can you stand it? You have a choice between conversation with people who have their wits and a room with a view, and you choose a room with a view." Mother raised her chin, pointed her nose in the air–a gesture she always made when she had no answer, but was determined on her course: "Your father and I always insisted on nice views. You know how nice the view was from our apartment." I knew there was no use in persisting. "You tell me when you're ready to move, *if* you're ready to move. You tell me."

As the weeks passed, I noticed a change: she seemed to accept her situation without, however, admitting it. The complaints and criticisms were now fewer and had lost their edge. She had even come to see the virtues of the place–the kindness of the staff, which she took for granted as an entitlement of her illness, was now appreciated for what it was: kindness. She admires the cleanliness, which for her would be next to godliness if she were a believer. "This is like a hotel, not a nursing home." She recalls the grim place where her younger brother ended his days a decade or more ago. She doesn't care for the food, but she no longer speaks with bitterness about it. Has the antidepressant Zoloft begun to do its work? Even the sight of twisted and vacuous faces doesn't seem to disturb her. "Everyone here is in her own world," she remarks with an almost Olympian detachment. Well, not everyone. There are others who have their wits about them. But the home has its share of the unhearing, the unseeing, the inarticulate, the half demented. How can she, in full possession of her faculties, bear it? Am I deluded into thinking that she derives a certain pleasure from being an observer of the scene, sanity in the midst of derangement and decrepitude? She seems even alive to the comedy of it all, though her conscience and compassion are alert to the suffering. She attends to the difficulties of her roommates, calling the attention of nurses and nurse's aides to their needs when they themselves are incapable of doing so.

While navigating the corridor with her walker, she looks left and right into rooms, noting the furniture, the decorations, and the views. She has become a *flaneur*, her curiosity aroused by everything she sees. There is now even the play of amusement on her face as she tells me the adventures of the day: "You see that woman over there? She takes off her clothes and appears naked in the corridor and scratches herself constantly as if she has a skin disease. That man over there. He enters my room when I'm elsewhere and rifles through my dresser. I caught him inspecting my underwear the other day. I waved him away." He left her room one day, leaving his flatulence behind. She wrinkles her nose in disgust, but cannot resist an outburst of hilarity. Where has the laughter been all these years? Is this too the work of the antidepressant? She tells me, not without vanity, of the old man, who declared his age to be ninety-seven, stopping her on walks up and down the corridor and serenading her with "When Irish Eyes Are Smiling." She has become amused and amusing in her very old age. "Such experiences," she says with a shrug. Even her disapprovals can't conceal her fascinated curiosity. "I have something interesting to tell you" was the first thing she said to me on one visit. "I was lying in bed reading. Suddenly I heard people running in the corridor. A nurse told me that a woman was visiting a man in his room. They shut the door. And when the nurses came, you know." I couldn't resist: "Good for them." Mother shook her head. "No, it's not fitting. These are old people. It's not right. The nurse scolded her. In the dining room the woman tried to sit with the man and hold hands, but they put her at a separate table. Can you imagine?" Of course, I can imagine, and so can Mother, whose prurience is close to the surface. She tells the story—with an unwitting smile.

Her favorite joke is the following: Sadie and Sara go on a safari in darkest Africa. Sadie is jumped by a gorilla who mauls and rapes her. Sarah runs away. Sadie is taken to the hospital, wrapped in bandages from head to toe. Sarah feels guilty and goes to the hospital to visit her.

She stands at Sadie's bedside, but Sadie doesn't say a word. "Sadie, I'm so sorry. I ran away in fear. Please forgive me." Not a word from Sadie. "Sadie, say something. I'll do anything you want." Silence. "Please, please . . ." Finally, Sadie speaks: "What should I say? He doesn't call, he doesn't write."

For all her frailty, she does not look her age. Staff and residents alike are astonished when she tells them that she is ninety-three. She could easily pass for someone in her eighties. What she cannot tell them is that she is ninety-six, two and a half years older than her official age. I found out her real age only recently. Her birth certificate was a creation for the purpose of emigration. To be allowed to emigrate to America in 1924, she would have had to be no older than twenty according to the new immigration law. My father was also a year older than his official age, and he and Mother took a vow of secrecy about their age, fearful perhaps that the false documents made them illegal aliens and that at any time, even decades after their arrival and naturalization, they might be deported. Even their son was not to know. What else haven't I been told? I have a copy of mother's "birth certificate" issued in Bucharest. It has yellowed into authenticity. I will need to produce it with her naturalization papers when the money she is paying in (six thousand dollars a month) runs out and she becomes eligible for Medicaid. I sometimes take it out of the drawer in my desk devoted to Mother's things and look upon it reverently. It made possible my own existence. I am the result of a false document. Without the document my mother would have remained in Europe only to be consumed by the ovens.

In my rush to find a nursing home, I had not considered the ethnicity or religious convictions of the residents. Though the home is ecumenical in its admission standards, the residents are mostly Irish and Italian Catholics, some WASPs, Greeks and Armenians and a few Jews, who can be guessed at from their names. After her stay in the rehabilitation section of the home, Mother had been moved into a room which she was to share with a devout Catholic who wanted her to accompany her on visits to the chapel. Mother told her that she is Jewish and not religious. All her life, she had lived among Jews—in

Bessarabia, in Brooklyn, in Forest Hills. Now she is among the goyim, and I have detected no distress. The bonds of senescence may be stronger than ethnicity. I would be surprised, but not astonished, if I saw her and her roommate "walkering" themselves down the corridor to chapel, my mother deciding to keep her roommate company, while privately reflecting on the nonsense of the services. My mother has refused every invitation to accompany her roommate to the chapel for rosary. If the Jewish God did not exist for her, what chance did the Christian God have? "Imagine," she says, "they believe that Mary remained a virgin after conceiving Jesus. The Holy Spirit entered her. Such nonsense."

She complains about the lack of activities. "There is not much to do here. The activities are bingo, religious services, rosary, crafts, and current events. Bingo is not for me. I went to crafts and current events. I didn't see anything I wanted to do in crafts. And the current events, I don't know. They talk about things I'm not interested in–the Celtics, the Red Sox." She gives me one of her disdainful looks. "So I read." And she has been reading up a storm. Willa Cather's *The Professor's House,* Edith Wharton's *Ethan Frome,* Michael Korda on the Kennedys, biographies of the Duchess of Windsor, the royal family, and Rose Kennedy. The ophthalmologist's diagnosis was "legally blind," so her reading must be illicit. She is full of information and indignation about what she has read. "Marilyn Monroe slept with everyone. The Duchess of Windsor was a clever crook. Some of the things she did are unheard of. Edward was impotent, probably homosexual. She went to a brothel in China where they taught her tricks to arouse Edward. Can you imagine? The book about the Kennedys has interesting things about politics. But the language, the word 'fuck' is throughout the book. Is it necessary?" Many years before, when I had returned from France after a year on a Fulbright, I had smuggled in an illegal copy of Henry Miller's *Tropic of Cancer.* Mother retrieved it from the bottom of the trunk while unpacking and confiscated it. A week later she called in mild indignation: "Is this literature? It's disgusting." "You don't have to read it." But she wouldn't give it up. She would read it to the end. "I want to see how long he can keep this up."

I am under orders to provide her with serious books. "I can't afford to waste my time with trash," she says. She reminds me of the pleasure she took in reading Ray Monk's Wittgenstein biography. Perhaps I could find her a biography of Pushkin or Tolstoy, writers she had read and loved in school. She remembered that Henri Troyat had written biographies of Russian writers. When I visit her, I find her so absorbed in what she is reading that she is unaware of my presence. She looks up at me with a rare look of pleasure on her face. She has been reading Henri Troyat's life of Tolstoy and her response is pure appreciation: "What a mind, what a character! He was so great that even the czar feared him. He dressed like a peasant and hated the ways of the city. He wanted to be useful, to do things with his hands, so he learned to make shoes. There is a pair of shoes in a museum signed 'made by the author of *War and Peace*.' " Scarcely a visit goes by when she doesn't recount what she has read with an untutored connoisseurship that astonishes me. My graduate students are no match for her. She knows her limitations, but the printed page doesn't intimidate her. She knows when she is in the presence of distinction and when in the presence of triviality and trash. And she knows how to make a book her own. I gave her Michael Ignatieff's life of Isaiah Berlin, whose early years in Riga carried her back to her own early life in Belz. Berlin's paternal line went back to the Shneersons, the family of the Lubavitcher rabbi, who, my mother informed me, had intermarried with the Liebsons of Belz. A Liebson had rescued her father, my grandfather, when he fell from a horse. Mother had read herself into the book, and the marvelous Shaya (Isaiah's Hebrew name) had become an acquaintance. Age has not dimmed her curiosity about others, in fact, has increased it. She has traveled very little in her seventy-plus years in America, preferring instead to remain at home, but in her reading she has become a traveler—and something more. She now resembles the Talmudic scholar who lives in books. She had prided herself on her independence and dreaded losing it. But now that she has lost it, it is as if something in her has been fulfilled. Her body is imprisoned by frailty, but her mind has been freed to enjoy itself.

I take her to see an exhibit of early Picasso in the Boston Museum of Fine Arts. On entering the first room, we are greeted by a plaque in which Picasso is quoted recalling what his mother said about him, to this effect: "If I had been a soldier I would have become Napoleon, if a priest, the pope. Instead I am a painter and became Picasso." My mother looks up at me from her wheelchair and says, "His mother didn't say that." I think that my mother's response should be affixed to the plaque. My mother knows mothers, and by the end of the show, she knew Picasso: "The man is an animal." I marvel at her judgment. I give her short stories by Bellow, and when I ask for her verdict she says, "He can write." I cannot give her inferior goods, because she can sense quality immediately, and she tells me again and again that she has no time to waste. I sometimes think that aging has purified her, allowed her to concentrate her mind. She has always had an eye for landscape: flowers, trees, greens and blues. But her main pleasure now is character. She has been reading mostly biographies: of Tolstoy, Turgenev, Chekhov, Napoleon, Disraeli, Churchill, Eleanor Roosevelt, Golda Meir. It is as if before she dies she want to know, if only vicariously, what human beings in their fullness can achieve. Unlike many of her companions in the home who have been reduced to their deteriorating bodies, she has achieved a certain freedom from her body in books.

And she has lost nothing of her authority in family matters, still insisting as she does on her role as matriarch. When she hears of a quarrel within the family, she will intervene if at all possible. If the younger generation cannot handle matters as she sees fit, she will do it for them. When I suggest that it may not be her business to interfere or, more diplomatically, that she has earned her rest, let others concern themselves in these matters, she insists on her role.

When my mother entered the nursing home, I was sixty-five-years old, the classic age of retirement. I am now sixty-nine, one year away from actual retirement. But what will I retire to? Daily visits to the nursing home, continual reminders of the ultimate retirement into death. When I visit, I greet some of the residents like old friends; occasionally, I am taken for one of the residents. While accompanying

my mother on her walk down the corridor, I am accosted by a resident, who tells me that my "head wrapping" is hanging from the bulletin board. I look puzzled and tell her that I am not staying at the
place. "Ah, too bad you have to leave." I tell my wife of the encounter
and we break into laughter. But what are we laughing about?

I am haunted by senescence these days. Not death or dying, but
senescence: the posture of the body in half-life, or should I say barely
life, the faces of bodies that stare ahead in wheelchairs, seemingly
without pain, with eyes marked by lives that they can no longer
remember. They have become a daily event in my visits from obligation and, to my surprise, affection. My mother has not yet achieved
that look of half-life, though I glimpse it when she lies in bed with
open eyes and shrunken cheeks. Right now, she sits and looks about
her, when not complaining, observing the common destiny, with the
equanimity of her longevity. Every visit to the nursing home is like a
preparation for a permanent stay. Like the demented woman with the
long bony fingers, the home pulls me in. The gloom dissipates when
my mother tells about her latest discoveries in the book she is reading.

What is the secret of my mother's longevity? Genes of course play
their part. Friends tell me that I am lucky to have a share of them. I too
may live forever. I have my mother's body, a complaining body, more
symptomatic than diseased. Symptoms are alarm signals, so the symptomatic body exists in a state of alarm. It is as if a siren goes off every
time there is smoke. Where there is smoke, there isn't always fire. But
genes are only part of the answer. In her will to survive, she will risk
nothing that will endanger her survival. Most of us pursue pleasures
knowing the risks, not because we are courageous, but because we
can't help ourselves. I have a friend with a heart condition who sits
five rows from the stage during a performance of a Mahler symphony.
I had another friend who tunneled his way through the caves of Las-
caux while in remission from lymphoma for a book he was writing,
only to suffer a relapse and die a week later in a Paris hospital. I know
a woman who risks a heart attack every time she flies, but will not
forgo the pleasures of traveling. My mother will deprive herself of
everything that threatens her safety. The drama of immigration was

enough for a lifetime. She exists in the economy of survival. It is not a matter of cowardice, for, as she tells me with a conviction that I believe, she is ready for anything that may befall her, but she will not conspire with it.

I have a recurrent dream that my father, ever faithful in life, abandoned my mother and me. In the dream we never speak of it, but I experience the abandonment as a profound absence. My breathing becomes constricted and I wake up desolated. In death my father abandoned us, and I have now taken his place. E. L. Doctorow has a story about a middle-aged man who dies, leaving behind his very elderly mother, who is in a nursing home. His sister wants to keep the fact of the son's death from her mother, so she tells her that he has moved to Arizona for health reasons. He is suffering from severe bronchitis. She then recruits her nephew, her deceased brother's son, to write letters from his father in Arizona to maintain the fiction. I don't have a sibling to conspire to keep me alive after my death, I worry that my mother may survive me. Nothing worse for a parent than surviving a child.

Eight: A Question of Identity

MY FRIEND THE Israeli novelist Aharon Appelfeld arrives from time to time in the States as a reproving voice of conscience. He wants to pack me up and take me back with him to Israel, where we would sit together in a café, drink coffee, and read the Bible, Talmud, Midrash, the Yiddish poems of Chaim Nachman Bialik, Chaim Grade, the stories of Sholem Aleichem, Mendele, and Peretz. He looks at my Jewish face, mounted on a body "too tall for a Jew," and regards me with a mixture of affection and pity. How could I bear to waste my cultural legacy? His lament is not only for me (more acute for me, because the legacy is a real possession of mine) but for a whole generation of assimilated and, if they are intellectual, universalizing Jews. His own Israel has its version of rejectionism. Anything that looks or sounds like *galut*, the exile, the diaspora, has for Israelis (particularly the native-born) something shameful about it. Appelfeld comes to the United States and Europe in search of a Yiddish Zion only to find it in a state of evaporation. Those Jews who have never known it don't want it, don't know what it means to want it.

I listen to Appelfeld, whose conviction and passion I can't begin to match, at once tempted by and resistant to his effort to define me. I can't tell him what Jewishness means to me. I know I would not want to be packed into his suitcase. I can't bring myself to go to a synagogue or temple (I can imagine Appelfeld's disdain if I went to a temple), even during high holy days. I belong to no Jewish clubs. I can't read Hebrew. I can read Yiddish, but I have looked at passages in Yiddish books and have not been inclined to read them. And yet, when a Jewish friend of mine, Alvin Kibel, Bronx-born, married to a gentile, said that he was not a Jew, that nothing in his theory and practice qualified him as one (his heroes were Homer, Dante, Cervantes, Tolstoy, and so on), I argued with some bitterness that of course he was one and that there was something shameful in his denial of it. "What am I denying? Tell me what makes me Jewish." I couldn't say, but was unwilling to allow him his self-description. My friend was like the German Jew who responded to the knock on the door by the Gestapo incredulously, disbelieving that he was not permitted to say who he was not and who he was. Like me, my friend is an atheist, but he lacks Yiddish, the substitute for religion that I possess. I might have quoted, but did not, Albert Memmi, who writes: "A man is not a Jew because he decides to be one: he discovers that he is a Jew, then he either consents or refuses . . . without ceasing to be one. Of course he is a Jew in a different way depending upon his refusal or approval, but he is still a Jew."

In fairness to my friend, his objection to Judaism has a moral basis. He dislikes what he sees as its arrogance, its sense of chosenness. He remembers my father's occasional judgment of behavior: *"Nur bei die goyim"* (you can expect this of the gentiles). Does the suffering and persecution of centuries entitle Jews to their inordinate self-love and contempt of gentiles? I believe my father was only half joking when he said *"Nur bei die goyim."* Ivan Shtink was an unforgettable part of his legacy. I might say it jokingly and not mean it, so I say to myself. But I wonder whether my friend is not on to something, for there is in every Jew a residual sense of spiritual privilege. Are we entitled to it? Is any nation or ethnic group entitled to it? Can ethnic identity survive without it? Can we hope for a decent fate for humanity with it? I have since expiated for my sin of coercion, but I feel a kind of sorrow for my friend or, if not for him, for my relation to him. At moments I feel what Appelfeld must feel for me—that mixture of affection and pity.

What is left of the Jew when he has abandoned Judaism, its religion and language? It's a question I ask about myself. Maybe a certain reflectiveness, an inability to take things for granted, a continuously nagging sense of difficulty and problem, anxiety, guilt. Christians have historically tried to make Jews feel guilty for the death of Christ; they have succeeded only in making them aggrieved victims. As the pope has recently acknowledged, it is the Christians who are guilty for making the accusation and for all the consequences that have ensued. We should at least be grateful that he has transferred the burden to his own tradition. If we are not and do not feel guilty for the death of Christ, of what are we guilty? . . . Jewish guilt! Does any other ethnic or racial group provide an adjective for guilt? I have never heard anyone speak of Italian guilt or French guilt or Irish guilt (Stephen Dedalus is all guilt, but not in his capacity as Irishman). Yes, there is German guilt, but it is a judgment passed on Germans for crimes committed, not a subjective state of indeterminate origins. God knows, there is enough guilt to go around. Christians, after all, are born in original sin, Jews are not. But there is something distinctive about the way Jews feel guilty about their parents or their children or their relation to the world. Is it that they lack the reserve of non-Jews and talk about it all the time? Why should Jews feel guilt if the Jews have been victims, not agents of oppression? If you blame yourself when you are punished, you must have done something to deserve it. My father told me of a time his father beat him for something he hadn't done. When he protested the injustice, his father showed no remorse, my father should accept the punishment for the times he had done something wrong and had gotten away with it.

Here is the crux of the matter. Jewish guilt is the motive for moral passion, the constant worrying about whether one has done right, done enough, done too much. How should one react to provocation, injustice, indifference, neglect? In matters large and small, mostly small, but no less significant to us, we find ourselves preoccupied with concern about conduct, about how to speak and act in all situations.

More than thirty years ago, I participated in a symposium on "the meaning of *galut* [exile] in America." The editor of the journal rounded up the usual suspects, most of whom found the concept either uncomfortable or irrelevant. Those who tried to make something of it connected or converted it to the fashionable (more fashionable then than now) idea of alienation: "a condition of the soul, bordered by tears," one contributor said. My own contribution (I was then in my early thirties) condescended to the very idea of *golus* (the Yiddish translation of *Galut*). *Golus* was for the Zionists, not for "progressive" Yiddishists like me. Of course, I had changed from what I once was, but I had retained the mistrust of exile talk I had acquired in my childhood. It was now connected in my mind with fashionable talk about alienation. "The contemporary piety," I wrote, "is that we are all alienated, Jews and Gentiles alike, and the idea has become so characteristic of our culture that the verb doesn't need a complement. Alienated from what?" The word, I argued, had become a catchall for "unhappiness, loneliness, and suffering," a secular translation of the expulsion from paradise. But my condescension to exile and alienation gave way to a recognition of a common anxiety shared by Zionists and Yiddishists alike, the assimilation of Jews into American life. How to resist the seductiveness of the melting pot, the melting out of differences? I confessed that it wasn't my anxiety.

At the age of thirty-two I was in a state of confusion about who I was or what I wanted, or not so much a state of confusion as a state of indifference. I would not have thought of having to define myself if the symposium had not obligated me. I knew that I didn't want to return to a country I had never seen, nor did I want a ghettoized Jewish existence. I wrote: "The young sensitive American Jew [who else but myself?] who is unhappy wants to find himself in Paris or Rome, not Jerusalem, because home is a place from which you want to escape at times [a cautious qualifier]; home (Orthodox, Zionist, or assimilationist) may rob a person of his fullness as a human being. Imagine a life in which one's friends were all members of one's family." But then I twisted and turned, worrying that an escape from home may become permanent, "an act of self-mutilation, a sacrifice of one's power."

The incoherence of my contribution was the incoherence of my (Jewish?) soul. I wanted to be the rare person who assumes his Jewishness gracefully, with an unconscious pride, and yet feels free to live outside the Pale of Settlement. "The Pale of Settlement," "the Ghetto": they were metaphors for living exclusively (even voluntarily) among Jews. And what would my graceful Jewishness be outside the Pale of Settlement and the unconscious pride in it? It was as if I wanted to leave and stay at home at the same time. Having abandoned the "faith" of the movement, I had no desire to embrace another faith. Though neither Zion nor the synagogue held any attraction for me, I appreciated the need for the state of Israel after the Holocaust. How could I not? And I even came to understand the need for a belief in a transcendent being as a recourse against political tyranny. Every Jew and gentile, believer or skeptic, should want to protect a space for the believer. Without such a space, there can be no freedom. But I did not share the need. A columnist in a Jerusalem newspaper, reviewing the symposium, remarked on my gracelessness about his city and made it clear that the city had no desire to welcome me.

Most of the other contributors were clearly uncomfortable with the subject; it forced them to think against the tendency of their lives, which was not to think about their Jewishness. The shortest contribution to the symposium was by the novelist Henry Roth, the celebrated author of *Call it Sleep,* who spoke of "Judaism as only one element in [his] culture–things being what they are, an inescapable element unfortunately, instead of a freely accepted one." And he concluded with the astonishing suggestion of what future-born Jews in America might confer on humanity in addition to the boons they had already conferred: "the last and greatest one: of orienting themselves toward ceasing to be Jews." Roth didn't explain himself, apparently didn't feel he had to. He assumed what most Jewish writers on the subject have assumed, that being Jewish is a misfortune. It is the relentless theme of Albert Memmi's *Portrait of a Jew* and *The Liberation of the Jew.* Hannah Arendt wrote: "The thing which all my life seemed to me the greatest shame, which was the misery and misfortune of my life–having been born a Jewess–this I should on no account now wished to have missed." Roth, American-born and of Arendt's generation—still a time when the Jewish experience in Europe powerfully affected American Jewish consciousness—agreed that being Jewish was a misfortune, but apparently felt differently about it. He would have wished to have missed his Jewish fate.

And who with any knowledge of history can deny that being a Jew has been a misfortune? But who of my generation or that of my children thinks of it as a misfortune? Even now when I read Memmi or Arendt, though I know of what they speak, I find that I cannot entirely enter the zone of their feeling. I have been reading Peter Novick's *Holocaust in America,* a critique of its exploitation mainly in the service of justifying the state of Israel and her practices. I am struck by the way he, an American-born Jewish historian, minimizes anti-Semitic expression in America. By the mid-sixties, he writes, "anti-Semitism in the United States was, by every measure, continuing its long-term decline, diminishing to the point that it presented no significant barriers or disadvantages to American Jews." He dismisses "a series of anti-Semitic remarks made by a few militant blacks in the late sixties" as "laughably trivial." But he offers no critieria by which we can judge whether the anti-Semitism was significant or trivial and fails to mention that the few militant blacks who made the remarks were leaders of organizations. Novick's complacency may have its own particular motives, but it also reflects a sense of security American Jews have achieved that is unparalleled in any other country of the diaspora. Even before the advent of multiculturalism here and abroad, America was unique in not demanding, in Arendt's phrase, "a homogeneity of population and an ethnic foundation for its state." Unlike their counterparts in the rest of the diaspora, American Jews now assimilate (it was not always the case) not because they have something to conceal. In its ideal expression, America invites you to declare whatever your hyphenate identity might be: Irish-American, Italian-American, African-American, Jewish-American. Then why has the secular American Jew lost touch with his Jewishness? The opportunities, temptations, and distractions of American life are irresistible. Judaism, rooted in an older, more oppressive way of life, can hardly be expected to compete. The secular American Jew who has not altogether rejected Judaism may perform an occasional ritualistic exercise: fast on Yom Kippur, attend synagogue or temple on the high holy days, attend a Passover seder, have his son circumsized, arrange for his son to be bar mitzvahed or, if he has a daughter, bat mitvahed, but none of these exercises is informed with the historical feeling of victimhood that has been the Jewish fate. I say *feeling*, because he doubtless knows something of that fate, but why should he want to possess a feeling that brings unhappiness?

Here lies a danger. What if there is a resurgence of anti-Semitism that is not "laughably trivial"? In her essay "The Pariah as Rebel," Hannah Arendt wrote: "For honor never will be won by the cult of success or fame, by cultivation of one's own self, nor even by personal dignity. From the 'disgrace' of being a Jew there is but one escape–to fight for the honor of the Jewish people as a whole." Having left his Jewishness behind, how will the assmilated Jew be expected to know where his honor lies? And he will be without resources to fight for it. To be a Jew in America is not a misfortune, but there is always the potential that it may become one. Zionism has been the great reminder that no Jew is completely safe in diaspora.

My radical Yiddishist upbringing innoculated me against the temptations of Zionism. That is an understatement, for Zionism was presented to us by our teachers as a reactionary cause to be combated. I may have rejected the Marxism of my youth, but not the *Yiddishkeit* and the mistrust of Zionism that accompanied it. After the Holocaust, one could not but support the state of Israel, and where would Israel be without Zionism? And yet the vaccine against Zionism has remained in my system, for I have never been comfortable with the idea of a Jewish state. Perhaps I've retained the binational ideal of my "progressive" childhood, the ideal of Moors and Jews living together in the Golden Age of Spain before the Inquisition. How can there be peace and harmony in Israel without genuine equality between Jews and Arabs? How can political equality exist in a state that calls itself Jewish? And what if the Arabs become the majority in Israel, would they be allowed to acquire power through the franchise? Questions with disturbing answers. I know of course that a binational state is, practically speaking, an impossibility and that the survival of the state of Israel trumps any answers to these questions. A binational state would not resolve the conflict between Arab and Jew; that conflict would have to be resolved before such a state could be rationally thought a possibility.

My wife and I did make a visit to Israel in 1981, when I was forty-nine, and stayed for a month at Mishkenot, the center for scholars and artists. The visit was an unqualified pleasure. My remarks about Jerusalem in the symposium article now seem to me like sophomoric foolishness. During my stay in Israel, I travelled to Hulda, the kibbutz where the writer Amos Oz lived, in order to interview him for an article for *Partisan Review.* We arrived on a bright March Sunday morning (a workday in Israel) and found ourselves among busy workmen. A worker in a hard hat pointed to a man who would show us the way to Oz's study. Our guide, short, unassuming, and friendly, turned out to be General Israel Tal, a former deputy defense minister and, as we later found out from Oz, the world's leading authority on tank warfare. Tal belonged to the Peace Now movement, of which Oz was a leading member. Young, well built, and ruggedly handsome, Oz greeted us with an old-world courtesy and excused himself for having to delay the interview with him. He and Tal had something to talk over.

My wife and I sat on the sofa while the two men talked. From time to time Tal would interrupt the conversation, conducted in Hebrew (which we did not understand), and ask us in English about our trip to Israel. Why had it taken me so long to make my first trip? He did not wait for an answer and guessed with absolute accuracy that I was a New Yorker from a Yiddishist anti-Zionist background and that my resistance to visiting Israel took longer to overcome than my commitment to radical ideology. He asked me whether I had come to talk to Oz about literature and when I said literature and politics, he smiled and said that Oz had great political ability, but he had urged him to stay out of politics, so that he could devote himself to what was eternal (art) rather than to what was transient (politics). This mild-mannered man in civilian clothes with an avuncular smile, the father of the Israeli tank, had traveled to the study of a young novelist to discuss the state of the union; he had expressed himself on the eternal value of art. One could expect to find such a combination of events only in an improbable fiction or in the reality of the state of Israel.

During the course of the interview Oz expressed an extraordinary version of Zionism that spoke to my own resistance to it: "Not that I am in love with the idea of little national states. When I listen to the brilliant anti-Zionist arguments of George Steiner or Noam Chomsky, to a certain degree I envy these people. Theirs is a simple world. We hear these people one way or another claiming that the Jews are destined to be the vitamin, the fertilizer, the stimulator of Western civilization, and as such they should be scattered—that's their way to make a 'contribution,' whatever they mean by this. I share his feeling. I'm not at all in love with the adolescent toys of nationhood—waving flags and so on. I could even share Steiner's or Chomsky's or whoever's vision of a world in which there are perhaps one hundred civilizations, not single nation-states. But as long as everyone else has locks on his doors and bars on his windows and machine guns and tanks and airplanes, I'm going to play the bloody game according to the bloody rules. The vision of the Jews as eternal pioneers of a multinational or nonnational or postnationalistic world is something which I think I cannot afford, not after Auschwitz. I'd be delighted to be the third one in the neighborhood or the fifth one in the world to join such an arrangement and abolish nation-states altogether. But I'm not going to remain the eternal pioneer of the next phase of world history. We Jews have played this role for a long time. Some have admired us for this, some persecuted us. Nobody followed. Hence my Zionism, A to Z, in a nutshell."

I was struck by Oz's confidence in his Israeli identity. Among other Israelis I met, whatever the differences and contentions of their politics and religious beliefs, there was none of the questioning of one's identity that one finds in the diaspora and particularly in America. Which is not to deny the conflicts, often fierce, within the state. Oz the dove was declaring his solidarity with the hawks in defense of his country on the eve of an election in which the Likud Party, under Menachem Begin, came to power for the first time. The campaign was characterized by a bitter division within Israeli Jewry between East European Ashkenazim and North African Sephardim (paradoxically, between the privileged left and the underprivileged right), a division that at the time was not common knowledge in America. The bitterness of the division was in evidence in the burning of Labor Party headquarters (symbol of Ashkenazi power in Israel) by Sephardic supporters of Begin during the election campaign. Should there be peace between Jew and Arab, the drama to which Oz said Israelis were addicted could be displaced to the conflict between East European Ashkenazim and North African Sephardim. Perhaps even more serious is the division between Orthodox and secular Jews.

The Orthodox and secular Jews in Israel contend over the fate of the country. Walking through the neighborhood of Mea Shearim in Jerusalem, my wife and I had the strange sensation that every visitor has of being thrust back into an earlier century. It is the Eastern European shtetl redivivus: bearded men with curled hair, wearing long *kapotes* and *shtramls,* their women following behind in dress that conceals their bodies from head to toe. On the walls of buildings, there is an occasional graffito that equates (secular) Zionism with Nazism. For the ultra-Orthodox, the state of Israel is a profanation against the messiah, who alone can bring Zion to fruition. And if the secular Zionist has betrayed Judaism, what of the American Jew in diaspora?

I read in the papers with revulsion that American Reform rabbis go to Israel and visit the Wailing Wall only to be abused by the Orthodox who believe they own Judaism. One of the Orthodox shouts that they have done more harm to the future of Jewry than the Holocaust. He may be right: Jewry is disappearing in assimilation. My daughter married a Protestant, my son a Catholic. Will my grandson be circumsized? My mother remembers how my grandfather admired my *mila* while my diaper was changed. My mother, atheist that she is, cannot invoke religion: her reasons are medical. Whatever vestigial religious feeling may exist is repressed or sublimated in hygiene. My Jewish identity (certain, but hard to define) exerts little hold on my children, certainly not in the form that it has taken in me. They are free to do as they like. I want that freedom for myself, so how could I deny it them, even if I prefer that they exercise it differently? I would not want to live in a country that would contest my self-identity, tell me what it means to be a Jew or anything else.

In the centuries of wandering, the Jew has learned to shift for himself, to adapt, to accommodate, to disappear and reappear, to invent and reinvent himself. He has been an expert in living on air, a *luft-mentsch*. This is what it has meant historically to be in diaspora. But as Americans, we (for I am not alone) cannot say that we are in diaspora, for we have no nostalgia for a home that we have never known; indeed, that my parents and grandparents had never known. Neither victims nor victimizers, we have known neither defeat nor triumph. Nor have we ceased to be Jews, though we are hard put to say what our Jewishness comes to. We experience it as a residuum of feelings, attitudes, attachments, and knowledge. Alain Finkielkraut speaks to me when he writes: "Our relationship with Mother is Jewish, and it's Jewish insomnia that we suffer, replete with feelings of guilt that attack in the night. Our vital need for books is Jewish as well, so too our need for Jewish concepts and for living and breathing the written word. And of course it almost goes without saying: there's our Jewish sense of humor, full of tenderness or despair." And I would add indignation at injustice and patience in the face of adversity. Which is not to say that only Jews have feelings of guilt or trouble sleeping or have the need for books or a sense of humor or indignation or patience. But there is a distinctive inflection in the way Jews combine these qualities. Osip Mandelstam had the poet's instinct for the right simile: "As a little musk fills an entire house, so the influence of Judaism overflows all of one's life." And yet I want to say that the kind of Jew I am doesn't exhaust the totality of my being.

What is missing in me is that sense of solidarity that one experiences in a synagogue or a *landsmanshaft* or an organization dedicated to Jewish causes. I would not congratulate myself on the feeling of independence that Hannah Arendt affirmed when she responded to Gershom Scholem's critique of her book *Eichmann in Jerusalem:* "I do not belong to any organization and always speak only for myself and . . . I have great confidence in Lessing's *selbstdenken* for which, I think, no ideology, no public opinion and no 'convictions' can ever be a substitute." I don't share Arendt's self-assurance in her *selbstdenken,* but she does describe a sense of separateness I feel from whatever is institutional or communal or ideological, whether it be Jewish or gentile or anything else. That feeling too is Jewish.

My father complained that I had failed to pass on my Jewish legacy to my children. His rebuke retains its sting when I learn that my son, married to a devout Catholic, has taken to reading books about the Jewish tradition. He began with the novels of Chaim Potok. For Christmas–not Hanukkah–I gave him a history of the Jewish people, as if in belated expiation for my earlier sins of omission. He even learned enough to conduct a seder and prepared Passover dishes with the advice of his grandmother. I suspect that in observing his wife's devotion to her religion, he experienced an absence in his own life. My daughter, married to a Protestant, has not felt the same challenge to learn about the Jewish tradition. She devotes herself to studying the plight of the working poor and advocating their cause, for which I take no credit–though at times she and her husband, who shares her passions, remind me of my younger self. Her grandmother's past is a source of fascination for her, but it is an exotic fascination for a past she does not possess. When I read her passages from this memoir, she is wide-eyed with interest and speaks of it as my legacy to her. She and her brother may have passed into another kind of American life in which their Jewish identity, whatever of it they retain, is at once unthreatened (at least for now), minimal and yet, I hope, unextinguished.

Acknowledgments

I am grateful to Daniel Aaron, Joan Bamberger, Leslie Epstein, Michael Gilmore, and Robert Nozick for not letting me off easy in their attentive and constructive readings of drafts of the book. Leslie was an endless source of support from the very beginning. I am also grateful to Ted Solataroff, who found promise in my essays early on. He put me in touch with Peter Mayer, who saw the possibility of a book in those essays and provided both the necessary encouragement and an acute editorial eye. My conversations with Saki Bercovitch about *Yiddishkeit* and related matters helped in the writing of the book. One could not ask for better group support. I have drawn upon previously published essays of mine in *Agni, Culturefront, Jewish Frontier, Partisan Review, Midstream*, the *Michigan Quarterly, The Sewanee Review*, and *The Gettysburg Review.*